4

Longman Academic Writing Series

FIFTH EDITION ESSAYS

Alice Oshima
Ann Hogue
with Lara Ravitch

Longman Academic Writing Series 4: Paragraphs to Essays, Fifth Edition

Pearson Education, 10 Bank Street, White Plains, NY 10606

Staff Credits: The people who made up the *Longman Academic Writing Series 4* team, representing editorial, production, design, and manufacturing, are Pietro Alongi, Margaret Antonini, Eleanor Barnes, Rosa Chapinal, Aerin Csigay, Ann France, Shelley Gazes, Amy McCormick, Lise Minovitz, Liza Pleva, and Joan Poole.

Cover image: jupeart/Shutterstock
Text Composition: TSI Graphics

Library of Congress Cataloging-in-Publication Data

Oshima, Alice
   [Writing academic English]
   Longman Academic Writing Series, Level 4 : Essays / Alice Oshima, Ann Hogue, Lara Ravitch.
      —Fifth edition.
      pages cm.
   ISBN-13: 978-0-13-291569-4
   ISBN-10: 0-13-291569-3
   1. English language—Rhetoric—Handbooks, manuals, etc. 2. English language—Grammar
   —Handbooks, manuals, etc. 3. English language—Textbooks for foreign speakers.
   4. Academic writing—Handbooks, manuals, etc. 5. Report writing—Handbooks, manuals, etc.
   I. Hogue, Ann. II. Ravitch, Lara. III. Title.

   PE1408.H6644 2013
   808'.042—dc23

                                                                    2013005061

ISBN 10: 0-13-291569-3
ISBN 13: 978-0-13-291569-4

Printed in the United States of America
3 4 5 6 7 8 9 10—V082—18 17 16 15

CONTENTS

iii

PART II: WRITING AN ESSAY

PART III: SENTENCE STRUCTURE

APPENDICES

TO THE TEACHER

Welcome to the new edition of Level 4 in the *Longman Academic Writing Series*, a five-level series that prepares English language learners for academic coursework. This book, formerly called *Writing Academic English*, is intended for high-intermediate students in university, college, or in secondary school programs. It offers a carefully structured approach that focuses on writing as a process. It teaches rhetoric and sentence structure in a straightforward manner, using a step-by-step approach, high-interest models, and varied practice types.

Like the previous editions, this book integrates instruction in essay organization and sentence structure with the writing process. It carefully guides students through the steps of the writing process to produce the well-organized, clearly developed essays that are essential to academic writing in English. You will find a wealth of realistic models to guide writers and clear explanations supported by examples that will help your students through typical rough spots. These explanations are followed by the extensive practice that learners need to assimilate writing skills and write with accuracy and confidence. There are interactive tasks throughout the text—pair work, small-group activities, and full-class discussions—that engage students in the learning process and complement the solitary work that writers must do. The tasks progress from recognition exercises to controlled production and culminate in communicative Try It Out activities.

In the first part of this book, you will find a quick review of paragraph writing and summarizing. The second part of the book offers comprehensive chapters on process, cause/effect, comparison/contrast, and argumentative essays. Sentence structure, with a special emphasis on subordinated structures, appears in the third part of the book. Finally, the extensive appendices and a thorough index make the text a valuable and easy-to-use reference tool.

What's New in This Edition

Instructors familiar with the previous edition will find these new features:

- **Chapter objectives** provide clear goals for instruction;
- **Two new vocabulary sections**, Noticing Vocabulary and Applying Vocabulary, explain vocabulary from the writing models and support its use in the Writing Assignment;
- **Selected writing models** have been updated or replaced, while old favorites have been retained and improved;
- **Try It Out!** activities challenge students to be creative and apply the skills they have studied;
- **Writing Tips** contain strategies that experienced writers use;
- **Self-Assessments** ask students to evaluate their own progress;
- **Timed Writing** practice develops students' writing fluency.

The Online Teacher's Manual

The Teacher's Manual is available at **www.pearsonELT.com/tmkeys**. It includes general teaching notes, chapter teaching notes, answer keys, reproducible writing assignment scoring rubrics, and reproducible chapter quizzes.

Acknowledgments

We sincerely appreciate the contributions of the many people who have helped shape the fifth edition of this book. First and foremost, we would like to acknowledge Lara Ravitch, for her tireless dedication to this book and the many new models, practices, activities, and assignments that she contributed.

We are also grateful to the members of the Pearson ELT team for the expertise and dedication they brought to this project, particularly Amy McCormick, Lise Minovitz, and Eleanor Kirby Barnes. I would also like to thank Barbara Weisberg and Meg Brooks for their time, support, and guidance in developing this book.

To the many reviewers who contributed to our planning for this edition and those whose thoughtful comments and suggestions on the previous editions also helped to shape this book, we extend our heartfelt thanks: **Mark Alves**, Montgomery College, Maryland; **Angelina Arellanes-Nuñez**, University of Texas at El Paso; **Dorrie Brass**, Annapolis, Maryland; **Robyn Brinks-Lockwood**, Stanford University, California; **Tony J. C. Carnerie**, University of California San Diego, California; **Marsha Gerechter Abramovich**, Tidewater Community College, Virginia Beach, Virginia; **Patty Heises**, University of Washington, Seattle, Washington; **Alex Jones**, Seattle, Washington; **Ruth Moore**, University of Colorado at Boulder, Colorado; **David Ross**, Intensive English Program, Houston, Texas; **Diana Savas**, Pasadena City College, Pasadena, California; **Jacqueline Smith**, Brooklyn, New York; **Barbara Smith-Palinkas**, Tampa, Florida; **Anita Sokmen**, Director, English Language Programs Extension Courses & Marketing, University of Washington, Seattle, Washington.

We would also like to thank the following people for their feedback on our online survey: **Eric Ball**, Langara College, British Columbia, Canada; **Mongi Baratli**, Al Hosn University, Abu Dhabi, United Arab Emirates; **Jenny Blake**, Culture Works ESL, London, Canada; **Karen Blinder**, English Language Institute, University of Maryland, Maryland; **Bob Campbell**, Academic Bridge Program, Doha, Qatar; **Nancy Epperson**, Truman College, Illinois; **Kemal Erkol**, Onsekiz Mart University, Çanakkale, Turkey; **Russell Frank**, Pasadena City College, California; **Jeanne Gross**, Cañada College, California; **Lisa Kovacs-Morgan**, English Language Institute, University of California at San Diego, California; **Mary Ann T. Manatlao**, Qatar Foundation, Academic Bridge Program, Doha, Qatar; **Brett Reynolds**, Humber Institute of Technology and Advanced Learning, Ontario, Canada; **Lorraine C. Smith**, CUNY Queens College, New York.

Alice Oshima
Ann Hogue

CHAPTER OVERVIEW

Longman Academic Writing Series, Level 4, Essays offers a carefully structured approach to high-intermediate academic writing. It features instruction on paragraph and essay organization, sentence structure, grammar, and the writing process.

Four-color design makes the lessons even more engaging.

CHAPTER 8

ARGUMENTATIVE ESSAYS

OBJECTIVES

To write academic texts, you need to master certain skills.

In this chapter, you will learn to:

- Analyze an argumentative essay
- Construct an introduction for an argumentative essay
- Use transitions of contrast
- Identify and rebut opposing arguments
- Support your ideas using statistics
- Write, revise, and edit an argumentative essay about space travel

Changes in technology have had a dramatic effect on many different areas of life, including the workplace.

152

Realistic writing models present the type of writing students will learn to produce in the end-of-chapter Writing Assignments.

INTRODUCTION

An **argumentative essay** is an essay in which you agree or disagree on an issue, using reasons to support your opinion. Your goal is to convince your reader that your opinion is right. Argumentation is a popular kind of essay question because it forces students to think on their own: They have to take a stand on an issue, support their stand with solid reasons, and support their reasons with solid evidence. At the end of this chapter, you will write an argumentative essay about whether it is wise or practical to attempt to send a human mission to Mars.

ANALYZING THE MODEL

The writing model is about the role of technology in the modern workplace.

Read the model. Then answer the questions.

✎ Writing Model

═══ REPLACED BY A ROBOT ═══

1   Ever since the invention of computers, technology has done more and more of the job of the average worker. From mathematical calculations to mailing lists, computers have become more efficient, in more areas, than their human colleagues. Although some argue that computers will never replace people, others are concerned about the advanced robotic technology that computers make possible. Indeed, it is likely that the use of more and better robots will someday result in fewer jobs for humans. However, this should not be seen as a problem. Rather, as technology improves, employers in all fields should look to maximize their robotic workforce and minimize human error.

2   Until now, many have argued that robots can only replace humans in certain less-skilled jobs. They might, for example, be able to perform routine tasks on an assembly line. These opponents of a mechanized workforce may not be aware that technology has progressed in the areas of decision-making and creativity. Some robots' work in these areas is almost equal to that of humans. In fact, some interactive computers are so well-designed that it will soon be possible to talk with them almost endlessly before realizing that they are not human (Loftus). A computer even won the game show *Jeopardy* not long ago. These computers are clearly capable of more than simple tasks.

3   Others argue that, even though computers may someday be able to approximate human behavior, humans will always be able to do the job better. While that may be true for a general-purpose robot, highly-specialized machines can often do specific tasks better than a

(continued on next page)

Chapter objectives provide clear goals for instruction.

Noticing Vocabulary points out useful words and phrases from the writing models.

Writing Tips provide useful strategies to help students produce better writing.

Applying Vocabulary allows students to practice the new vocabulary and then use it in their writing assignments.

✏ **Noticing Vocabulary: Word Families**

Good writers use a wide range of vocabulary. You can quickly improve your vocabulary by studying **word families**. Word families are groups of words that are related. Words in a word family often have similar meanings but are different parts of speech. For example, notice the word *successful* in the model. The words *success, succeed, successful,* and *successfully* belong to the same word family.

PRACTICE 1 Identifying Words in Word Families

Ⓐ Look at the writing model again. Find and underline the words in the chart. Then complete the chart. Use a dictionary as needed.

VERB	ADJECTIVE	ADVERB
----------	aggressive	*aggressively*
agree		
create		
----------	disrespectful	
dominate		
influence		
----------	passive	
submit		
----------	unproductive	
use		

Ⓑ Notice the word endings in the chart in Part A. List the ending(s) for each part of speech.

Verbs: *-ate*_____

Adjectives: _____

Adverbs: _____

4 CHAPTER 1

✏ **Applying Vocabulary: Using Word Families**

You have learned that recognizing words in word families can help you build your vocabulary. You also identified several patterns for word endings. This information can help you use the correct form of a word in your writing.

PRACTICE 10 Reviewing Words in Word Families

Before you begin your writing assignment, review the word families chart on page 4. Then fill in the blank in each sentence with the word from the chart that best fits. Think about the meaning and part of speech.

1. My neighbor's dog is very _____. He bites everyone who comes near him.

2. The team took a(n) _____ approach to the negotiations, agreeing to everything the other side proposed, and making no demands.

3. Some people try to _____ the conversation; they never let anyone else speak.

4. Employees who behave _____ in salary negotiations do not point out how they can contribute to the company, do not clearly state their financial expectations, and, as a result, are not likely to receive a competitive wage.

5. In American culture, it is not appropriate to try to _____ a teacher's decision about your grade by giving him or her presents or compliments.

Writing Tip

If there's a word you want to use in your writing, but it's the wrong part of speech, check your dictionary. You may be able to find a word from the same word family that fits your sentence.

THE WRITING PROCESS

Writing is a process, and like any process, it consists of a series of steps. While the exact number of steps in the process may vary, this book will take you through six of them. You will be following these steps as you do the writing assignments in each chapter, so it is important that you have an idea of how each step in the process works.

Step 1: Prewrite to get ideas.

The first step in the writing process is to choose a topic and generate ideas. This is called **prewriting** because you do it before you begin writing. Even if a topic has already been assigned, you will still need to generate ideas about it in order to decide what you want to write.

There are many different methods you can use to come up with ideas to get started. You will have an opportunity to practice different techniques in your chapter assignments.

Paragraph Structure **17**

Organization sections explore essay structure in a variety of organizational patterns.

CHAIN ORGANIZATION

The other organizational pattern you can use to write about causes and effects is chain organization. Writing Model 2 on page 119 uses this organizational style.

In Writing Model 2, causes and effects are linked to each other in a continuous chain. One event (a change in seasons), causes another event (decreased sunlight), which causes a third event (disturbance in both hormonal balance and the body's natural clock), which in turn causes a fourth event (the development of depressive symptoms), and so on. Each new cause and its effect are links in a chain, with the effect of one event becoming the cause of the next event. Depending on the complexity of the ideas in each link, you can devote an entire paragraph to one link, or you may include several links in one paragraph, or you may describe the entire chain in one paragraph. Chain organization usually works better than block organization when the causes and effects are too closely linked to be separated. Notice the chain pattern in this diagram.

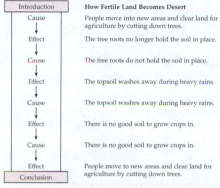

How Fertile Land Becomes Desert

Introduction	
Cause	People move into new areas and clear land for agriculture by cutting down trees.
Effect	The tree roots no longer hold the soil in place.
Cause	The tree roots do not hold the soil in place.
Effect	The topsoil washes away during heavy rains.
Cause	The topsoil washes away during heavy rains.
Effect	There is no good soil to grow crops in.
Cause	There is no good soil to grow crops in.
Effect	People move to new areas and clear land for agriculture by cutting down trees.
Conclusion	

Writing Tip

The type of organization you choose depends on your topic.

- A chain pattern is usually easier if the causes and effects are very closely interrelated, as in an explanation of a natural phenomenon such as a thunderstorm.
- The block pattern is usually easier with larger, complex topics such as global warming or homelessness.
- Sometimes you will want to use a combination of block and chain organization. Writing Model 1 on pages 117–119 uses mostly block organization, but in paragraphs 4, 5, and 6, you will find chain organization.

Cause / Effect Essays **123**

Practice activities reinforce learning and lay the groundwork for the end-of-chapter Writing Assignment.

PRACTICE 3 Analyzing Chain Organization

Fill in the boxes to complete the flowchart, which illustrates the cause / effect chain described in Writing Model 2.

Less sunlight

Body produces
more _____ and   +   _____
less _____

Lack of energy, oversleeping, weight gain, anxiety

TRY IT OUT! Choose one of the topics and, on a separate sheet of paper, write two outlines: one for block organization and one for chain organization.

TOPICS
- The psychological causes of Internet addiction
- The effect of job loss on mental health
- The psychological effects of violent video games and movies

TRANSITION SIGNALS FOR CAUSE / EFFECT RELATIONSHIPS

Just as certain transition signals show time order and logical division, certain words and phrases signal cause / effect relationships. You may already know many of them. This chart and the one on page 126 will help you review them.

CAUSE SIGNAL WORDS	
Coordinators	**Examples**
for	Bison were indispensable to the Native American tribes, for this one animal provided them with nearly everything they needed for survival: meat, clothing, shelter, tools, and weapons. (*Note:* When used in this way, *for* has the same meaning as *because*.)
	However, you must use a comma in front of *for*, and you must not use a comma in front of *because*.
Subordinators	**Examples**
because since as	Bison were indispensable to the Native American tribes as this one animal provided them with nearly everything they needed for survival: meat, clothing, shelter, tools, and weapons.

124 CHAPTER 6

NEW!

Try It Out! activities challenge students to apply what they have learned.

Transition Signals sections provide tools for improving the flow of ideas in different types of essays.

Chapter 3 provides instruction on **using and citing outside sources** and **avoiding plagiarism**.

CORRECT CITATIONS

The purpose of a citation is not only to avoid plagiarism, but also to refer your readers to the source of your information. That way, they can read the original source if they want to learn more about the topic. It is important to be accurate in your citations.

There are a number of different ways of citing information. In general, you will want to follow whatever guidelines your instructor gives you to complete an assignment. However, for most of your academic work, you will find this two-stage process useful and sufficient for citing your sources:

1. Insert a short reference in parentheses at the end of each piece of borrowed information. This short reference is called an *in-text citation*.

2. Prepare a list describing all your sources completely. This list is titled "Works Cited" and appears as the last page of your paper.

In-Text Citations

Here are three examples of in-text citations and of their corresponding entries in a works-cited list. In the first example, notice the position and punctuation of the citation—at the end of the last sentence of the borrowed information, before the final period.

According to the National Geographic "Enduring Voices" project, a language dies every two weeks ("Disappearing Languages").

The phrase "Disappearing Languages" in quotation marks and parentheses at the end of this sentence is the first element of the title of an article from which the preceding information was taken. There was no author. If there had been an author, the author's last name—rather than part of a title—would have appeared inside the parentheses, with no quotation marks. Because the article was found on the Internet, it did not have a page number.

Here is an example of an in-text citation for an article with an author and page number:

(Bryson 17)

If you include a quotation in your writing that you found in someone else's work, indicate the source of that quotation. Your in-text citation will say *qtd. in*, which is an abbreviation for *quoted in*:

(qtd. in Bryson 17)

The same chapter teaches other essential tools for research-based writing, such as **paraphrasing**, **quoting**, and **summarizing**.

WRITING A SUCCESSFUL PARAPHRASE

To paraphrase correctly, you first need to make sure that you fully understand the original passage. Use this method to write a good paraphrase.

- Read the original passage several times until you understand it fully. Underline the key words. Look up unfamiliar words and find synonyms for them. It is not always possible to find synonyms for every word, especially technical vocabulary. In this case, use the original word.
- Take notes while you read. Write down only a few words for each idea—not complete sentences. Here are one writer's notes on the original passage about universal language:

language—people use to communicate—but so many— difficult to understand one another—people wish— universal international language—reasons: cultural, economic bonds, better feelings between countries

- Make a brief outline:

A. Language—people use to communicate
   1. So many languages make it difficult to understand one another.
   2. People wish for one universal international language.
B. Reasons
   1. Cultural, economic bonds
   2. Better feelings between countries

- Write your paraphrase from your notes. Don't look at the original while you are writing.
- Check your paraphrase against the original to make sure you have not copied vocabulary or sentence structure too closely. Above all, make sure that you have not changed the meaning of the original or given any wrong information.
- Add in-text citations. Also add a works-cited list if appropriate.

Step-by-step Writing Assignments make the writing process clear and easy to follow.

WRITING ASSIGNMENT

Your assignment for this chapter is to write an essay of five or more paragraphs on a topic related to education. Choose one of the topics from the list to write about. Use the writing model on pages 75–76 to help you. To complete the assignment, follow the steps in the writing process.

TOPICS

- Criteria to consider when choosing a major
- Qualities of a successful student
- Factors that make a class productive and enjoyable

Prewrite — **STEP 1: Prewrite to get ideas.**

- After selecting your topic, use a prewriting strategy such as listing (Chapter 1) or clustering (Chapter 2) to generate ideas.
- Look for related points in your list or cluster diagram. If you find anything that is completely off topic or repeated, cross it out.
- Group similar ideas together. These groups will become your body paragraphs.

Organize — **STEP 2: Organize your ideas.**

- Decide how you want to organize your essay. Do you want to use a comparison / contrast pattern? A logical division of ideas?
- Write a thesis statement for your essay. Be sure it indicates the organization pattern you plan to use.
- Use ideas from your prewrite to make an outline as you did in Practice 10. Put your thesis statement at the top. Then, next to letters A, B, and C, write sentences that will form the topic sentences of your body paragraphs.
- In the spaces under A, B, and C, add details you will use in your body paragraphs.

Write — **STEP 3: Write the first draft.**

- Use your outline to write your first draft. Remember to include the three parts of the essay that you studied in this chapter: an introductory paragraph (including the thesis statement), body paragraphs, and a conclusion.
- Don't worry if you think of new ideas as you write. You can add or delete ideas later. Just be sure that your new ideas support your thesis.

Revise — **STEP 4: Revise the draft.**

- Review the content and organization of your draft. Do not try to correct errors in format, mechanics (capitalization, punctuation, and spelling), grammar, and sentence structure at this stage. You will do this in Step 5.

98   CHAPTER 4

Peer Review and **Writer's Self-Check Worksheets** at the back of the book help students collaborate and sharpen their revision skills.

- Begin by reading over your essay to get a general overview. As you read, make sure that
  - your essay has a thesis statement;
  - the thesis is developed with enough supporting information;
  - you support your opinions with facts and examples;
  - your conclusion supports your thesis statement.
- Make notes in the margin about anything you want to improve.
- Ask a classmate to read and give you feedback on your first draft using the Chapter 4 Peer Review on page 327.
- Discuss your classmate's suggestions and decide which ones to take.

Proofread — **STEP 5: Edit and proofread the draft.**

- Make sure that you have identified all of the changes you want to make in content and organization. Then review your essay for errors in format, mechanics, grammar, and sentence structure. Use the Chapter 4 Writer's Self-Check on page 328 to help you.
- When you find an error, make a note on your paper using the correction symbols from Appendix D on pages 309–311.

Write — **STEP 6: Write a new draft.**

- In your new draft, include the changes you identified in Steps 4 and 5.
- Proofread your new draft again carefully. Make sure it is neat and error free.
- Hand in your essay to your teacher.

 NEW!

Self-Assessment encourages students to evaluate their progress.

SELF-ASSESSMENT

In this chapter, you learned to:

- ○ Identify the parts of an essay
- ○ Analyze an essay's introduction and conclusion
- ○ Construct an appropriate thesis statement
- ○ Support the thesis statement with body paragraphs
- ○ Organize an essay, using transition signals as necessary
- ○ Write, revise, and edit an essay about education

Which ones can you do well? Mark them ✓

Which ones do you need to practice more? Mark them ✗

EXPANSION

🕐 **TIMED WRITING** ◀

In this expansion, you will write an essay in class. As you write, focus on using the techniques for logical division essays that you learned in this chapter. You will have 50 minutes. To complete the expansion in time, you will need to budget your time accordingly. Follow this procedure.

1. Read the writing prompt (or the prompt your teacher assigns) carefully. Choose one topic to write about. Make sure you understand the question or task. You may want to underline the key words in the prompt. (5 minutes)

2. Brainstorm to get ideas, write a thesis statement, and make a rough outline to organize your ideas. (10 minutes)

3. Write your essay. Be sure to include an introductory paragraph with your thesis statement, body paragraphs, and a concluding paragraph. (25 minutes)

4. Check your essay for errors. Correct any mistakes. (10 minutes)

5. Give your paper to your teacher.

Prompt: Write a logical division essay about one of these topics:
- Different kinds of teachers
- Benefits of learning a new language
- Three educational experiences that inspired you

● **USING QUOTES AND PARAPHRASES TO SUPPORT IDEAS** ◀

Write an essay about the challenges of education in a new culture. Use information given by students who have had this experience and experts in the field of international education. Quote, summarize, and paraphrase your outside sources as appropriate.

- If possible, interview individuals about the topic of your essay. Write down their answers. Then look at their answers to see which will help to explain and expand the ideas you are discussing in your essay.
- Use the Internet to find information about your topic. Find two or three websites with detailed information or expert opinions that you think will make your ideas clearer to the reader.

Remember to include in-text citations and a works-cited list to inform your readers about your sources. In doing so, you not only show your readers that you can speak authoritatively on the topic, but you also give them a chance to do further reading themselves.

100 CHAPTER 4

NEW!

Timed Writing activities help prepare students to write well on tests.

NEW!

Additional writing tasks encourage students to further develop the writing skills in each chapter.

PART III SENTENCE STRUCTURE

169

NEW!

Separate chapters on **Sentence Structure** provide practice with the most challenging structures for high-intermediate students. The chapters can be taught in any order.

Questions about the Model

1. When do people with a fear of public speaking become paralyzed? Underline the adverb clause in sentence 3 that provides this information. What word introduces this clause?

2. Why do individuals with this fear sometimes take classes? Double underline the adverb clauses in sentences 7 and 8 that provide this information. What words introduce each clause?

3. Where do these individuals see unfriendly faces? Triple underline the clause in sentence 4 that provides this information. What word introduces this clause?

4. What contrast is established by the adverb clause in sentence 9? What words introduce this clause?

KINDS OF ADVERB CLAUSES

These are the various kinds of adverb clauses. In the pages that follow, you will study and practice each kind.

- **Time clauses** answer the question "When?"
- **Place clauses** answer the question "Where?"
- **Clauses of manner** answer the question "How?"
- **Distance clauses** answer the question "How far?"
- **Frequency clauses** answer the question "How often?"
- **Purpose clauses** answer the question "For what intention?"
- **Result clauses** answer the question "For what effect?"
- **Conditional clauses** answer the question "Under what circumstance?"
- **Contrast clauses of direct opposition** show how one thing differs from another.
- **Contrast clauses of concession** show an unexpected result.

Punctuation of Adverb Clauses

The punctuation of an adverb clause depends on the order of the clauses. When an adverb clause comes first in a sentence, put a comma after it. When an adverb clause follows an independent clause, do not separate the clauses with a comma.

ADVERB CLAUSE
Because humans are curious animals,

INDEPENDENT CLAUSE
they constantly explore their world.

INDEPENDENT CLAUSE
Humans constantly explore their world

ADVERB CLAUSE
because they are curious animals.

Adverb Clauses **223**

EDITING PRACTICE

Find and correct eleven more errors in adjective clauses in this essay. Look for these kinds of errors:

INCORRECT RELATIVE PRONOUN — I telephoned the student who his wallet I found in the parking lot. *whose*

DISAGREEMENT OF VERB AND ANTECEDENT — People who lives in earthquake zones need earthquake insurance. *live*

INCORRECT REPETITION OF NOUNS OR PRONOUNS — My friend whom I loaned my car to him returned it with several dents.

INCORRECT COMMA USAGE — Cell phones, which always seem to ring at inappropriate times, should be turned off during concerts, lectures, and naps.

El Niño

1 Scientists have been studying an ocean event who is the cause of drastic changes in weather around the world. 2 This event is an increase in the temperature of the Pacific Ocean that occur *occurs* around Christmas off the coast of Peru. 3 Hence, the Peruvian fishermen whom first noticed it named it El Niño, a name that means "the Christ child" in Spanish. 4 The causes of this rise in ocean temperatures are unknown, but its effects are obvious and devastating.

5 For example, El Niño threatens Peru's anchovy harvest, which could mean higher prices for food. 6 The warm water of El Niño keeps the nutrient-rich cold water which provides anchovies with food down at the bottom of the ocean. 7 Anchovies are the primary source of fish meal which is the main ingredient in animal feed.

8 In addition, guano[1] from birds who feed off the anchovies is a major source of fertilizer. 9 As a result of decreasing supplies of anchovies and guano, the prices of animal feed, and fertilizer rise. 10 This causes farmers, who they must pay more for feed and fertilizer, to charge more for the food they produces. 11 Food prices have soared as a result of El Niños in past years.

12 El Niño has other global effects. 13 It can cause heavy rains, floods, and mudslides along the coasts of North and South America and droughts in other parts of the world. 14 In the 1982–1983 El Niño, West Africa suffered a terrible drought which caused crop failures and food shortages. 15 Lack of rain also created problems for Indonesia whose forests burned for months during the 1997–1998 El Niño. 16 Indeed, El Niño is an unpredictable and uncontrollable phenomenon of nature, that we need to study it in order to prepare for and perhaps lessen its devastating effects in the future.

---

[1] **guano:** droppings from birds and bats

262 CHAPTER 13

WRITING A PARAGRAPH

PARAGRAPH STRUCTURE

OBJECTIVES

To write academic texts, you need to master certain skills.

In this chapter, you will learn to:

- Identify the parts of a paragraph
- Construct an appropriate topic sentence
- Support the topic sentence with details and examples
- Distinguish facts from opinions
- Use a concluding sentence to complete a paragraph
- Write, revise, and edit a paragraph about communication

It is important to pay attention to your communication style if you want to be successful.

INTRODUCTION

In this chapter, you will focus on the structure of a good paragraph. A **paragraph** is a group of related sentences that discusses one (and usually only one) main idea. A paragraph can be as short as one sentence or as long as ten sentences or more. The number of sentences is unimportant; however, the paragraph should be long enough to develop the main idea clearly. At the end of this chapter, you will write a well-structured paragraph on the topic of communication. For an example of a well-structured paragraph, look at the model.

ANALYZING THE MODEL

The writing model discusses communication styles.

Read the model. Then answer the questions.

Writing Model

Communication Styles That Don't Communicate

1 Studies show that certain styles of interpersonal communication are less effective than others. **2** Which styles are the ones to avoid? **3** These same studies indicate that the two least effective styles are aggressive and passive communication. **4** On the one hand, an aggressive style involves speaking in a disrespectful manner, expressing anger, or trying to dominate the conversation. **5** For example, a business executive might tell her coworker that his ideas for a new product are terrible. **6** Then she might interrupt him when he tries to explain his ideas. **7** This approach hinders successful communication. **8** It also creates barriers between people. **9** A passive communication style, on the other hand, can be equally unproductive. **10** A passive style might lead a person to hide his or her beliefs, speak quietly, and submit to all demands. **11** Someone working on a fashion design project, for instance, might agree to use a fabric that he thinks is unattractive. **12** He would not express his true feelings to the group. **13** In short, ineffective communicators can fail to influence others either by being too forceful or by hiding their opinions.

Questions about the Model

1. What is the main idea of the paragraph?

2. In which sentence does the writer state the main idea?

3. How does sentence 3 support the main idea?

4. What points does the writer make about an aggressive style?

5. In which sentence does the writer introduce an example of an aggressive style?

6. What points does the writer make about a passive style?

7. In which sentence does the writer introduce an example of a passive style?

✎ Noticing Vocabulary: Word Families

Good writers use a wide range of vocabulary. You can quickly improve your vocabulary by studying **word families**. Word families are groups of words that are related. Words in a word family often have similar meanings but are different parts of speech. For example, notice the word *successful* in the model. The words *success*, *succeed*, *successful*, and *successfully* belong to the same word family.

| PRACTICE 1 | **Identifying Words in Word Families** |

A Look at the writing model again. Find and underline the words in the chart. Then complete the chart. Use a dictionary as needed.

VERB	ADJECTIVE	ADVERB
----------	aggressive	aggressively
agree		
create		
----------	disrespectful	
dominate		
influence		
----------	passive	
submit		
----------	unproductive	
use		

B Notice the word endings in the chart in Part A. List the ending(s) for each part of speech.

Verbs: ___-ate_____

Adjectives: _____

Adverbs: _____

PARTS OF A PARAGRAPH

Paragraphs generally include three parts. All paragraphs have a **topic sentence** and **supporting sentences**. Most paragraphs also have a **concluding sentence**.

THE TOPIC SENTENCE

Every good paragraph has a topic sentence. A topic sentence is the most important sentence in a paragraph.

The topic sentence briefly indicates what the paragraph is going to discuss. For this reason, the topic sentence is a helpful guide to both the writer and the reader. The writer can see what information to include (and what information to exclude). The reader can see what the paragraph is going to be about and is therefore better prepared to understand it. For example, in the writing model, the topic sentence alerts the reader to look for communication styles that are ineffective.

Here are three important points to remember about a topic sentence:

- A topic sentence is a **complete sentence**; that is, it contains at least one subject and one verb. These examples are not complete sentences because they do not contain a subject and a verb:

  INCOMPLETE Communicating with colleagues.

  INCOMPLETE How to improve online social networks.

- A topic sentence contains two parts: a **topic** and a **controlling idea**. It names the topic and then limits the topic to a specific area to be discussed in the space of a single paragraph.

  |——— TOPIC ———||——— CONTROLLING IDEA ———|
  Communication with colleagues requires sensitivity and understanding.

  |——— TOPIC ———||——— CONTROLLING IDEA ———|
  Improving online social networks can help professionals communicate.

- A topic sentence is the most general statement in the paragraph because it gives only the topic and the controlling idea. It does not give any specific details.

  This is a general statement that could serve as a topic sentence:

  The Arabic origin of many English words is not always obvious.

  This sentence is *too general*. It doesn't provide much guidance about what the paragraph will be about.

  English has been influenced by other languages.

  On the other hand, this sentence is *too specific*. It could serve as a supporting sentence but not as a topic sentence.

  The slang expression *so long* (meaning "good-bye") is probably a corruption of the Arabic *salaam*.

The Position of Topic Sentences

The topic sentence is usually (but not always) the first sentence in a paragraph. Experienced writers sometimes put topic sentences in other locations, but the best spot is usually right at the beginning. Readers who are used to the English way of writing want to know what they will read about as soon as they begin reading.

Synonyms, words with the same basic meaning, do not always have the same emotional meaning. For example, *stingy* and *frugal* both mean "careful with money." However, calling someone stingy is an insult, but calling someone frugal is usually a compliment. Similarly, a person wants to be slender but not skinny. Therefore, you should be careful in choosing words as many so-called synonyms are not completely synonymous.

At times, a topic sentence comes at the end of the paragraph. In this case, the paragraph might begin with a series of examples or facts. Then the topic sentence at the end would be the conclusion drawn from these examples or facts.

Mediation is now a popular way to solve disagreements between children in school. A mediator can also help a divorcing couple discuss finances or improve communication between employees and company executives. These are a few ways that mediators can help opposing parties come to agreement.

PRACTICE 2   **Choosing Topic Sentences**

Decide which sentence in each group is the best topic sentence and label it *best*. Then look at the other sentences in the group and label them *TG* (too general), *TS* (too specific), or *I* (incomplete).

GROUP 1

_TS___ a. A lunar eclipse is an omen of a coming disaster.

_TG___ b. Superstitions have been around forever.

_best__ c. People hold many superstitious beliefs about the moon.

_I____ d. Is made of green cheese.

GROUP 2

_____ a. The history of astronomy is interesting.

_____ b. Ice Age people recorded the appearance of new moons by making scratches in animal bones.

_____ c. For example, Stonehenge in Britain was built 3,500 years ago to track the movement of the sun.

_____ d. Ancient people recorded lunar and solar events in different ways.

GROUP 3

_____ a. It is hard to know which foods are safe to eat nowadays.

_____ b. In some large ocean fish, there are high levels of mercury.

_____ c. Undercooked chicken and hamburger may carry *E. coli* bacteria.

_____ d. Not to mention mad cow disease.

_____ e. Food safety is an important issue.

GROUP 4

_____ a. Hybrid automobiles more economical to operate than gasoline-powered cars.

_____ b. The new hybrid automobiles are very popular.

_____ c. Hybrid cars have good fuel economy because a computer under the hood decides to run the electric motor, the small gasoline engine, or the two together.

_____ d. The new hybrid automobiles are popular because of their fuel economy.

PRACTICE 3 **Recognizing Topic Sentences**

Read the sentences in each group and decide which is the topic sentence. Label it *TS* (topic sentence). (*Hint:* Remember that the topic sentence is the most general statement in a paragraph.)

PARAGRAPH 1

_____ a. A notes / memo function lets you make quick notes to yourself.

_____ b. Other capabilities include word processing, spreadsheets, and email.

_____ c. A voice recorder that uses a built-in microphone and speaker works like a tape recorder.

_____ d. Basic tools include an appointment calendar, an address book, to-do lists, and a calculator.

_____ e. MP3 playback lets you listen to digital music files, and a picture viewer lets you look at digital photos.

_____ f. Most smart phones have tools for basic tasks as well as for multimedia functions.

_____ g. A few models also include a built-in digital camera and keyboard.

PARAGRAPH 2

_____ a. Twelve years after *Sputnik*, the United States caught up by becoming the first nation to land a man on the moon.

_____ b. The Europeans have joined the competition, vowing to land European astronauts on the moon by 2025 and on Mars by 2035.

_____ c. The number of nations competing in the "space race" has grown since the early days of space exploration.

_____ d. China joined the competition in 2003 when it launched *Shenzhou 5*.

_____ e. Initially, the former Soviet Union took the lead when it sent the first man into Earth orbit in the spaceship *Sputnik* in 1957.

_____ f. For almost 50 years, the United States and Russia were the only competitors in the contest to explore space using manned spacecraft.

(continued on next page)

PARAGRAPH 3

_____ a. Another important change was that people had the freedom to live and work wherever they wanted.

_____ b. The earliest significant change was for farming families, who were no longer isolated.

_____ c. The final major change brought by the automobile was the building of superhighways, suburbs, huge shopping centers, and theme parks such as Disney World in Florida.

_____ d. The automobile revolutionized the way of life in the United States.

_____ e. The automobile enabled them to drive to towns and cities comfortably and conveniently.

_____ f. In fact, people could work in a busy metropolitan city and drive home to the quiet suburbs.

PARAGRAPH 4

_____ a. In time, this melted part rises as magma[1].

_____ b. The formation of a volcanic eruption is a dramatic series of events.

_____ c. As the plate[2] sinks, friction and Earth's heat cause part of it to melt.

_____ d. The magma produces heat, steam, and pressure.

_____ e. First of all, most volcanoes are formed where two plates collide[3].

_____ f. Then one of the plates is forced under the other and sinks.

_____ g. When the heat, steam, and pressure from the magma finally reach the surface of Earth, a volcanic eruption occurs.

The Two Parts of a Topic Sentence

As noted earlier, a topic sentence has two essential parts: the topic and the controlling idea. The topic names the subject of the paragraph. The controlling idea limits or controls the topic to a specific area that you can discuss in the space of a single paragraph.

The reader immediately knows that this paragraph will discuss how easy it is to prepare convenience foods and perhaps will give some examples (canned soup, frozen dinners, and so on).

┌─── TOPIC ───┐ ┌─ CONTROLLING IDEA ─┐
Convenience foods are easy to prepare.

The reader of this topic sentence expects to read about various ethnic foods popular in the United States: tacos, egg rolls, sushi, baklava, pizza, and so on.

┌─────── CONTROLLING IDEA ───────┐ ┌─ TOPIC ─┐
Immigrants have contributed many delicious foods to U.S. cuisine.

---

[1] **magma:** hot melted rock below the surface of the Earth

[2] **plate:** one of the very large sheets of rock that forms the surface of the Earth

[3] **collide:** (to) crash violently into someone or something

A topic sentence should not have controlling ideas that are unrelated. The three parts of the controlling idea in this topic sentence are too unrelated for a single paragraph. They require three separate paragraphs to explain fully.

TOO MANY IDEAS Advanced communication technologies have improved dramatically, and they have also enhanced business relationships and nurtured social interactions.

GOOD Advanced communication technologies have improved dramatically.

PRACTICE 4 **Identifying the Topic and Controlling Idea**

Read each sentence. Circle the topic and underline the controlling idea.

1. (Driving on freeways) requires skill and alertness.

2. Driving on freeways requires strong nerves.

3. Driving on freeways sometimes requires an aggressive attitude.

4. The Caribbean island of Trinidad attracts tourists because of its calypso music.

5. Spectacular beaches make Puerto Rico a tourist paradise.

6. Moving away from home can be a stressful experience for young people.

7. Owning an automobile is a necessity for me.

8. It is an expensive luxury to own an automobile in a large city.

9. A major problem for many students is the high cost of tuition and books.

10. Participating in class discussions can be a problem for some students.

PRACTICE 5 **Writing Topic Sentences**

A Write a topic sentence for each paragraph with a topic and a controlling idea.

PARAGRAPH 1

_____

_____ English speakers relaxing at home, for example, may put on *kimonos*, which is a Japanese word. English speakers who live in a warm climate may take an afternoon *siesta* on an outdoor *patio* without realizing that these are Spanish words. They may even relax on a *chaise* while snacking on *yogurt*, words of French and Turkish origin, respectively. At night, they may *shampoo* their hair and put on *pajamas*, words from the Hindi language of India.

(continued on next page)

PARAGRAPH 2

_____

_____ In many European universities, students are not required to attend classes. In fact, professors in some countries generally do not know the names of the students enrolled in their courses. In the United States, however, students are required to attend all classes and may be penalized if they do not. Furthermore, in the European system, students usually take just one comprehensive examination at the end of their entire four or five years of study. In the North American system, on the other hand, students usually have numerous quizzes, tests, and homework assignments, and they almost always have to take a final examination in each course at the end of each semester.

PARAGRAPH 3

_____

_____ For example, the Eskimos, living in a treeless region of snow and ice, sometimes build temporary homes out of thick blocks of ice. People who live in deserts, on the other hand, use the most available materials, mud or clay, which provide good insulation from the heat. In Northern Europe, Russia, and other areas of the world where forests are plentiful, people usually construct their homes out of wood. In the islands of the South Pacific, where there is an abundant supply of bamboo and palm, people use these tough, fibrous plants to build their homes.

B On a separate sheet of paper, write two or three topic sentences for each topic. Each topic sentence should have a different controlling idea.

TOPICS
- Cell phones
- Movies
- Text messaging
- Advertising
- Online social networks

Example

Topic: _cell phones_

Topic sentences: 1. _Using a cell phone while driving can be dangerous._

2. _There are cell phone manners that everyone should know._

3. _Cell phones have changed the way we communicate._

Communication today is instantly possible from almost anywhere.

TRY IT OUT! Work in a small group. Choose three topics that interest you. Be sure that they are different topics from the ones in Practice 5B. Write a topic sentence for each one. Be sure to include a controlling idea.

SUPPORTING SENTENCES

Supporting sentences explain or prove the topic sentence. One of the biggest problems in student writing is that student writers often fail to support their ideas adequately. You need to use specific details to be thorough and convincing.

There are several kinds of specific supporting details such as examples, facts and statistics, and quotations.

PRACTICE 6   **Identifying Supporting Details**

Work with a partner. Read two versions of the same paragraph. Then answer the questions.

Version 1: Paragraph without Support

Cell Phones and Driving

1 Many governments are responding aggressively to the threat that cell phones pose to safety on the road. 2 Cell phones cause accidents all the time. 3 Sometimes people are injured and have to go to the hospital. 4 People don't pay attention while they are talking on the phone, so they run into other cars. 5 A lot of governments are tired of dealing with the problem. 6 If you are caught with a cell phone while driving, you might have to pay a fine. 7 In conclusion, driving while on the phone is a bad idea.

(continued on next page)

Cell Phones and Driving

1 Many governments are responding aggressively to the threat that cell phones pose to safety on the road. **2** In 2009, almost 1,000 automobile deaths occurred in the United States alone because drivers were distracted by cellular phones (Snyder). **3** Cell phone use increases the chance of an accident resulting in hospitalization by a factor of four (Nikkel). **4** These problems can be blamed on the fact that using cell phones dramatically slows drivers' reaction times. **5** "If you put 20-year-old drivers behind the wheel with a cell phone, their reaction times are the same as 70-year-old drivers who are not using a cell phone," said University of Utah psychology professor David Strayer. **6** "It's like instantly aging a large number of drivers (Britt)." **7** Because studies show that the use of cell phones while driving is so dangerous, it has been banned in dozens of countries around the world. **8** For example, in Australia, Bahrain, the United Kingdom, and Brazil, drivers are now required to pay a fine if they are caught texting or talking on a mobile device. **9** Governments are hopeful that these laws will lead to safer communication practices and fewer fatal accidents.

Sources:
1. Britt, Robert Roy. "Drivers on Cell Phones Kill Thousands, Snarl Traffic."
2. Edgar Snyder & Associates. "Cell Phone Texting and Accident Statistics."
3. Nikkel, Cathy. "Notes from the Road."

Questions about the Paragraphs

1. What is the topic sentence of each paragraph? Circle the topic. Underline the controlling idea.

2. Which supporting sentences in Version 2 contain these details? Write the sentence numbers.

   An example: _____   A statistic: _____   A quotation: _____

3. How do the details in Version 2 improve the paragraph? Write your ideas on a separate sheet of paper.

Opinions vs. Facts

When supporting your ideas, it is important to distinguish between facts and opinions. **Opinions** are subjective statements based on a person's beliefs or attitudes as in these examples:

Women are better communicators than men.

Smoking is a bad habit.

English is an easy language to learn.

Opinions are not acceptable as support. It is certainly suitable to express opinions in academic writing. In fact, most professors want you to express your own ideas. However, you may not use an opinion as support, and if you express an opinion, you must support it with facts. **Facts** are objective statements of truths.

At sea level, water boils at 100 degrees Celsius.

Women live longer than men.

Cigarettes are addictive.

Sometimes even facts need proof. While all three statements above are facts, the last two need proof. Your readers may not believe that women live longer than men, or they may not agree that cigarettes are addictive. You have to use specific supporting details such as examples, statistics, and quotations to prove that these statements are true facts.

OPINION
Photographs of ultrathin fashion models send the wrong message to girls and young women.

FACT BUT NEEDS PROOF
Fashion models are extremely thin.

SPECIFIC SUPPORTING DETAIL
The average model weighs 23 percent less than the average woman of the same height.

Using Examples as Support

Examples are perhaps the easiest kind of supporting detail to use because you can often take examples from your own knowledge and experience. You don't always have to search the library or the Internet for supporting material. Furthermore, examples make your writing lively and interesting, and your reader is more likely to remember your point if you support it with a memorable example.

Words and phrases that introduce examples include *for example*, *for instance*, and *such as*. See Transition Signals on pages 31–34 in Chapter 2 for more information about introducing examples.

| PRACTICE 7 | **Using Specific Supporting Details** |

A Read each sentence and label it *O* (opinion), *F–NP* (fact that needs proof), or *SSD* (specific supporting detail).

F–NP **1.** People who steal identities do a lot of damage before their victims become aware of it. *(The writer could give an example of a person who was victimized before noticing it.)*

O **2.** Punishment for identity thieves is not severe enough. *(The writer could give an example of a typical punishment.)*

SSD **3.** As of 2010, credit card fraud accounted for 17 percent of reported identity theft.

_____ **4.** Identity theft is more serious than any other type of theft.

_____ **5.** Identity theft is increasing at a rapid pace.

(continued on next page)

_____ 6. In 2000, 31,000 cases of identity theft were reported to the Federal Trade Commission (FTC); in 2009, the number was 278,000.

_____ 7. Many people do not report identity theft to the police.

_____ 8. In 2009, 28 percent of identity theft victims did not notify the police, according to the FTC.

_____ 9. Identity theft happens to ordinary people, not just to the wealthy.

_____ 10. It is easy for a thief to use the U.S. Postal Service to steal identities.

_____ 11. For example, thieves steal credit card statements from mailboxes, and then send a change-of-address card to the postal service to have future statements sent to a different address.

_____ 12. Most victims of identity theft are young adults.

_____ 13. The FTC reports that there were more victims in the age group 20–29 than in any other group.

_____ 14. The police should do more to protect citizens from identity theft.

B Work with a partner or in a small group. Discuss what specific supporting details you might use to support the sentences you labeled *O* and *F–NP*.

THE CONCLUDING SENTENCE

A concluding sentence serves two purposes: It signals the end of the paragraph, and reminds the reader of the important ideas. It can do this either by summarizing the main points of the paragraph or by repeating the topic sentence in different words (paraphrasing).

A paragraph does not always need a concluding sentence. For example, not every paragraph in a multi-paragraph essay needs one. However, for single paragraphs, especially long ones, a concluding sentence is helpful to the reader because it is a reminder of the important points.

Never introduce a new idea in the concluding sentence. For example if this sentence were in a paragraph about different kinds of greeting cards, adding a comment about the cost of cards would add a new idea.

> In conclusion, we now have a greater variety of greeting cards to choose from, but they are also becoming very expensive.

You may want to begin your concluding sentence with one of the signals in this list. You may also end a paragraph without a formal signal.

END-OF-PARAGRAPH SIGNALS		
Followed by a Comma		**Not Followed by a Comma**
In brief,	Lastly,	The evidence suggests that . . .
In conclusion,	Therefore,	There can be no doubt that . . .
Indeed,	Thus,	These examples show that . . .
In short,	To sum up,	We can see that . . .
Finally,		

Read the paragraphs. Decide whether each concluding sentence summarizes the main points or repeats the topic sentence in different words. Then answer the questions.

Paragraph 1

Greeting Cards

Have you noticed how many different kinds of greeting cards you can buy these days? In the old days, the local drugstore had one rack displaying maybe five or six basic kinds of cards. You could walk into the store and choose an appropriate card in five minutes or less. Today, however, the display space for greeting cards is as big as a soccer field, and it may take an hour or two to hunt down the right card with exactly the right message. There are at least 30 categories of birthday cards alone: birthday cards for different ages, from different ages, for different relatives, from different relatives, for different genders, from different genders, from a couple, from the office, for dog owners, for cat owners, and so on. There are cards for getting a job, for retiring from a job, for acquiring a pet, for losing a pet, for becoming engaged, for breaking up. There are also greeting cards to send for no reason—"Thinking of you" or "Just because" cards. The newest type of card is the "encouragement card." An encouragement card offers comforting thoughts and helpful advice to someone who is sad or distressed in these troubled times. These examples clearly show that these days there is a greeting card for every possible life event and for a few nonevents as well.

Paragraph 2

A Hawaiian Legend

Native people create legends to explain unusual phenomena in their environment. A legend from the Hawaiian island of Kauai explains how the naupaka flower, a flower that grows on beaches there, got its unusual shape. The flower looks like half a small daisy—there are petals on one side only. The legend says that the marriage of two young lovers on the island was opposed by both sets of parents. The parents found the couple together on a beach one day, and to prevent them from being together, one of the families moved to the mountains, separating the young couple forever. As a result, the naupaka flower separated itself into two halves. One half moved to the mountains, and the other half stayed near the beach. This story is a good example of a legend invented by native people to interpret the world around them.

Questions about the Paragraphs

1. In which paragraph does the concluding sentence summarize the main points of the paragraph, which are not specifically stated in the topic sentence?

2. In which paragraph does the concluding sentence paraphrase (repeat in different words) the topic sentence?

3. What are the conclusion signals in each paragraph? Circle them.

Read the paragraphs and underline the topic sentences. Then add a good concluding sentence to each paragraph by paraphrasing the topic sentence or summarizing the main points. Remember to use an end-of-paragraph signal.

Paragraph 1

A person can be a good communicator by being a good listener. When speaking with someone, a good listener pays close attention to the speaker's words while looking at his or her face. A good listener also shows interest by smiling and nodding. Also, posture is important; it can affect communication for both the speaker and the listener. For instance, sitting slumped in a chair makes a person seem passive, while a relaxed posture with the body bent slightly forward shows interest in the speaker and the conversation. Remember, too, that good communicators do not interrupt while someone is speaking; although interruption is active participation, it can be impolite. _____

_____

_____

Paragraph 2

Modern communication technology is raising the stress level for corporate workers. They feel buried under the large number of messages they receive daily. In addition to telephone calls, office workers receive dozens of email, voice mail, and text messages daily. In fact, U.S. managers receive on average more than 200 email messages a day. Because they do not have enough time to respond to these messages during office hours, it is common for them to do so in the evenings or on weekends at home. _____

_____

_____

✎ Applying Vocabulary: Using Word Families

You have learned that recognizing words in word families can help you build your vocabulary. You also identified several patterns for word endings. This information can help you use the correct form of a word in your writing.

| PRACTICE 10 | Reviewing Words in Word Families |

Before you begin your writing assignment, review the word families chart on page 4. Then fill in the blank in each sentence with the word from the chart that best fits. Think about the meaning and part of speech.

1. My neighbor's dog is very _____. He bites everyone who comes near him.

2. The team took a(n) _____ approach to the negotiations, agreeing to everything the other side proposed, and making no demands.

3. Some people try to _____ the conversation; they never let anyone else speak.

4. Employees who behave _____ in salary negotiations do not point out how they can contribute to the company, do not clearly state their financial expectations, and, as a result, are not likely to receive a competitive wage.

5. In American culture, it is not appropriate to try to _____ a teacher's decision about your grade by giving him or her presents or compliments.

Writing Tip

If there's a word you want to use in your writing, but it's the wrong part of speech, check your dictionary. You may be able to find a word from the same word family that fits your sentence.

THE WRITING PROCESS

Writing is a process, and like any process, it consists of a series of steps. While the exact number of steps in the process may vary, this book will take you through six of them. You will be following these steps as you do the writing assignments in each chapter, so it is important that you have an idea of how each step in the process works.

Step 1: Prewrite to get ideas.

The first step in the writing process is to choose a topic and generate ideas. This is called **prewriting** because you do it before you begin writing. Even if a topic has already been assigned, you will still need to generate ideas about it in order to decide what you want to write.

There are many different methods you can use to come up with ideas to get started. You will have an opportunity to practice different techniques in your chapter assignments.

Step 2: Organize your ideas.

Once you have chosen your topic and generated your ideas, the next step is to decide which ideas to use and how you will organize them. You need to create a plan of the main ideas and the supporting information for each of your paragraphs. Your plan can be a rough list of ideas or a formal outline. Organizing your ideas will make writing a paragraph with a topic sentence and supporting points and details much easier.

Step 3: Write the first draft.

The next step is to follow your plan and write a first draft. As you write, it is important to focus on making your ideas clear. Don't worry about grammar, punctuation, or spelling. A first draft is not supposed to be perfect.

Step 4: Revise the draft.

Once you have written your first draft, you can focus on revising it. When you revise, you change what you have written to improve it by checking the content and organization. At this stage, it is helpful to have another person's perspective on your writing. This person, usually a classmate, is called a **peer reviewer**. A peer reviewer's job is to read, ask questions, and comment on what is good and what might be changed or made clearer. In Appendix F, pages 320–336, there are Peer Reviews for each chapter in this book that can be used for this purpose.

Step 5: Edit and proofread the draft.

In this step, you proofread your paragraph to check for possible mistakes in grammar, punctuation, spelling, and sentence structure. It helps to have a checklist. In Appendix F, pages 320–336, there are Writer's Self-Checks for each chapter to help you with this part of the step. After proofreading, edit your paper to correct your mistakes.

Step 6: Write a new draft.

The last step of the process is to write a new, final draft. Before you hand in your draft to your instructor, read it once more and don't be surprised if you decide to make changes. Remember, the writing process involves continuous writing, revising, and rewriting until you are satisfied with the final product.

WRITING ASSIGNMENT

Your writing assignment for this chapter is to write a paragraph of 10 to 15 sentences on the topic of communication. Use the writing model on page 3 to help you. Follow the steps in the writing process.

Prewrite

STEP 1: Prewrite to get ideas.

- One technique you can use for prewriting is called **listing**. Listing is a brainstorming technique in which you quickly make a list of any words or phrases that are related to your topic. To list ideas for this writing assignment, follow this procedure:
  - Write *Communication* at the top of your paper.
  - Make a list of everything that comes to your mind about this topic. Don't worry about spelling or grammar at this point. Try to stay on this topic; however, don't worry if you write something that is off topic.

COMMUNICATION	
many many different ways	letters—write grandma
what's best?	different purposes?
cell phones—photos	problems communicating?
texting—too much! addiction in society?	~~smart phones~~
talking—fun, face to face, friends	

This is the beginning of a list that one student brainstormed before writing her paragraph.

 Organize

STEP 2: Organize your ideas.

- Look for related points in the list you brainstormed in Step 1. If you find anything completely off topic, or repeated, cross it out.

- Rewrite your list and group similar ideas together. This will help to narrow your topic into something that you can put into a single paragraph.

- Choose one main idea to focus on and choose related points as support for your main idea.

 Write

STEP 3: Write the first draft.

- Using your list, begin writing your first draft. Remember to include the three parts of the paragraph that you studied in this chapter: a topic sentence, supporting sentences that contain examples or facts, and a concluding sentence.

- Don't worry if you think of new ideas that are not on your list as you write. You can add or delete ideas later. Just be sure that your new ideas support your topic.

Revise

STEP 4: Revise the draft.

- Review the content and organization of your draft. Do not try to correct errors in format, mechanics (capitalization, punctuation, and spelling), grammar, and sentence structure at this stage. You will do this in Step 5.
- Begin by reading over your paragraph to get a general overview. As you read, check to make sure that
  - your paragraph has a topic sentence;
  - the topic is developed with enough supporting information;
  - you support your opinions with facts;
  - your concluding sentence is on the topic.
- Make notes in the margin about anything you want to improve.
- Ask a classmate to read and give you feedback on your first draft using the Chapter 1 Peer Review on page 321.
- Discuss your classmate's suggestions and decide which ones to take.

Proofread

STEP 5: Edit and proofread the draft.

- Make sure that you have identified all of the changes you want to make in content and organization. Then review your paragraph for errors in format, mechanics, grammar, and sentence structure. Use the Chapter 1 Writer's Self-Check on page 322 to help you.
- When you find an error, make a note on your paper using the correction symbols from Appendix D on pages 309–311.

Write

STEP 6: Write a new draft.

- In your new draft, include the changes you identified in Steps 4 and 5.
- Proofread your new draft again carefully. Make sure it is neat and error free.
- Hand in your paragraph to your teacher.

SELF-ASSESSMENT

In this chapter, you learned to:

- ○ Identify the parts of a paragraph
- ○ Construct an appropriate topic sentence
- ○ Support the topic sentence with details and examples
- ○ Distinguish facts from opinions
- ○ Use a concluding sentence to complete a paragraph
- ○ Write, revise, and edit a paragraph about communication

Which ones can you do well? Mark them ✓

Which ones do you need to practice more? Mark them ⊗

TIMED WRITING

To succeed in academic writing, you often need to write quickly. For example, sometimes you have to write a paragraph in class or for a test and you only have 30 minutes.

In this expansion, you will write a paragraph in class. You will have 30 minutes. To complete the expansion in time you will need to budget your time accordingly. Follow this procedure.

1. Read the writing prompt (or the prompt your teacher assigns) carefully. Make sure you understand the question or task. You may want to underline the key words in the prompt. (2 minutes)

2. Brainstorm to get ideas. Then group related ideas from your list together to organize them. (5 minutes)

3. Write a topic sentence. (3 minutes)

4. Write your paragraph. Be sure to include support for your topic sentence and a conclusion. (15 minutes)

5. Check your paragraph for errors. Correct any mistakes. (5 minutes)

6. Give your paper to your teacher.

Prompt: Choose one of the topics in Practice 5B on page 10 and write a well-organized paragraph. Focus on writing a paragraph with detailed support for the topic sentence.

WRITING ON AN ASSIGNED TOPIC

Sometimes, your instructor will assign a specific topic. You will not be allowed to choose what you would like to write about. Instead, you will need to focus on the topic assigned. Read the prompt and write on the topic.

Prompt: Think about a positive or negative experience you had with someone talking on his or her cell phone in a public place. Perhaps you saw someone use a cell phone to help out a person in need. Or perhaps you overheard someone discussing a very private matter in a very loud voice. Write a well-organized paragraph discussing your experience with the cell phone user. Be sure to state what you learned from your experience.

CHAPTER 2

UNITY AND COHERENCE

OBJECTIVES

To write academic texts, you need to master certain skills.

In this chapter, you will learn to:

- Organize a unified paragraph around one central idea

- Construct a coherent paragraph by

  - Repeating key nouns

  - Using consistent pronouns

  - Using transition signals to link ideas

  - Arranging ideas in logical order

- Write, revise, and edit a paragraph about health and medicine

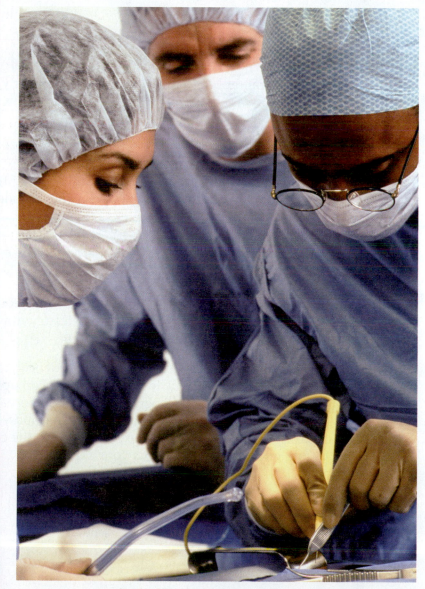

Medical advances have saved many lives.

In this chapter, you will learn about the importance of **unity** and **coherence** in constructing a good paragraph. When a paragraph is unified, it is focused exclusively on one main idea. When it is coherent, information flows logically, and readers can easily follow your ideas. Your final assignment will be to write a unified and coherent paragraph about a topic related to health and medicine.

ANALYZING THE MODEL

The writing model is a unified, coherent paragraph on the topic of public health.

Read the model. Then answer the questions.

✏ Writing Model

Public Health Successes

1 Although it is difficult to solve public health problems, great success has been achieved with certain illnesses. 2 For example, the eradication[1] of smallpox was one of the most significant accomplishments of the 20th century. 3 When the campaign against smallpox was launched in 1967, about 10 to 15 million people contracted the disease each year. 4 Of these, two million died. 5 More than 10 million individuals were disfigured. 6 However, a little more than a decade later, the smallpox program had met its goal; the last case of this terrible illness occurred in Somalia in 1977. 7 Following this important achievement, the World Health Organization tried to recreate its success. 8 The focus of the next campaign was polio, which can paralyze or kill its victims if it is untreated. 9 The elimination of this disease is not yet complete, but the number of cases has greatly decreased. 10 As the battles against smallpox and polio show, remarkable advances can be made in the field of public health.

Source: Paragraph adapted from Buckingham, Robert. *A Primer on International Health.*

[1] **eradication:** completely getting rid of or destroying something, such as a disease or a social problem

Questions about the Model

1. What is the topic sentence of this paragraph? Underline it.

2. What two examples develop and support the topic sentence?

3. Which sentence introduces the first example? Which sentence introduces the second example?

4. Are all the sentences related to the topic sentence?

5. What is the purpose of the concluding sentence?

✏ Noticing Vocabulary: Synonyms 1

Developing a rich and varied vocabulary can help you become a stronger writer. When you are writing about a complex topic, you want to be able to connect ideas and information in a way that will make sense to your reader. **Synonyms** can help you do this. Synonyms are words that mean the same or almost the same thing. You can use synonyms in your writing to discuss concepts, examples, and opinions without being repetitious.

If you want to use a synonym in your writing, but you cannot think of one, consult a print or online **thesaurus**. A thesaurus is a reference work that provides synonyms for many different words. Remember, however, that synonyms can sometimes have slightly different meanings from one another. When you choose a synonym to use in your writing, be sure that it means exactly what you want to say.

| PRACTICE 1 | Noticing Synonyms |

Ⓐ Find these words and their synonyms in the model. Write the synonyms.

1. eradication _____

2. significant _____

3. people _____

4. disease _____

Ⓑ These words are also in the model. Write a synonym for each word. Use a dictionary or thesaurus as needed.

1. difficult _____

2. problems _____

3. launched _____

4. recreate _____

UNITY

As mentioned earlier, a key element in a well-written paragraph is **unity**. A unified paragraph focuses on one main idea. For example, if you are writing an essay about the advantages of different kinds of pain medications, you might have a paragraph about the advantages of taking aspirin. In your paragraph, you should discuss only the advantages of aspirin. Do not discuss the disadvantages or begin to discuss other kinds of medicine. If you are writing an entire essay about the advantages of taking aspirin, then discuss only *one* advantage, such as heart health, in each paragraph. If you begin to discuss another advantage, start a new paragraph.

The second feature of unity is that every supporting sentence must directly explain or prove the main idea. For example, in a paragraph about the high cost of prescription drugs in the United States, you could mention buying generic brands as an alternative to brand-name drugs, but if you write several sentences about how generic drugs are made, you are getting off topic, and your paragraph will not have unity.

<table>
<tr><td>PRACTICE 2</td><td>**Staying on Topic**</td></tr>
</table>

PRACTICE 2 **Staying on Topic**

These paragraphs contain one or more sentences that are off topic. Underline the topic sentence. Cross out any sentences that are off topic.

Paragraph 1

The cloning of genes[1] has made many medical advances possible. Human growth hormone (HGH) is a good example. This hormone stimulates the growth of bones and muscles during childhood. Cloning the gene for HGH has provided an increase in the availability of the hormone. However, the availability of HGH and other products of biotechnology[2] raises an ethical question. The hormone is used widely to treat children with dwarfism, a condition that results in an adult height of 4'10" or shorter. There have been several interesting television shows recently about individuals with dwarfism. Many of these shows are very popular. Should HGH be available to anyone who wants taller children or only those who have children with dwarfism? Suppose parents want their average-size son to be taller so he will have a better chance of making his high school varsity team? Doctors do not have any evidence that exposure to HGH affects average-size children negatively, but many feel it is unethical to provide it to children with no serious medical need.

Paragraph 2

Advances in medicine can come from surprising places, including water. Many scientists are interested in the medical uses of small aquatic[3] animals. They believe these animals are useful for new medical products. Some ancient civilizations used berries and grasses for medical purposes. These plant-based medicines were often quite effective. In the future, important drugs may be made from aquatic organisms. In addition, these organisms may be used as models to understand human diseases. Many years from now, sea creatures may help people lead healthier and longer lives.

Source: Paragraphs 1 and 2 adapted from Thieman, William, and Michael Palladino, *Introduction to Biotechnology.*

---

[1] **genes:** a part of a cell in a living thing that controls what it looks like, how it grows, and how it develops. People get their genes from their parents.

[2] **biotechnology:** using living things for new purposes, such as making medicine

[3] **aquatic:** growing or living in or near water

This paragraph not only has sentences that are off topic but also discusses more than one topic. Decide where the paragraph should be divided into two. Underline each topic sentence. Then cross out any sentences that are off topic.

Polite or Not?

Even when you try to be polite, it is easy to do the wrong thing accidentally in a new culture. For example, in the United States, when someone offers you food or a beverage, accept it the first time it is offered if you want it. If you say, "No, thank you" because it is polite to decline the first one or two offers in your culture, you could become very hungry and thirsty. In the United States, a host thinks that "no" means "no" and will usually not offer again. Meals in the United States are usually more informal than meals in other countries, and the times of meals may be different. Although Americans are usually very direct in social matters, there are a few occasions when they are not. If an American says, "Please drop by sometime," he may or may not want you to visit him in his home. Your clue that this may not be a real invitation is the word "sometime." In some areas of the United States, people do not expect you to visit them unless you have an invitation for a specific day and time. In other areas of the United States, however, "dropping by" is a friendly, neighborly gesture. Idioms are often difficult for newcomers to understand.

COHERENCE

Although paragraph unity is important, it is not the only factor that you need to consider in writing a successful paragraph. In order for paragraphs to be well-structured, they must also be **coherent**. The word coherence comes from the Latin verb *cohere*, which means "to hold together." For coherence in writing, the sentences must hold together; that is, the movement from one sentence to the next must be logical and smooth. There must be no sudden jumps. Each sentence should flow smoothly into the next one.

Here are four ways to achieve coherence:

- Repeat key nouns.
- Use consistent pronouns.
- Use transition signals to link ideas.
- Arrange your ideas in logical order.

REPETITION OF KEY NOUNS

The easiest way to achieve coherence is to repeat key nouns. In this paragraph, the repetition of the noun *fear* smooths the flow of the sentences and creates coherence.

PARAGRAPH WITH COHERENCE

> ### The Health Consequences of Fear
>
> When worry escalates, the result is fear. Everyone has experienced fear. A swimmer of only moderate skill might be afraid of swift waters; a child might fear the dark. A hiker will probably feel fear when hearing the distinctive warning of a rattlesnake; a jogger might experience it when confronted with an angry dog. According to the author Norman Cousins, "Fear . . . create[s] negative expectations. One tends to move in the direction of one's expectations." Fear causes the heart to race, the head to spin, the palms to sweat, the knees to buckle, and breathing to become labored. Its physical effects are such that the human body can't withstand it indefinitely.

In this version of the paragraph, the word *fear* has been replaced by the pronoun *it* after the first use. This overuse of the pronoun makes the paragraph confusing and less coherent. The reader will forget what "it" stands for.

PARAGRAPH WITHOUT COHERENCE

> ### The Health Consequences of Fear
>
> When worry escalates, the result is fear. Everyone has experienced it. A swimmer of only moderate skill might be afraid of swift waters; a child might fear the dark. A hiker will probably feel it when hearing the distinctive warning of a rattlesnake; a jogger might experience it when confronted with an angry dog. According to the author Norman Cousins, "It . . . create[s] negative expectations. One tends to move in the direction of one's expectations." It causes the heart to race, the head to spin, the palms to sweat, the knees to buckle, and breathing to become labored. Its physical effects are such that the human body can't withstand it indefinitely.

There is no fixed rule about how often to repeat key nouns or when to use pronouns as a substitute. You should repeat a key noun instead of using a pronoun when the meaning is unclear.

Source: Paragraph based on Karren, Keith, Lee Smith, Brent Hafen, and Kathryn Frandsen. *Mind Body Health: The Effects of Attitudes, Emotions, and Relationships.*

A Find problems with the pronoun *it* in this paragraph. Replace *it* with the key noun *English* as necessary to make the paragraph more coherent.

English

    English has almost become an international language. Except for Chinese, more people speak it than any other language. Spanish is the official language of more countries in the world, but more countries have ~~it~~ *English* as their official or unofficial second language. More than 70 percent of the world's mail is written in it. It is the primary language on the Internet. In international business, it is used more than any other language, and it is the language of airline pilots and air traffic controllers all over the world. Moreover, although French used to be the language of diplomacy, it has displaced it throughout the world. Therefore, it is a useful language to know.

B Find problems with the subject pronouns. Replace them with key nouns as necessary to make the paragraph more coherent.

Dolphins

    Dolphins display almost human behavior at times. For example, they display the human emotions of joy and sadness. During training, when they do something correctly, they squeal excitedly and race toward their trainer. When they make a mistake, however, they droop[1] and mope[2] around their pool. Furthermore, they help each other when they are in trouble. If one is sick, it sends out a message, and others in the area swim to help it. They push it to the surface of the water so that it can breathe. They stay with it for days or weeks until it recovers or dies. They have also helped trapped or lost whales navigate their way safely out to the open sea. They are so intelligent, in fact, that the U.S. Navy is training them to become underwater bomb disposal experts.

---

[1] **droop:** sink down

[2] **mope:** act depressed

Key Noun Substitutes

Although repeating key words can make a paragraph more coherent, you don't want to repeat the same word too often. As you learned in Noticing Vocabulary: Synonyms on page 24, you can substitute synonyms or expressions with the same meaning if you do not wish to repeat a key word again and again. Pronouns, when used correctly, are also good substitutes for key nouns.

PRACTICE 5 **Identifying Key Noun Substitutes**

Read the paragraph. Then answer the questions.

A Mardi Gras Custom

1 "Throw me something, mister," is the customary plea for a Mardi Gras "throw." 2 In the final days of Mardi Gras—the season of parties, parades, and revelry[1] that precedes the Christian period of fasting and penance[2] called Lent—crowds of spectators line the streets of New Orleans. 3 They hope to catch a Mardi Gras souvenir tossed from parading floats. 4 Mardi Gras organizations called "krewes" build the floats and sponsor the parades, and, while cruising along parade routes, these costumed krewe members throw plastic trinkets to the crowds below. 5 The trinkets, which are called "Mardi Gras throws," consist of bead necklaces, coins, cups, toys, Frisbees, and figurines stamped with the krewe's symbol or the parade theme. 6 Mardi Gras throws are big business for the companies that supply them. 7 Krewe members spend an average of $800 on them, and some spend $2,000 or more. 8 By far the most treasured of the Mardi Gras mementos are gaudy bead necklaces. 9 Originally made of glass, they are now made of plastic.

Source: Roach, John. "The Rich History of Mardi Gras's Cheap Trinkets."

1. How many times does the writer use the expresssion *Mardi Gras throw* in

   the paragraph? _____

2. What three words does the writer use as substitutes for *Mardi Gras throw*?

   (*See sentences 3, 4, and 8.*) _____ _____

   _____

3. What does the pronoun *them* refer to in sentences 6 and 7? _____

4. What does the pronoun *they* refer to in sentence 9? _____

---

[1] **revelry:** celebration, festivities

[2] **penance:** punishment that you accept to say that you are sorry for doing a bad thing

CONSISTENT PRONOUNS

When you use pronouns, make sure that you use the same person and number throughout your paragraph. For example, don't change from *you* to *he* (change of person) or from *he* to *they* (change of number).

Notice the changes the writer makes for consistency.

> The root of a word is ~~their~~ *its* most basic part. A prefix is another word part. Prefixes can be added to the beginning of words to change ~~its~~ *their* meaning. Students who know a few Latin and Greek roots and prefixes have an advantage over ~~a student~~ *students* who ~~does not~~ *do not* know them. They can often guess the meaning of new words. If, for example, ~~you~~ *students* know that the prefix *omni* means "all," ~~you~~ *they* have a better chance of guessing the meanings of words such as *omnibus*, *omnipresent*, and *omnidirectional*. Furthermore, ~~a student~~ *students* who ~~knows~~ *know* that the root *sci-* comes from *scire*, "to know," can guess that *omniscient* means "all-knowing."

PRACTICE 6   **Using Consistent Pronouns**

Find errors with pronoun consistency. Make corrections.

Olympic Athletes

Olympic athletes must be strong both physically and mentally. First of all, if you hope to compete in an Olympic sport, you must be physically strong. Furthermore, those who want to compete in the Olympics must train for many years. For the most demanding sports, they train several hours a day, five or six days a week, for ten or more years. In addition to being physically strong, athletes must also be mentally tough. This means that you have to be totally dedicated to your sport, often giving up a normal school, family, and social life. Being mentally strong also means that he or she must be able to withstand the intense pressure of international competition with its accompanying media coverage. Finally, not everyone can win a medal, so Olympians must possess the inner strength to live with defeat.

TRANSITION SIGNALS

Another element of a smooth and coherent paragraph is the use of **transition signals**. Transition signals can be single words such as *first, finally,* and *however,* or phrases such as *in conclusion, on the other hand,* and *as a result.* There are different kinds of transition signals such as subordinators (*when, although*), coordinators (*and, but*), adjectives (*another, additional*), and prepositions (*because of, in spite of*).

Transition signals are like traffic signs; they tell your reader when to go forward, turn around, slow down, and stop. In other words, they tell your reader when you are presenting, for example, a similar idea (*similarly, and, in addition*), an opposite idea (*on the other hand, but, in contrast*), an example (*for example*), a result (*therefore, as a result*), or a conclusion (*in conclusion*).

Transition signals give a paragraph coherence because they guide your reader from one idea to the next.

| PRACTICE 7 | Using Transition Signals |

Compare these paragraphs. Circle the transition signals in paragraph 2. How do they make the paragraph more coherent?

PARAGRAPH 1

One difference among the world's seas and oceans is that the salinity[1] varies in different climate zones. The Baltic Sea in northern Europe is only one-fourth as salty as the Red Sea in the Middle East. There are reasons for this. In warm climates, water evaporates[2] rapidly. The concentration[3] of salt is greater. The surrounding land is dry and does not contribute much freshwater to dilute[4] the salty seawater. In cold climate zones, water evaporates slowly. The runoff created by melting snow adds a considerable amount of freshwater to dilute the saline seawater.

PARAGRAPH 2

One difference among the world's seas and oceans is that the salinity varies in different climate zones. For example, the Baltic Sea in northern Europe is only one-fourth as saline as the Red Sea in the Middle East. There are two reasons for this. First of all, in warm climate zones, water evaporates rapidly; therefore, the concentration of salt is greater. Second, the surrounding land is dry; consequently, it does not contribute much freshwater to dilute the salty seawater. In cold climate zones, on the other hand, water evaporates slowly. Furthermore, the runoff created by melting snow adds a considerable amount of freshwater to dilute the saline seawater.

---

[1] **salinity:** salt content

[2] **evaporates:** dries up

[3] **concentration:** percentage of

[4] **dilute:** reduce the concentration

Paragraph 2, in Practice 7, is more coherent because it contains transition signals. Each transition signal has a special meaning; each shows how a sentence relates to the one that precedes it.

- *For example* tells you that an example of the preceding idea is coming.
- *Two* tells you to look for two different reasons.
- *First of all* tells you that this is the first reason.
- *Second* and *furthermore* indicate that additional ideas are coming.
- *Therefore* and *consequently* indicate that the second statement is a result of the first statement.
- *On the other hand* tells you that an opposite idea is coming.

Some transition signals are listed in the chart on page 33. Most groups of transition signals have different rules for punctuation and their position in a sentence, so it's good to examine these rules by groups.

See Appendix B, Transition Signals, pages 296–298, for a more complete list.

Transition Phrases and Conjunctive Adverbs

Most of the transition phrases and conjunctive adverbs in the Transition Signals chart can appear at the beginning, in the middle, or at the end of an independent clause. They are usually set off by commas. You may remember that an independent clause is a group of words that contains a subject and a verb and expresses a complete thought.

For example, the Baltic Sea in northern Europe is only one-fourth as saline as the Red Sea in the Middle East.

The runoff created by melting snow**, furthermore,** adds a considerable amount of freshwater to dilute the saline seawater.

The Mediterranean Sea is more saline than the Red Sea**, however**.

EXCEPTIONS

- The words and phrases in the groups for listing ideas in order, introducing a conclusion or summary, and introducing a result usually appear only at the beginning of a sentence, not in the middle or at the end.
- *Too* usually appears only at the end of a sentence, sometimes preceded by a comma.
- The time words *then*, *now*, and *soon* usually do not need commas.

Meaning / Function	Transition Phrases	Conjunctive Adverbs	Coordinating Conjunctions	Subordinating Conjunctions	Other Signals
To introduce an **additional idea**	in addition	furthermore moreover besides also too	and		another (+ noun) an additional (+ noun)
To introduce an **opposite idea** or **contrast**	on the other hand in contrast	however nevertheless instead still nonetheless	but yet	although though even though whereas while	in spite of (+ noun) despite (+ noun)
To introduce a **choice** or **alternative**		otherwise	or	if unless	
To introduce a **restatement** or **explanation**	in fact indeed	that is			
To list in **order**	first, second, third next, last, finally				the first, second, third, etc. (+ noun) the next, last, final (+ noun)
To introduce an **example**	for example for instance				an example of (+ noun) such as (+ noun)
To introduce a **conclusion** or **summary**	clearly in brief in conclusion indeed in short in summary				
To introduce a **result**	accordingly as a result as a consequence	therefore consequently hence thus	so		

The words in the Transition Phrases and Conjunctive Adverbs columns of the chart can also connect two independent clauses. In this case, use a semicolon and a comma.

—————— INDEPENDENT CLAUSE ——————   —————— INDEPENDENT CLAUSE ——————
In warm climate zones, water evaporates rapidly**;** **therefore,** the concentration of salt is greater.

————————— INDEPENDENT CLAUSE —————————
Both the Red Sea and the Mediterranean have narrow outlets to the ocean**;**

————— INDEPENDENT CLAUSE —————
however, the Mediterranean's is narrower.

——————— INDEPENDENT CLAUSE ———————   ——————— INDEPENDENT CLAUSE ———————
A few societies in the world are matriarchal**;** **that is,** the mother is head of the family.

———————— INDEPENDENT CLAUSE ————————
Some English words have no exact equivalents in other languages**;** **for example,**

——————— INDEPENDENT CLAUSE ———————
there is no German word for the adjective *fair*, as in *fair play*.

See Appendix B, Conjunctive Adverbs, pages 294–295, for more examples.

Coordinators

This group of transition signals includes the seven coordinating conjunctions *and, but, so, or, nor, for,* and *yet* and the five correlative ("paired") conjunctions *both . . . and, not only . . . but also, neither . . . nor, either . . . or,* and *whether . . . or.* When coordinators connect two independent clauses, use a comma.

————— INDEPENDENT CLAUSE —————
In a matriarchy, the mother is the head of the family**,** **and**

————— INDEPENDENT CLAUSE —————
all the children belong to her extended family group.

———— INDEPENDENT CLAUSE ————   ———— INDEPENDENT CLAUSE ————
In warm climate zones, water evaporates rapidly**,** **so** the concentration of salt is greater.

—— INDEPENDENT CLAUSE ——   —— INDEPENDENT CLAUSE ——
Children **not only** need love**,** **but** they **also** need discipline.

When coordinators connect two words or phrases, do not use a comma.

Would you rather take a written **or** an oral exam?

Children need **not only** love **but also** discipline.

Exception

Some writers use a comma before *but* and *yet* even when they do not connect independent clauses to emphasize the contrast of the connected ideas.

The poem is solemn**,** **yet** optimistic in tone.

See Appendix B, Coordinators, page 291, for more examples.

Subordinators

A subordinator (subordinating conjunction) is the first word in a dependent clause. As you may remember, a dependent clause is a group of words containing a subject and a verb that does not express a complete thought. A dependent clause always begins with a subordinator and must be connected to an independent clause to form a sentence. The sentence may or may not have a comma. The general rule is this: Put a comma after a dependent clause but not in front of one.

DEPENDENT CLAUSE — INDEPENDENT CLAUSE
Although the company's sales increased last year**,** its net profit declined.

INDEPENDENT CLAUSE — DEPENDENT CLAUSE
The company's net profit declined last year **although** its sales increased.

See Appendix B, pages 292–294, for more information about subordinators.

Other Signals

The transition signals in this group include nouns such as *example*, adjectives such as *additional*, prepositions such as *in addition to*, verbs such as *cause*, and adverbs such as *too*. There are no punctuation rules for this group, but it is important to notice what kinds of words follow these signals.

Additional is an adjective, so it is followed by a noun.

An **additional** reason for the company's bankruptcy was the lack of competent management.

In addition to is a preposition, so it is followed by a noun or noun phrase.

In addition to increased competition, the lack of competent management caused the company's bankruptcy.

Such as is followed by a noun or noun phrase and no comma.

Vocabulary differences between British and American English include words **such as** *bonnet / hood*, *petrol / gasoline*, *windscreen / windshield*, and *lorry / truck*.

A truck or a lorry? It depends on what version of English you are using.

Read the paragraphs and circle the transition signals. Punctuate them as needed.

Genetic[1] Engineering

Genetic research has produced both exciting and frightening possibilities. Scientists are now able to create new forms of life in the laboratory because of the development of gene splicing[2]. On the one hand, the ability to create life in the laboratory could greatly benefit humankind. Indeed agriculture has already benefited from applications of gene splicing. For example researchers have engineered a more nutritious type of rice that could help alleviate the serious problem of vitamin A deficiency. It is estimated that more than 124 million children worldwide lack vitamin A, which puts them at risk for permanent blindness and other health issues. In addition genetic engineers have created larger fish, frost-resistant strawberries, and cows that produce more milk.

On the other hand some people feel that gene-splicing technology could have terrible consequences. In fact a type of corn engineered to kill a certain insect pest also threatened to annihilate[3] desirable monarch butterflies. In another accident, a genetically engineered type of corn that was approved only for animal consumption because it was toxic to humans accidentally cross-pollinated with corn grown for humans. As a result many countries banned imports of genetically modified corn for several years. Furthermore the ability to clone human beings is a possibility that frightens many people. In 2004, two South Korean scientists reported that they had successfully cloned a human embryo (Dreifus). The embryo did not develop into a baby however it is possible that one could do so in the future, a possibility that not everyone is comfortable with.

Source: Dreifus, Claudia. "2 Friends, 242 Eggs and a Breakthrough."

---

[1] **genetic:** from gene, the unit of heredity
[2] **gene splicing:** gene joining
[3] **annihilate:** wipe out, destroy completely

Genetic engineering has an important but controversial role in agriculture.

A Write the transition signal that best shows the relationship between the sentences. Make punctuation and capitalization changes as needed.

1. A recent article in *Era* magazine suggested ways to reduce inflation. The article suggested that the president reduce the federal budget _; furthermore_ (*however / in contrast / furthermore*) it suggested that the government reduce federal, state, and local taxes.

2. The same article said that the causes of inflation were easy to find _____ (*however / for example / therefore*) the cure for inflation was not so easy to prescribe.

3. *Era* also suggested that rising wages were one of the primary causes of inflation _____ (*however / therefore / for example*) the government should take action to control wages.

4. In physics, the weight of an object is the gravitational force[1] with which Earth attracts it; _____ (*moreover / therefore / for example*) if a man weighs 150 pounds, this means that Earth pulls him down with a force of 150 pounds.

5. The farther away from Earth a person is, the less the gravitational force of Earth. _____ (*in conclusion / therefore / however*) a man weighs less when he is 50,000 miles from Earth than when he is only 5,000 miles away.

6. A **tsunami** is a tidal wave produced by an earthquake on the ocean floor. The waves are very long and low in open water, but when they get close to land, they encounter friction[2] because the water is shallow _____ (*on the other hand / as a result / for example*) the waves increase in height and can cause considerable damage when they finally reach land.

---

[1] **gravitational force:** the force that pulls things toward Earth
[2] **friction:** resistance

B Complete the paragraph. Use the transition signals from the box. Use each word once. Add punctuation as needed. In some cases, more than one answer is possible.

also		for example	in fact	similarly
final and most convincing		indeed	second	third

Time

One stereotype about Americans says that they are overly concerned with time. One of the first things you notice is that for Americans, time seems as valuable as money. _____ they even have a saying, "Time is money." _____ have you noticed how many verbs can be followed by both *time* and *money*? _____ you can *spend time, save time, lose time, find time, make time, waste time,* and *run out of time.* _____ you can *spend, save, lose, find, make, waste,* and *run out of* money. _____ Americans seem to regard time as a "thing" that one can own. You can *have time, buy time,* and *take time.* (One wonders how much it costs and where it is taken.) A _____ piece of evidence that Americans are obsessed with time is their obsession with being on time. _____ people who are habitually late risk punishment ranging from frowning disapproval to losing their jobs. The _____ proof is that these poor people sometimes take courses in time management! That is really overdoing it. Don't you agree?

1. **2.** **3.** **4.** **5.** **6.** **7.** **8.**

TRY IT OUT! On a separate sheet of paper, write a paragraph using Topic Sentence 1 or 2. Use the suggested transition signals, supporting points, and examples given or your own ideas.

Topic Sentence 1: There are some noticeable differences between British and American English.

TRANSITION SIGNALS

another difference	such as	for instance
for example	finally	in conclusion

SUPPORTING POINTS	EXAMPLES
Pronunciation	Speakers of British English do not always pronounce *r*.
	schedule: British = [shed-u-al]; American = [sked-u-al]
Spelling	colour / color; realise / realize; defence / defense
Vocabulary	petrol / gas; biscuit / cookie; pocket money / allowance

Topic Sentence 2: Sometimes I enjoy being alone.

TRANSITION SIGNALS

for instance   on the other hand
moreover   therefore

Writing Tip

Read your writing aloud and pay attention to your own language. Are you using too many transition signals? Too many can be distracting rather than helpful. There is no rule about how many to use in one paragraph. Use them only when they will help your reader follow your ideas.

PRACTICE 10   **Correcting Too Many Transition Signals**

Delete extra, unhelpful transition signals from this paragraph. Then rewrite the paragraph on a separate sheet of paper. Change the capitalization and punctuation as needed. Discuss your changes in a small group.

How to Grow an Avocado Tree

After you have enjoyed that delicious avocado, do not throw out the seed! You can grow a beautiful houseplant by following these simple steps. **First,** wash the seed. **Second,** dry it. **Third,** insert three toothpicks into its thickest part. **Then** fill a glass or empty jar with water. **After that,** suspend the seed in the water with the pointed end up and the broad end down. The water should cover about an inch of the seed. **Next,** put the glass in a warm place, but not in direct sunlight. Add water when necessary to keep the bottom of the seed under water at all times. In two to six weeks, you should see roots begin to grow. **Furthermore,** the seed will crack open, and **then** a stem will emerge from the top. **However,** wait until the stem is 6 to 7 inches long. **Then** cut it back to about 3 inches. **Now** wait until the roots are thick and the stem has leafed out again. **Then** fill an 8- to 10-inch diameter clay pot with enriched potting soil. Plant the seed, leaving the top half exposed. **Then** water it well. **After that,** water frequently but lightly; **also** give the plant an occasional deep soaking. **Then** place the potted plant in a sunny window and watch it grow. **Then, when** the stem is 12 inches high, cut it back to 6 inches to encourage the growth of side branches. In just a few more weeks, you will have a beautiful indoor plant. **In conclusion,** enjoy your new plant, but do not expect it to bear fruit. Avocados grown from seed occasionally flower and bear fruit; **however, first** you will have to plant it outside and **then** wait anywhere from five to thirteen years.

Source: "Grow Your Own Tree." California Avocado Commission.

LOGICAL ORDER

In addition to repeating key nouns and pronouns and using transition signals, a fourth way to achieve coherence is to arrange your sentences in some kind of logical order.

Your choice of one kind of logical order over another will, of course, depend on your topic and your purpose. You may even combine two or more different types of logical order in the same paragraph. The important point to remember is to arrange your ideas in some kind of order that is logical to a reader accustomed to the English way of writing.

Some common kinds of logical order in English are *chronological order*, *the logical division of ideas*, and *comparison / contrast*.

- *Chronological order* is order by time—a sequence of events or steps in a process. The paragraph "How to Grow an Avocado Tree" (page 39) uses time order to organize the steps.

- In a *logical division of ideas*, a topic is divided into parts, and each part is discussed separately. The writing model "Communication Styles That Don't Work" on page 3 uses logical division of ideas. First, it discusses passive communication and then it discusses active communication.

- In a *comparison / contrast* paragraph, the similarities and/or differences between two or more items are discussed. The paragraph about synonyms on page 6 compares and contrasts word meanings.

PRACTICE 11	**Recognizing Kinds of Logical Order**

Work with a partner. Read the paragraphs and decide which kind of logical order is used in each. Discuss the reasons for your choice. Underline the transition signals.

PARAGRAPH 1

The process of machine translation of languages is complex. To translate a document from English into Japanese, for example, the computer first analyzes an English sentence, determining its grammatical structure and identifying the subject, verb, objects, and modifiers. Next, the words are translated by an English-Japanese dictionary. After that, another part of the computer program analyzes the resulting awkward jumble of words and meanings and produces an intelligible sentence based on the rules of Japanese syntax[1] and the machine's understanding of what the original English sentence meant. Finally, a human bilingual editor polishes the computer-produced translation.

Kind of logical order: _____

---

[1] **syntax:** sentence structure, grammar

PARAGRAPH 2

Although there has been some success in decreasing the spread of polio, this campaign has not been as successful as the smallpox campaign. The slower progress against polio is due to differences between the viruses. These differences can cause difficulty for polio eradication. The main difference involves visibility of the disease. Unlike smallpox, polio does not always show symptoms. Smallpox symptoms were immediately visible to health professionals. For some cases of polio, on the other hand, the disease is difficult to identify. Doctors may have to do a lengthy examination to find it. Thus, some cases may go unnoticed. Compared to smallpox, then, it is easier for poliovirus to circulate.

Kind of logical order: _____

PARAGRAPH 3

The many different calendars used throughout the world are all based on the phases of the moon, on the revolution of Earth around the sun, or on a combination of the two. The first kind of calendar is the lunar calendar, based on the phases of the moon. A month is calculated as the time between two full moons, 29.5 days, and a year has 354 days. The Islamic calendar used in Muslim countries is a lunar calendar. It has 12 months and a cycle of 30 years in which the 2nd, 5th, 7th, 10th, 13th, 16th, 18th, 21st, 24th, 26th, and 29th years have 355 days, and the others 354 days. A second kind of calendar is the solar calendar, which is based on the revolution of Earth around the sun. The ancient Egyptians used a solar calendar divided into 12 months of 30 days each, which left five uncounted days at the end of each year. A very accurate calendar developed by the Mayan Indians in North America was also a solar calendar. It had 365 days, 364 of which were divided into 28 weeks of 13 days each. The new year began on the 365th day. Because the solar year is exactly 365 days, 5 hours, 48 minutes, and 46 seconds long, however, a solar calendar is not totally accurate, so many cultures developed a third kind of calendar, the lunisolar calendar. In a lunisolar calendar, extra days are added every so often to reconcile the lunar months with the solar year. The Chinese, Hebrew, and Gregorian calendars used today are lunisolar calendars.

Kind of logical order: _____

Source: Paragraph 2 adapted from Buckingham, Robert. *A Primer on International Health.*

✎ Applying Vocabulary: Using Synonyms 1

In your writing assignment for this chapter, you are going to write a paragraph about a topic related to health and medicine. You will probably want to use synonyms to connect ideas without being repetitive.

PRACTICE 12 **Using Synonyms**

A Write synonyms for the words. You may want to use some of these words and their synonyms in your writing assignment.

1. doctor _____

2. sick _____

3. injured _____

4. recover _____

B On a separate sheet of paper, write four pairs of sentences. Use the words from Part A in your sentences. Include one of the words in the first sentence of each pair and then use a synonym in the second sentence.

EXAMPLES:

You should see a doctor about that cough.

Dr. Herkimer works as a physician at Memorial Hospital.

WRITING ASSIGNMENT

Your assignment for this chapter is to write a paragraph of 10 to 15 sentences on a topic related to health and medicine. Choose one of the topics to write about. Use the writing model on page 23 to help you. Follow the steps in the writing process.

TOPICS
- Describe a medical advance that has been important to society.
- Compare and contrast two medical advances.
- Compare and contrast two types of illness or injury.
- Explain the process of recovery from an illness or injury.

Prewrite **STEP 1: Prewrite to get ideas.**
- Collect information and generate ideas about your topic. One technique you can use is called **clustering**. Clustering is a brainstorming technique in which you create a diagram of related ideas.
  - Write your topic in the center of your paper and circle it.
  - Place any ideas that come to you about the topic in separate circles around the topic. Draw lines from these ideas to the topic.

- Think about each of these ideas and add further thoughts in circles around them. Draw lines from your new ideas to each first idea.
- From the ideas that you have circled, choose at least three points to use in your paragraph. Think of one example or piece of support for each point.

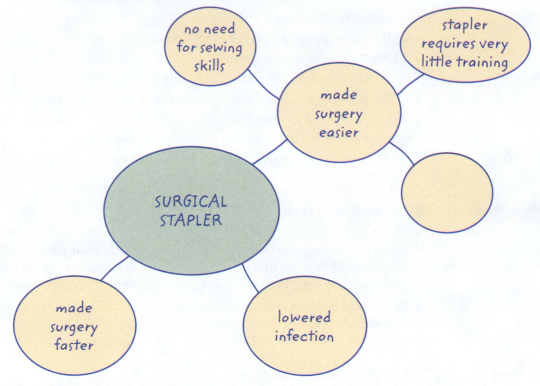

A student made a cluster diagram to prepare for her paragraph about the effects of a medical advance.

Organize **STEP 2: Organize your ideas.**

- Choose one main idea from the prewriting that you think will be a strong focus for your paragraph. Use it to write a topic sentence for your paragraph. Be sure your topic sentence states both your topic and controlling idea.
- Look back at your cluster diagram. Based on the ideas you selected for your paragraph, decide which kind of logical organization your paragraph requires: chronological order, the logical division of ideas, or comparison / contrast.

Write **STEP 3: Write the first draft.**

- Organize your paragraph around one central idea.
- Include a topic sentence, supporting sentences, and a concluding sentence. Use facts, examples, and details to support your opinions.
- Repeat nouns and use consistent pronouns to ensure coherence.

Revise

STEP 4: Revise the draft.

- Review the content and organization of your draft. Do not try to correct errors in format, mechanics (capitalization, punctuation, and spelling), grammar, and sentence structure at this stage. You will do this in Step 5.
- Read over your paragraph to get a general overview. As you read, make sure that
  - all your supporting sentences relate to your topic sentence. Delete any sentences that are off topic;
  - the paragraph is coherent. Add transition signals as needed.
- Make notes in the margin about anything you want to improve.
- Ask a classmate to read and give you feedback on your first draft using the Chapter 2 Peer Review on page 323.
- Discuss your classmate's suggestions and decide which ones to take.

 Proofread

STEP 5: Edit and proofread the draft.

- Make sure that you have identified all of the changes you want to make in content and organization. Then review your paragraph for errors in format, mechanics, grammar, and sentence structure. Use the Chapter 2 Writer's Self-Check on page 324 to help you.
- When you find an error, make a note on your paper using the correction symbols from Appendix D on pages 309–311.

Write

STEP 6: Write a new draft.

- In your new draft, include the changes you identified in Steps 4 and 5.
- Proofread your new draft again carefully. Make sure it is neat and error free.
- Hand in your paragraph to your teacher.

SELF-ASSESSMENT

In this chapter, you learned to:

- ○ Organize a unified paragraph around one central idea
- ○ Construct a coherent paragraph by
  - Repeating key nouns
  - Using consistent pronouns
  - Using transition signals to link ideas
  - Arranging ideas in logical order
- ○ Write, revise, and edit a paragraph about health and medicine

Which ones can you do well? Mark them ✓

Which ones do you need to practice more? Mark them ✗

TIMED WRITING

In this expansion, you will write a paragraph in class. As you write, focus on using the techniques for unity and coherence that you learned in this chapter. You will have 30 minutes. To complete the expansion in time, you will need to budget your time accordingly. Follow this procedure.

1. Read the writing prompts (or the prompt your teacher assigns) carefully. Choose one to write about. Make sure you understand the question or task. You may want to underline the key words in the prompt. (2 minutes)

2. Brainstorm or make a cluster diagram to generate ideas. Then group related ideas together and organize them. (5 minutes)

3. Write a topic sentence. (3 minutes)

4. Write your paragraph. Be sure to include a topic sentence, supporting ideas, and a conclusion. (15 minutes)

5. Check your paragraph for errors. Correct any mistakes. (5 minutes)

6. Give your paper to your teacher.

Prompt: Write a unified and coherent paragraph about one of these topics:

- Discuss a medical development that is important to your life.

- Write about an experience that you have had with a medical professional.

- Explain what is necessary to have a healthy lifestyle.

RESPONDING TO A READING

One common type of academic writing involves responding to what you read. When you write a response, you need to read the passage carefully to understand all of the ideas. If you are given a prompt, you need to read it carefully as well, and use the prompt to focus your writing. Reread the paragraphs in "Genetic Engineering" on page 36 and write a one-paragraph response. In your response, explain whether you think genetic engineering is a more positive or more negative development and why.

CHAPTER 3

USING OUTSIDE SOURCES

OBJECTIVES

To write academic texts, you need to master certain skills.

In this chapter, you will learn to:

- Cite sources of outside information used for reference
- Use direct and indirect quotations as supporting details
- Correctly paraphrase information from outside sources
- Summarize outside sources used as support
- Write, revise, and edit a summary of an article about language

Many languages will soon die out if the older generations do not teach them to the children.

In this chapter, you will practice using information from outside sources to support your ideas. **Outside sources** are materials you refer to other than your own knowledge and experience. Outside sources can include information you gain from reliable online websites, books, other print materials such as newspapers, or interviews.

There are three ways to insert outside information into your own writing: You can quote it; you can paraphrase it; or you can summarize it. Whichever way you choose, you must tell your readers where you found the information you use. In this chapter, you will learn more about each method. Your final assignment will be to write an academic summary on the topic of language.

ANALYZING THE MODEL

The writing model discusses an Alaskan language that is on the edge of extinction.

Read the model. Then answer the questions.

✎ Writing Model

Hope for Dying Languages

1 Inupiaq, an Alaskan language, has been threatened with extinction, but new educational initiatives may bring it back to life. 2 The threat to Inupiaq is very serious. 3 According to the National Geographic "Enduring Voice" project, a language dies every two weeks ("Disappearing Languages"). 4 Since Inupiaq has only 1,500 remaining speakers, it is in grave danger of following this trend (Hopkins). 5 The decline began under a harsh policy of assimilation in the last century. 6 This directive forced Native Americans to attend English language schools. 7 At these schools, they were discouraged from speaking their native tongues. 8 Now, however, that policy has been changed. 9 Inupiaq is currently taught at the University of Alaska. 10 Similarly, software developers are writing computer programs to help children learn Inupiaq and other endangered languages.
11 These efforts may increase Inupiaq use in the younger generation. 12 As Henry Goodman, a young Inupiat man, comments, "Listening to the elders . . . speak the language, I couldn't understand; it's part of our culture, and I never did learn [the] language growing up" (qtd. in Woodroof). 13 Happily, the new Inupiaq language projects will give him a chance to learn it now.

Sources:
1. "Disappearing Languages." *National Geographic*.
2. Hopkins, Kyle. "Alaska Natives Team with Rosetta Stone."
3. Woodroof, Martha. "Endangered Alaskan Language Goes Digital."

Questions about the Model

1. What is the topic sentence? Underline it.

2. How do sentences 2 and 11 develop the topic sentence?

3. What key supporting fact is included in sentence 3? Where did the author of this paragraph find this information?

4. How do you think this paragraph might have been different if the author had relied only on information from his or her personal experience?

✎ Noticing Vocabulary: Synonyms 2

In Chapter 2, you learned about using synonyms to avoid repetition. Using synonyms can also add interest, specificity, and nuance to your writing. When you are looking for a synonym, remember that you can use a thesaurus.

| PRACTICE 1 | Identifying Synonyms |

Ⓐ **Find these words and their synonyms in the model. Write the synonyms.**

1. threat _____

2. initiatives _____

3. serious _____

4. languages _____

Ⓑ **Find the word *happily* in the last sentence of the writing model. Circle the synonym that best fits the meaning of *happily* as it is used in the model.**

1. cheerfully   2. joyfully   3. gladly   4. luckily

USING AND CITING SOURCES

Using reliable outside sources can help your writing, but there are many things you need to know before you start using the words and ideas of others to support and expand your ideas.

PLAGIARISM

When you use information from an outside source without acknowledging that source, you are guilty of plagiarism. Plagiarism is using someone else's words or ideas as if they were your own, and it is a serious offense. Students who plagiarize may fail a class or even be expelled from school.

To avoid plagiarism, you should always put quotation marks around words that you copy exactly. You do not need to use quotation marks if you change the words. However, whether you copy the words exactly or state an idea in your own words, you must cite the source. To cite a source means to tell where you got the information.

CORRECT CITATIONS

The purpose of a citation is not only to avoid plagiarism, but also to refer your readers to the source of your information. That way, they can read the original source if they want to learn more about the topic. It is important to be accurate in your citations.

There are a number of different ways of citing information. In general, you will want to follow whatever guidelines your instructor gives you to complete an assignment. However, for most of your academic work, you will find this two-stage process useful and sufficient for citing your sources:

1. Insert a short reference in parentheses at the end of each piece of borrowed information. This short reference is called an *in-text citation*.

2. Prepare a list describing all your sources completely. This list is titled "Works Cited" and appears as the last page of your paper.

In-Text Citations

Here are three examples of in-text citations and of their corresponding entries in a works-cited list. In the first example, notice the position and punctuation of the citation— at the end of the last sentence of the borrowed information, before the final period.

> According to the National Geographic "Enduring Voices" project, a language dies every two weeks ("Disappearing Languages").

The phrase "Disappearing Languages" in quotation marks and parentheses at the end of this sentence is the first element of the title of an article from which the preceding information was taken. There was no author. If there had been an author, the author's last name—rather than part of a title—would have appeared inside the parentheses, with no quotation marks. Because the article was found on the Internet, it did not have a page number.

Here is an example of an in-text citation for an article with an author and page number:

> (Bryson 17)

If you include a quotation in your writing that you found in someone else's work, indicate the source of that quotation. Your in-text citation will say *qtd. in*, which is an abbreviation for *quoted in*:

> (qtd. in Bryson 17)

Entries in Works-Cited List

If readers want more information about your sources, they can turn to the works-cited list at the end of the essay, report, or paper and find these entries:

"Disappearing Languages: Enduring Voices—Documenting the World's Endangered Languages." *National Geographic*. Nationalgeographic.com. 2012. Web. 14 Jun. 2012. <http://travel.nationalgeographic.com/travel/enduring-voices/>

This entry tells us that the complete title of the article is "Disappearing Languages: Enduring Voices—Documenting the World's Endangered Languages." It was published online in 2012 by *National Geographic*. *Nationalgeographic.com* is the name of the website on which it was published. The date *14 Jun 2012* is the date the writer found the article while researching the topic. The information in angle brackets (< >) is the website address (URL) where the article can be found. The URL is not required, but it can be helpful to provide it.

Entries for print publications are a little different. At the end of the reference, give the city of publication, the publisher's name, the date of publication, and the word *Print*. This shows that this is not an online source.

Bryson, Bill. *The Mother Tongue: English and How It Got That Way.* New York: Avon, 1991. Print.

See Appendix E: Research and Documentation of Sources, page 312, for more information on strategies for doing and citing research.

For each source, write a parenthetical in-text citation and the information that you would include in a works-cited list.

1. A quote from page 152 of the book *Go Tell It on the Mountain*, by James Baldwin, published in 1953, in New York, by Dell Publishing, in print.

   In-text citation: _(Baldwin 152)_

   Works cited: _Baldwin, James. Go Tell It on the Mountain._
   New York: Dell Publishing, 1953. Print.

2. A paraphrase from page 33 of the article "Can Minority Languages Be Saved?" by Eric Garland, published on pages 31–36 in the July–August 2006 edition of the magazine The Futurist.

   In-text citation: _____

   Works cited: _____

   _____

3. Information from the article "Olympic Table Tennis Grunts Are Athlete's Universal Language" by Jodi Jill, published in 2012 on the website examiner.com and retrieved on August 15, 2012.<www.examiner.com/article/olympic-table-tennis-grunts-are-athlete-s-universal-language>

   In-text citation: _____

   Works cited: _____

   _____

4. A quote from page 152 of the book *The Argument Culture: Stopping America's War of Words*, by Deborah Tannen, published in 1999 by Ballantine Books in New York.

   In-text citation: _____

   Works cited: _____

   _____

5. Information from the article "Becoming an Independent Language Learner" by Aaron G. Myers, published on July 25, 2012, on the website The Everyday Language Learner and accessed on October 15, 2012.

   In-text citation: _____

   Works cited: _____

   _____

QUOTATIONS

Quotations from reliable and knowledgeable sources are good supporting details. There are two different types of quotations: direct and indirect. When you use a direct quotation in academic writing, you copy another person's exact words (spoken or written) and enclose them in quotation marks. When you use an indirect quotation, the speaker's or writer's words are reported indirectly, without quotation marks. For this reason, indirect quotations are sometimes called reported speech.

In academic writing, you should *never* use an indirect quotation without paraphrasing, or rephrasing information in your own words. In this chapter, you will learn more about paraphrasing on pages 58–65.

PRACTICE 3 **Analyzing Direct Quotations**

Work with a partner. Reread the writing model "Hope for Dying Languages," on page 47. Then answer the questions.

1. Who spoke the words in quotation marks?

2. What verb introduces the quotation?

3. What information is provided by the in-text citation at the end of the quotation?
   - Who wrote the article in which the quotation originally appeared?
   - Is the source a printed article or an online article? How do you know?
   - Why do you think the author of the paragraph included the quotation? How does the quotation support the main idea?

REPORTING VERBS AND PHRASES

As you probably noticed, the verb *comments* introduced the quotation in the writing model on page 47. To introduce borrowed information—direct quotations, indirect quotations, or specific facts or ideas—from someone else's work, use the phrase *according to* or a reporting verb such as *comment* or one of these verbs:

assert	insist	note	state
claim	maintain	report	suggest
declare	mention	say	write

Here are some rules for their use.

RULES	EXAMPLES
1. Reporting verbs can appear before, in the middle of, or after a quotation.	One instructor says, "It is impossible to teach language without teaching grammar" (Jones 12).
	"It is impossible to teach a language," says one instructor, "without teaching grammar" (Jones 12).
	"It is impossible to teach language without teaching grammar," says one instructor (Jones 12).

RULES	EXAMPLES
2. The reporting phrase *according to* usually appears at the beginning or end, but not in the middle of a sentence.	<mark>According to</mark> one instructor, teaching language without teaching grammar is impossible (Jones 12). Teaching language without teaching grammar is impossible, <mark>according to</mark> one instructor (Jones 12).
3. Use *according to* with a reporting verb only when two separate people are saying two separate things.	<mark>According to</mark> **linguist Deborah Tannen**, journalist **David Broder** <mark>claims</mark> that more news coverage is devoted to political analysis of events than to the events themselves (Tannen 34).
4. Reporting verbs can be used either with or without the subordinator *as*.	<mark>As</mark> one middle school teacher <mark>says</mark>, when discussing the teaching of grammar, "When you learn your first language, your mind automatically understands the grammar" (Jones 15). One middle school teacher <mark>says</mark>, when discussing the teaching of grammar, "When you learn your first language, your mind automatically understands the grammar" (Jones 15).
5. Reporting verbs can be in any tense. However, a past tense reporting verb may cause changes in verbs, pronouns, and time expressions in an indirect quotation. See Sequence of Tenses Rules, page 56, for more information on these types of changes.	Some critics <mark>claim / have claimed</mark> that certain programs have not provided enough grammar teaching in ESL classes for young children ("English for Tots Not So Hot"). Some critics <mark>claimed</mark> that certain programs had not provided enough grammar teaching in ESL classes for young children ("English for Tots Not So Hot").

Writing Tip

Including the source of the borrowed information with the reporting expression gives authority to your writing because it lets your reader know immediately that your information is from a credible source.

PUNCTUATING DIRECT QUOTATIONS

Follow these general rules for punctuating direct quotations.

RULES	EXAMPLES
1. Put quotation marks around information that you copy word-for-word from a source. Do not use quotation marks with paraphrases, summaries, or indirect quotations.	According to *Language / Brain Magazine*<mark>,</mark> "Many people believe that some people have more talent for learning language than others<mark>."</mark>

(continued on next page)

RULES	EXAMPLES
2. Normally, place commas (and periods) before the first mark and also before the second mark in a pair of quotation marks.	"Many people believe that some people have more talent for learning language than others," according to *Language / Brain Magazine*.
Exceptions: If you insert only a few quoted words into your own sentence, do not use commas.	Susanna Wong, a professor at Upper Midwest State University, argues that "a large percentage" of language learners never fully acquire proficiency (128).
When you add an in-text citation after a quotation, put the period after the closing parenthesis mark.	The Association for Childhood English Learning warns, "A solely grammatical curriculum can prevent the children from learning how to communicate, yet grammar in some amount is required for a learner to become highly proficient" (qtd. in Torralba 26).
3. When quoting a complete sentence, capitalize the first word of the quotation as well as the first word of your sentence.	The Association for Childhood English Learning warns, "A solely grammatical curriculum can prevent the children from learning how to communicate, yet grammar in some amount is required for a learner to become highly proficient" (qtd. in Torralba 26).
4. If you break a quoted sentence into two parts, enclose both parts in quotation marks and separate the parts with commas. Capitalize only the first word of the sentence.	"A solely grammatical curriculum can prevent the children from learning how to communicate," warns The Association for Childhood English Learning, "yet grammar in some amount is required for a learner to become highly proficient" (qtd. in Torralba 26).
5. If you omit words, use an ellipsis (three spaced periods).	As Henry Goodman, a young Inupiat man, comments, "Listening to the elders . . . speak the language, I couldn't understand."
6. If you add words, put square brackets around the words you have added.	He added, "It's part of our culture and I never did learn [the] language growing up" (qtd. in Woodroof)
7. Use single quotation marks to enclose a quotation within a quotation.	A student said, "When I first started learning English, I would say things like 'he go' or 'I no have.'" (qtd. in Jones 14).
8. If your quotation is four lines or longer, do not use quotation marks. Introduce this type of quotation with a colon and indent it one inch from the left-hand margin.	A national news agency reported these survey results: Several years ago [when] 198 teachers in the city were asked how much time they spend on grammar teaching in the classroom, 75 teachers said they spent more than 90% of their time on grammar, 90 said they spent less than 10% of their time on grammar, and only 10 said they spent about 50% of their time on grammar (qtd. in Torralba 34).

See Appendix C: Punctuation Rules, page 299, for more information.

Add punctuation to the direct quotations, and change the capitalization as necessary.

1. Dr. Yixuan Ma, a well-known astrophysicist who has been studying black holes, said they are the most interesting phenomena we astrophysicists have ever studied.

2. As she explained in black holes the laws of nature do not seem to apply.

3. A black hole is a tiny point with the mass 25 times the mass of our sun explained Ma's associate, Chun-Yi Su. Black holes are created by the death of a very large star she stated.

4. It is an invisible vacuum cleaner in space she added with tremendous gravitational pull.

5. According to Dr. Su, if a person falls into a black hole, he will eventually be crushed due to the tremendous gravitational forces.

6. Time will slow down for him as he approaches the point of no return she said and when he reaches the point of no return, time will stand still for him.

USING DIRECT QUOTATIONS AS SUPPORT

The purpose of learning to write quotations is to be able to use them as supporting material in your writing. Quotations from experts in a field or people with particular experience can serve as useful details and examples when explaining a point.

TRY IT OUT!   On a separate sheet of paper, write a short paragraph using the material presented here comparing computers with the human brain. Follow the instructions.

1. Copy the topic sentence exactly as it is given.

2. Write several supporting sentences, using the main points and quotations supplied. Add supporting details such as examples if you can. Use the techniques and rules you have learned for quotations.

3. Add an in-text citation in the proper format after each quotation.

TOPIC SENTENCE Computers cannot be compared to human brains.

MAIN POINT A The human brain is more powerful than any computer.

QUOTATION "The human brain has information processing capabilities that are infinitely beyond anything that can be conceived of by a computer."

MAIN POINT B The kinds of processing in a human brain and a computer are different, too.

(continued on next page)

QUOTATION "A computer can easily calculate complicated numerical equations, which is difficult for a human being to do independently. On the other hand, humans easily discuss the relationships among ideas in a text and summarize stories. These are exceedingly difficult tasks for a computer."

SOURCE Both quotations are from an article entitled "Computers and the Human Brain" by Sasha Moskovski. The article was published on the website topictalk.com on May 3, 2009.

CHANGING DIRECT QUOTATIONS TO INDIRECT QUOTATIONS

When you change a direct quotation to an indirect quotation, use this method:
- Omit the quotation marks.
- Add the subordinator *that*.*
- Change the verb tense if necessary. Follow the sequence of tenses rules.
- Change pronouns (and time expressions if necessary) to keep the sense of the original.

The subordinator that *is often omitted in reported speech, especially in spoken language.*

Sequence of Tenses Rules

If the reporting verb is in a past tense, the verbs in an indirect quotation may change tense according to the rules. Also, pronouns (and sometimes time expressions) may change.

TENSE CHANGES		
Rules	**Direct Quotations**	**Indirect Quotations**
1. Simple present changes to simple past.	Susan said, "The exam is at eight o'clock."	Susan said (that) the exam was at eight o'clock.
2. Simple past and present perfect change to past perfect.	She said, "We didn't have time to eat breakfast." He said, "The exam has just started."	She said (that) they hadn't had time to eat breakfast. He said (that) the exam had just started.
3. *Will* changes to *would*, *can* to *could*, *may* to *might*, and *must* to *had to*.	Sam mentioned, "Today I will eat Chinese food, and tomorrow I'll eat French food if I can find a good restaurant."	Sam mentioned that today he would eat Chinese food and that tomorrow he'd eat French food if he could find a good restaurant.
4. Time expressions may change if the meaning requires it.	The teacher said, "You must finish the test right now."	The teacher said (that) we had to finish the test right then.

Notes

These are a few additional points about indirect quotations.

- When the reporting verb is simple present, present perfect, or future, the verb tense in the quotation does not change.

  He says, "I **can finish** it today."

  He says that he **can finish** it today.

- When the reporting phrase is *according to,* the verb tense does not change.

  The lawyer said, "My client **is** innocent."

  According to the lawyer, his client **is** innocent.

- When the quoted information is a fact or general truth, the verb tense in the quotation does not change.

  He said, "Water **boils** at a lower temperature in the mountains."

  He said that water **boils** at a lower temperature in the mountains.

| PRACTICE 5 | **Changing Direct Quotations to Indirect Quotations** |

On a separate sheet of paper, rewrite the direct quotations as indirect quotations.

1. OnlineEd, Inc., General Manager Jim Burns said, "Not everyone can attend college in the traditional way; therefore, taking courses via the Internet will offer many more students the chance to earn a college degree."

2. Premed student Alma Rodriguez commented, "I miss being on campus, but I have to work and take care of my family."

3. Other students noted, "Last year, we spent several hours a day commuting to and from school. Now, we don't have to do that."

4. Computer engineering student Amir Mehdizadeh stated, "I can choose when to study and how to study without pressure." He also said, "I will take two more online classes in the fall."

Writing Tip

Notice that all the examples of indirect quotation are from conversation. This is because indirect quotation is forbidden in academic writing. If you use the same words as a source, changing only the verb tense, it is considered plagiarism and can be cause for serious punishment. Instead of indirect quotation, in academic writing use paraphrase, an important strategy that you will learn about in the next section.

PARAPHRASING

When you paraphrase, you rewrite information from an outside source in your own words without changing the meaning. Unlike when you use indirect quotation or reported speech, you do not simply change verb tense. In addition, when you paraphrase, you convey the author's idea but change the author's words and sentence structure. You think about the message the author is trying to send in the text, and then try to express that idea in your own way. A paraphrase may be shorter and more concise than the original, but only slightly. Because you include in your rewrite all or nearly all of the content of the original passage—including many of the details—a paraphrase is almost as long as the original.

ANALYZING THE MODEL

The writing model consists of two passages about language. One is an excerpt from an encyclopedia entry about language by an author named Robert Kispert. The other is a paraphrase of the excerpt.

Read the models. Then answer the questions.

✏ Writing Model

ORIGINAL PASSAGE

1 Language is the main means of communication between peoples. 2 But so many different languages have developed that language has often been a barrier rather than an aid to understanding among peoples. 3 For many years, people have dreamed of setting up an international universal language which all people could speak and understand. 4 The arguments in favor of a universal language are simple and obvious. 5 If all peoples spoke the same tongue, cultural and economic ties might be much closer, and good will might increase between countries (Kispert).

Source: Kispert, Robert J. "Universal Language."

There are almost 7,000 living languages in the world today.

PARAPHRASE

1 Humans communicate through language. 2 Because there are so many different languages, however, people around the world have a difficult time understanding one another. 3 Some people have wished for a universal international language that speakers all over the world could understand. 4 Their reasons are straightforward and clear. 5 A universal language would build cultural and economic bonds. 6 It would also create better feelings among countries (Kispert).

Questions about the Model

1. How many sentences are there in the original passage? In the paraphrase?

2. How do the original passage and the paraphrase differ sentence by sentence? What are the differences between them in sentence structure and words?

   a. What is the first word of the first sentence in the original passage? Where does this word appear in the first sentence of the paraphrase?

   b. What is the first word of the second sentence in the original passage? What word replaces it in the second sentence of the paraphrase?

   c. What words replace *have dreamed of* in the third sentence? What word replaces *arguments in favor of* in the fourth sentence?

   d. Which sentence in the original becomes two sentences in the paraphrase?

PLAGIARISM AND PARAPHRASING

Learning to paraphrase properly can help you use information from outside sources accurately and ethically. It is essential to avoid committing plagiarism.

There are two kinds of plagiarism that you need to consider when paraphrasing.

1. When you use information from an outside source without citing the source (telling where you got the information), you are guilty of plagiarism.

2. Even when you cite your source, if your paraphrase is too similar to the original, you are guilty of plagiarism.

Reread the model on pages 58–59. Pay attention to the paraphrase. Then read these two paraphrases and decide which kind of plagiarism each example is guilty of.

UNACCEPTABLE PARAPHRASE 1

> Humans communicate through language. However, because there are so many languages in the world, language acts as an obstacle instead of as an aid to understanding. People have long wished for a universal international language that speakers all over the world could understand. A universal language would certainly build cultural and economic bonds. It would also create better feelings among countries.

UNACCEPTABLE PARAPHRASE 2

> Language is the principle means of communication between peoples. However, because there are numerous languages, language itself has frequently been a barrier rather than an aid to understanding among the world population. For many years, people have envisioned a common universal language that everyone in the world could communicate in. The reasons for having a universal language are clearly understandable. If the same tongue were spoken by all countries, they would undoubtedly become closer culturally and economically. It would probably also create good will among nations (Kispert).

Paraphrase 1 is plagiarism because the source is not cited. Paraphrase 2 is plagiarism because it is too similar to the original passage. For example, in the first sentence, only one word has been changed: *principle* replaces *main*. In the second sentence, only a few words have been changed. You can avoid the first kind of plagiarism by always citing your sources. You can avoid the second kind of plagiarism by learning to paraphrase correctly.

WRITING A SUCCESSFUL PARAPHRASE

To paraphrase correctly, you first need to make sure that you fully understand the original passage. Use this method to write a good paraphrase.

- Read the original passage several times until you understand it fully. Underline the key words. Look up unfamiliar words and find synonyms for them. It is not always possible to find synonyms for every word, especially technical vocabulary. In this case, use the original word.

- Take notes while you read. Write down only a few words for each idea—not complete sentences. Here are one writer's notes on the original passage about universal language:

> language—people use to communicate—but so many—
> difficult to understand one another—people wish—
> universal international language—reasons: cultural,
> economic bonds, better feelings between countries

- Make a brief outline:

> A. Language—people use to communicate
>   1. So many languages make it difficult to understand one another.
>   2. People wish for one universal international language.
> B. Reasons
>   1. Cultural, economic bonds
>   2. Better feelings between countries

- Write your paraphrase from your notes. Don't look at the original while you are writing.

- Check your paraphrase against the original to make sure you have not copied vocabulary or sentence structure too closely. Above all, make sure that you have not changed the meaning of the original or given any wrong information.

- Add in-text citations. Also add a works-cited list if appropriate.

Choosing the Best Paraphrase

Read each original passage. Then read the paraphrases in each group and decide which is the best. Label it *Best*. Label the others *Too sim.* (too similar), *No cit.* (no in-text citation), or *Inc. / Inacc.* (incomplete and / or inaccurate information).

ORIGINAL PASSAGE 1

Source: A passage titled "Late-blooming or Language Problem," published in 2012 on the website of the American Speech-Language-Hearing Association. There are no authors listed.

> The stages that children pass through in the development of language are very consistent. However the exact age when they hit these milestones varies a lot.

_____*Best*_____ **a.** As children develop language skills, they usually go through the same stages, but they may reach the stages at different ages ("Late-blooming").

_____*No cit.*_____ **b.** Developing children may pass through linguistic stages at different ages although they will generally pass through each stage at some point.

_____*Too sim.*_____ **c.** The stages that are passed through by children in language development are very consistent. However the exact time when they hit these milestones can be different ("Late-blooming").

_____*Inc. / Inacc.*_____ **d.** Language development is very different for different children, and there can be variation in the stages they go through ("Late-blooming").

ORIGINAL PASSAGE 2

Source: The same as Passage 1.

> The kind of language the child hears and how people respond to the child can affect the speed of language development.

_____ **a.** People's response to the child and the kind of language the child hears can affect his rate of language development ("Late-bloomer").

_____ **b.** Language can develop at different rates depending on the child's exposure to language and the response he or she gets when using it ("Late-bloomer").

_____ **c.** Rate of language development can be influenced by children's exposure to language and response to their language use.

_____ **d.** Language develops more quickly if children are exposed to different languages and if they receive a response ("Late-bloomer").

ORIGINAL PASSAGE 3

Source: A passage titled, "Speech and Language Disorders in the School Setting" from the same website as Passages 1 and 2.

> Children with communication disorders frequently do not perform at grade level. They may struggle with reading. Similarly, they may have difficulty understanding and expressing spoken language. Individuals with reading and writing problems also may have trouble using language to think and learn.

_____ a. Communication disorders prevent children from learning and are evidence of low intelligence ("Speech and Language Disorders").

_____ b. Children with speech and language challenges can fall behind in school because of trouble processing text or comprehending and using speech. Difficulty reading and writing can lead to problems with thinking and learning.

_____ c. Children with communication disabilities often do not work at grade level. They may have challenges with reading or have trouble comprehending and using spoken language. People with reading and writing problems also may have trouble using language to process ideas ("Speech and Language Disorders").

_____ d. Communication disabilities can cause problems for children in the areas of reading, writing, speaking, listening, thinking, and learning, which can result in poor performance in school ("Speech and Language Disorders").

PRACTICE 7   Writing a Paraphrase

Read the passage from an article that supports bilingual education. Write a paraphrase on a separate sheet of paper. Follow the method for writing a paraphrase described on page 61.

ORIGINAL PASSAGE

Source: An editorial in the *Houston Chronicle*, published Thursday, February 16, 2012, and accessed online August 5, 2012. The title of the article is "Editorial: Children can, and should, learn more than one language." There is no author listed.

> A powerful body of data shows that speaking more than one language arms kids with crucial real-world abilities. People who master two or more languages in childhood enjoy better cognitive development, leading to better academic performance across the board. Learning languages at a young age is also associated with better problem-solving, heightened verbal skills, and mental agility.

USING PARAPHRASES AS SUPPORT

You previously learned how to use quotations as support for your ideas. Similarly, the purpose of learning to paraphrase is to be able to use paraphrases as supporting material in your writing. In fact, paraphrase is usually preferred over quotation in academic writing because it shows that the writer truly understands the information, and it is often easier to understand how the information relates to the writer's points. Thus, whenever the exact words of your source are not important, you should use paraphrase.

Notice how a student in a sociolinguistics class used a paraphrase of a passage from an online article about a dying language in Chile called *Huilliche* or *Huillichesungun* to support her idea.

ORIGINAL PASSAGE

> Wequetrumao village hosts a kindergarten that teaches children elements of the language and culture. Ethnic and linguistic pride are extremely strong in this community, as evidenced by two young hip-hop performers who composed indigenous protest lyrics including words in Huillichesungun ("Disappearing Languages").

Source: *"Disappearing Languages." National Geographic.*

PARAPHRASE

> According to research by National Geographic, many people in the community find the language to be an important part of their identity. Some members of the younger generation actually use Huilliche in hip-hop music. One village has a kindergarten where children can learn about their linguistic and cultural heritage ("Disappearing Languages").

> Revitalizing dying languages is important for several reasons. First of all, language diversity makes life on earth more interesting. Just as it would be boring to have only few kinds of trees or flowers, a world with few languages would feel empty. Secondly, revitalizing dying languages is important to the communities who speak (or spoke) those languages. One example of this is Huilliche, the language of a native community in Chile. According to research by National Geographic, it has only a few remaining fluent speakers, most of whom are over 70. However, many people in the community find the language to be an important part of their identity. Some members of the younger generation actually use Huilliche in hip-hop music. One village has a kindergarten where children can learn about their linguistic and cultural heritage ("Disappearing Languages"). Clearly, it would be a mistake to deprive the world, and individual communities, of the beauty of these languages.

TRY IT OUT! Write a paragraph in which you agree with this statement.

Some people feel that children who immigrate to a new country should not be taught only the language of the new country. They believe these children should be educated bilingually, that is, both in their first language and in the language of their new country.

1. Write a topic sentence that states your opinion.

2. Include all or part of your paraphrase from Practice 7: Writing a Paraphrase on page 63 as one of your supporting points. Make sure to add an in-text citation at the end of the paraphrase.

3. Include additional supporting sentences using your own ideas and personal supporting example, if possible.

4. Use transition signals to connect the ideas and make your paragraph flow smoothly.

SUMMARIZING

Another way to use borrowed information from an outside source is to summarize the material. What is the difference between a paraphrase and a summary? When you retell a story that someone has told you, you repeat the story in your own words. If your retelling is about the same length as the original and includes many of the details, it is a paraphrase. If you shorten the story—retelling only the most important points and leaving out the details—it is a summary.

Summaries have many uses in academic writing. Like paraphrases, they can be used to support a point. They can also be part of a longer piece of writing, such as a book report. You might summarize a book before going on to write a response to it. Writing a summary can also be a good strategy for remembering things that you've read. For example, your teacher may ask you to summarize a textbook chapter.

ANALYZING THE MODEL

You previously read these writing models on pages 58–59. Here you will also read a summary of the same material.

Read the model. Then answer the questions.

✏️ **Writing Model**

ORIGINAL PASSAGE (85 WORDS)

> Language is the main means of communication between peoples. But so many different languages have developed that language has often been a barrier rather than an aid to understanding among peoples. For many years, people have dreamed of setting up an international universal language which all people could speak and understand. The arguments in favor of a universal language are simple and obvious. If all peoples spoke the same tongue, cultural and economic ties might be much closer, and good will might increase between countries (Kispert).
>
> **Source:** Kispert, Robert J. "Universal Language."

PARAPHRASE (63 WORDS, ABOUT THE SAME LENGTH AS THE ORIGINAL)

Humans communicate through language. Because there are so many different languages, however, people around the world have a difficult time understanding one another. Some people have wished for a universal international language that speakers all over the world could understand. Their reasons are straightforward and clear. A universal language would build cultural and economic bonds. It would also create better feelings among countries (Kispert).

> People communicate through language; however, having different languages creates communication barriers. A universal language could bring countries together culturally and economically as well as increase good feelings among them (Kispert).

Questions about the Model

1. How many sentences are there in the original passage? In the paraphrase? In the summary?

2. What are some other differences between the paraphrase and the summary? What two details were left out of the summary?

WRITING A SUCCESSFUL SUMMARY

To write a successful summary, you must focus on the most important points of the original passage. These are strategies for writing a good summary.

- Use your own words and your own sentence structure.
- Remember that a summary is much shorter than a paraphrase. Include only the main points and main supporting points, leaving out most details.
- Do not change the meaning of the original.

The method for writing a summary is similar to the one for writing a paraphrase.

- Read the original passage several times until you understand it fully. Look up any words that you don't understand.
- Decide what the most important points are. It helps to underline them. It also helps to take notes on the passage. Write down only a few words for each idea—not complete sentences.
- Write your summary from your notes. Don't look at the original while you are writing.
- Include a sentence that sums up the main idea of the article.
- Use transition signals between sentences as needed.
- Check your summary against the original to make sure you have used different words but have not changed the meaning.
- Add an in-text citation at the end of the summary.

Read the original passage and the two summaries. Then answer the questions.

ORIGINAL PASSAGE

Bilingualism and Its Advantages

It was once believed that learning to speak two languages at an early age could create confusion between them. However, research today indicates that bilingualism, or speaking two or more languages, has many advantages. One very obvious benefit is that individuals who speak several languages can communicate with more people.

Being bilingual also can have a deep impact on how the brain functions. Research shows that bilingual children are often better able to learn words, form rhymes, and solve problems than monolingual children. Children who are bilingual are adept as well at categorizing words ("The Advantages of Being Bilingual"). This is because the brains of bilingual children, according to experts, are able to process information with great efficiency. Having to switch between two languages on a constant basis seems to help these children develop a capacity to focus and ignore distractions. At the same time, they are able to retain information (Cuda-Kroen).

Bilingualism has been shown to have advantages for adults as well as children. At St. Michael's Hospital in Toronto, researchers found that being bilingual can delay the onset of Alzheimer's symptoms. Alzheimer's disease, an illness that affects the brain and memory, seems to progress more slowly in bilingual adults. This may be because their brains are better prepared to compensate for changes in brain function (Bhattacharjee). Based on these and other findings, it seems clear that being bilingual is not only beneficial for children. It may also be vital to a person's health and wellness later in life.

Sources:
1. "The Advantages of Being Bilingual." *American Speech-Language-Hearing Association.*
2. Bhattacharjee, Yudhijit. "The Benefits of Bilingualism"—NYTimes.com.
3. Cuda-Kroen, Gretchen. "Being Bilingual May Boost Your Brain Power": NPR.

SUMMARY A

Research suggests that speaking more than one language has many benefits. First, a person who speaks another language can communicate with more people. Also, learning another language can help brain development. Bilingual children are better at learning vocabulary, rhyming, problem solving, and analyzing words. Experts think bilingual children's brains are better at these tasks because changing from one language to another helps the brain become better at focusing. Being bilingual also has an advantage when a person is older. Researchers in Toronto found that Alzheimer's disease progressed more slowly in bilingual adults. In conclusion, bilingualism is great for both children and adults.

> Being bilingual is advantageous in many ways. Bilingual people can speak to more people around the world. Children that are bilingual are smarter, too. They can learn words, rhyme, and problem solve better than monolingual children. Their brains process information better because they have to go back and forth between languages. Being bilingual is also good for adults and helps stop diseases such as Alzheimer's.

Questions about the Summaries

1. Which summary is better? Why?

2. Which summary contains an idea that was not in the original passage?

Applying Vocabulary: Using Synonyms 2

You have learned that knowing and using a variety of synonyms can help you to avoid repetition in your writing and to add interest and nuance to it. You have also learned that synonyms can have slight variations in meaning or connotation, and that you therefore need to be careful about which synonyms you choose to include in a particular passage. Reference works such as a dictionary and thesaurus can be helpful guides when you need to find a synonym or to confirm a synonym's precise meaning.

PRACTICE 9 **Using Synonyms**

A Write synonyms for the words. You will see these words again in your Chapter 3 Writing Assignment. Use a dictionary or thesaurus as needed.

1. technology _____

2. software _____

3. languages _____

4. communicate _____

5. revive _____

B On a separate sheet of paper, write four pairs of sentences with the words from Part A. Include one of the given words in the first sentence of each pair and its synonym in the second sentence.

Your assignment for this chapter is to write a one-paragraph summary of an article entitled "How Technology Aids Language." Use the summary models on pages 66–67 to help you.

The reading that you will summarize for this assignment can be found in Appendix A: Chapter Readings, on page 279. To complete the assignment, first read the article. Then follow the steps in the writing process.

Prewrite

STEP 1: Prewrite to get ideas.

- After you have read the article on page 279 in Appendix A once, reread it several times until you are sure that you fully understand its meaning. Underline important points.
- Make notes on a separate sheet of paper. Summarize the author's main idea in your own words at the top.
- Then list the other important points, changing vocabulary words wherever possible. Write down only a few words for each point.

Organize

STEP 2: Organize your ideas.

- Review your list of important points. Arrange them in a logical order. Which point will you discuss first in your summary? Which will you discuss second?
- Ask yourself whether each point on your list is essential to understanding the article. If a reader could understand your summary without that point, then it may be a detail that you could leave out.

Write

STEP 3: Write the first draft.

- Write your summary from your notes. Don't look at the original while you are writing.
- Sum up the main idea of the article in your paragraph's topic sentence, using your own words.
- Use transition signals between sentences as needed.
- Check your summary against the original to make sure you have used different words but have not changed the meaning.
- Add an in-text citation at the end of the summary.

Revise

STEP 4: Revise the draft.

- Ask yourself whether someone who has not read the original text could understand your summary.
- Remember that a summary should be brief and focus only on the most important points. Is there anything you want to leave out of your summary? If so, delete that word, detail, or sentence.
- Make notes in the margin about anything you want to improve.
- Ask a classmate to read and give you feedback on your first draft using the Chapter 3 Peer Review on page 325.
- Discuss your classmate's suggestions and decide which ones to take.

Proofread

STEP 5: Edit and proofread the draft.

- Make sure that you have identified all of the changes you want to make in content and organization. Then review your summary for errors in format, mechanics (capitalization, punctuation, and spelling), grammar, and sentence structure. Use the Chapter 3 Writer's Self-Check on page 326 to help you.
- When you find an error, make a note on your paper using the correction symbols from Appendix D on pages 309–311.

Write

STEP 6: Write a new draft.

- In your new draft, include the changes you identified in Steps 4 and 5.
- Proofread your new draft again carefully. Make sure it is neat and error free.
- Hand in your summary to your teacher.

SELF-ASSESSMENT

In this chapter, you learned to:

- ○ Cite sources of outside information used for reference
- ○ Use direct and indirect quotations as supporting details
- ○ Correctly paraphrase information from outside sources
- ○ Summarize outside sources used as support
- ○ Write, revise, and edit a summary of an article about language

Which ones can you do well? Mark them ☑

Which ones do you need to practice more? Mark them ⊗

TIMED WRITING

In this expansion, you will write a one-paragraph summary of a reading. You will have 45 minutes to complete the expansion in class. You will need to budget your time accordingly. Follow this procedure.

1. Read the passage "The Challenge of Many Languages" on page 280 in Appendix A. Underline the points that you think will be most important to use in your summary (15 minutes)

2. Write a topic sentence for your summary that includes the main idea of the passage. Make sure to paraphrase. (5 minutes)

3. Write your summary. Be sure to include only the most important points, use paraphrase, connect ideas with appropriate transition signals, and include a citation. (20 minutes)

4. Check your paragraph for errors. Correct any mistakes. (5 minutes)

5. Give your paper to your teacher.

RESPONDING TO A READING

In Chapter 2, you learned to respond to a reading using your opinion. Now, you will again respond to a reading, but this time you will use your skills at quoting, paraphrasing, and summarizing to make sure that your ideas are closely connected to the ideas in the reading.

Reread "The Challenge of Many Languages" on page 280 in Appendix A, a passage that you previously summarized in your Chapter 3 Timed Writing. Your assignment is to write a response to the text. Explain whether you believe that an ideal society should be monolingual (in which everyone speaks only one language) or multilingual (in which people speak more than one language). Use information from the reading to discuss your view. You can use quotes, paraphrases, and a summary of ideas from the reading to support your ideas.

PART II

WRITING AN ESSAY

FROM PARAGRAPH TO ESSAY

OBJECTIVES

To write academic texts, you need to master certain skills.

In this chapter you will learn to:

- Identify the parts of an essay

- Analyze an essay's introduction and conclusion

- Construct an appropriate thesis statement

- Support the thesis statement with body paragraphs

- Organize an essay, using transition signals as necessary

- Write, revise, and edit an essay about education

A classroom can be an exciting learning environment.

In Chapters 1 through 3, you studied the key elements of a well-written academic paragraph. In this chapter, you'll do the same for an **essay**. An essay is a piece of writing several paragraphs long. It is about one topic, just as a paragraph is. However, because the topic is too complex to discuss in one paragraph, you need to divide it into several paragraphs, one for each major point. Then you need to tie the paragraphs together by adding an introduction and a conclusion. At the end of this chapter, you will write an essay on the topic of education.

ANALYZING THE MODEL

The writing model discusses the advantages of same-sex classes in middle school.

Read the model. Then answer the questions.

✎ **Writing Model**

Separating the Sexes, Just for the Tough Years

1   The middle school years (grades 6, 7, and 8) are known to be the "tough years." These are the years when the different rates of girls' and boys' physical, emotional, and cognitive[1] development are most noticeable. Girls develop ahead of boys in every area, and both suffer. Educators debate whether the separation of boys and girls into single-sex classes might improve students' academic performance. Single-sex classes were against the law in public schools until several years ago, but now they have become more common (Bonner and Hollingsworth). Although some parents, educators, and civil liberties groups continue to oppose single-sex classes, there is some evidence that separating boys and girls in middle school produces positive results.

2   First of all, it is difficult to say whether single-sex education leads to higher test scores, but it may make a difference in more important areas. Although some research shows no improvement in test scores, other research shows opposite results (Blum). More important, many psychologists believe that test scores are not a good measure of success. They suggest that self-confidence and self-esteem issues are more important. For example, in same-sex classes, girls report increased confidence and improved attitudes toward math and science ("Study"). New York University professor Carol Gilligan believes girls are more likely to be "creative thinkers and risk-takers as adults if educated apart from boys in middle school" (qtd. in Gross). Boys, too, gain confidence when they do not have to compete with girls. Boys can feel inferior when compared to girls, who literally "out-think" them. This feeling can cause them to become angry and fight back. In contrast, with no girls in the classroom, they are more relaxed and more open to learning (Gross).

(continued on next page)

---

[1] **cognitive:** related to the process of knowing, understanding, and learning something

3   In addition to these benefits, it is also necessary to examine how single-sex education will affect students' careers in the future. Opponents of the practice note that when students go into the workforce, they will have to work side-by-side with the opposite sex. They worry that attending all-girl or all-boy schools could deny children the chance to learn how to do so ("North"). However, this argument ignores the fact that children constantly interact with members of the opposite sex outside of school. This interaction can range from playing and arguing with siblings to negotiating allowances, chores, and privileges with their opposite-sex parent. Children learn and practice on a daily basis the skills they will need in their future workplaces.

4   Finally, opponents of same-sex education say that it is discriminatory[2]. However, research supports the opposite conclusion: that discrimination is widespread in mixed classes. Several studies have shown that boys dominate discussions and receive more attention than girls. Studies also indicate that teachers call on boys more often than on girls, even when girls raise their hands ("North"). Clearly, this is discriminatory.

5   For all these reasons, the arguments against same-sex classes are not valid. On the contrary, many people say that same-sex classes provide a better learning environment. Boys and girls pay less attention to each other and more attention to their schoolwork (Marquez). Girls are less fearful of making mistakes and asking questions in math and science; boys are less shy about sharing their ideas in language and literature. Furthermore, schoolchildren do not lack contact with the opposite sex. Indeed, they have many opportunities outside school to interact with one another. Finally, discrimination occurs in mixed classes, so discrimination is not a valid argument. Therefore, in my opinion, the policy of allowing single-sex classes in public schools should be continued and encouraged.

Sources:
1. Blum, Justin. "Scores Soar at D.C. School with Same-Sex Classes."
2. Bonner, Jessie and Heather Hollingsworth. "Single Sex Classes Popular as More Public Schools Split Up Boys and Girls."
3. Gross, Jane. "Splitting Up Boys and Girls, Just for the Tough Years."
4. Marquez, Laura. "Should girls, boys be in separate classrooms?"
5. "North Carolina School Stops Same-Sex Classes." *American Civil Liberties Union News.*
6. "Study: All Girls Schools Don't Improve Test Scores." *CNNinteractive.*

---

[2] **discriminatory:** treating a person or a group of people differently from other people, in an unfair way

Questions about the Model

1. How many paragraphs does this essay contain?

2. What are the topic sentences of paragraphs 2, 3, and 4? Underline each topic sentence. (*Note:* The topic sentence is not necessarily the first sentence.)

3. What key phrase appears three times in the introduction? Circle each repetition of this key phrase, or synonyms for this phrase, in the other paragraphs of the essay.

4. What is one fact or example that supports the opinion expressed in the concluding sentence?

✏️ Noticing Vocabulary: Nouns and Noun Suffixes

In Chapter 1, you completed a word families chart that included verbs, adjectives, and adverbs. You also learned that different ending patterns, or **suffixes**, can be added to a word to change its part of speech.

In this chapter, you will learn about some of the suffixes for nouns in word families. For example, notice the verb *improve* and the noun *improvement* in the first two paragraphs of the model. They belong to the same word family. The suffix *-ment* has been added to the end of the verb *improve* to create a noun.

Sometimes the end of a word changes slightly when you add a suffix to it. If you have any questions about how to spell a word form, check your dictionary.

| PRACTICE 1 | Identifying Nouns and Noun Suffixes |

A Work with a partner. Find the noun forms of these words in the model and write them in the word families chart.

VERB	NOUN	ADJECTIVE	ADVERB
argue	*argument*	argumentative	argumentatively
attend		attentive	attentively
develop		developmental	----------
discriminate		discriminatory	----------
improve		improved	----------
interact		interactive	interactively
perform		----------	----------
separate		separate	separately

B List the noun suffixes used in Part A.

1. _____

2. _____

3. _____

Writing an essay is no more difficult than writing a paragraph except that an essay is longer. The principles of organization are the same for both, so if you can write a good paragraph, you can write a good essay.

An essay has three main parts: an **introduction** (introductory paragraph), a **body** (at least one, but usually two or more paragraphs), and a **conclusion** (concluding paragraph).

The chart shows you how the parts of a paragraph correspond to the parts of an essay.

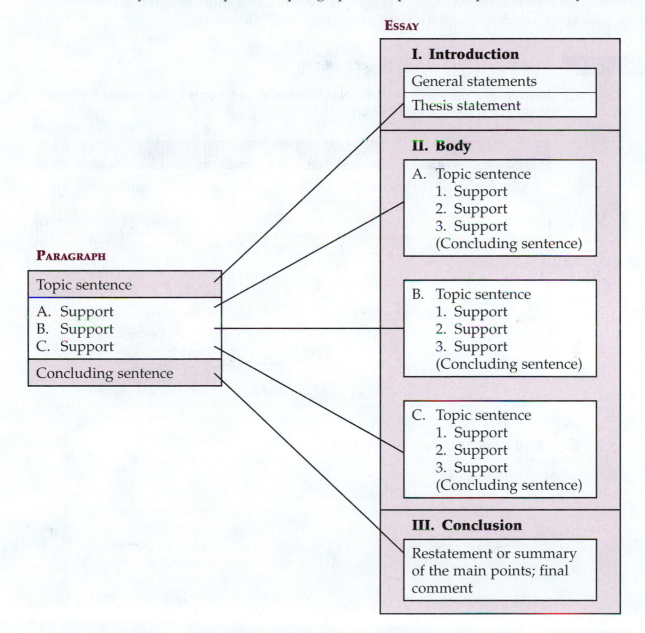

As the chart shows, an essay **introduction** consists of two parts: a few general statements to attract your reader's attention and a **thesis statement** to state the main idea of the essay. The thesis statement of an essay is like the topic sentence of a paragraph: It names the specific topic and gives the reader an idea of the contents of the essay. It may also suggest the writer's point of view on the topic.

The **body** consists of one or more paragraphs. Each body paragraph develops a subdivision or subtopic of the topic, so the number of paragraphs in the body will vary with the number of subtopics. The **conclusion**, like the concluding sentence in a paragraph, is a summary or review of the main points discussed in the body. However, although every essay needs a concluding paragraph, a concluding sentence is often not necessary for each body paragraph, especially when the ideas in consecutive paragraphs are closely related.

An essay has unity and coherence, just as a paragraph does. Transition signals and the repetition of key nouns help link the paragraphs and make the essay more coherent.

THE INTRODUCTORY PARAGRAPH

The general statements and the thesis statement in an introductory paragraph each play a specific role in the essay.

General statements
- introduce the general topic of the essay;
- capture the reader's interest.

The **thesis statement**
- states the specific topic;
- may list subtopics of the main topic;
- may indicate the pattern of organization of the essay;
- may indicate the writer's position or point of view;
- is usually the last sentence in the introductory paragraph.

Notice how the general statements in the introductory paragraph of the writing model (see below) introduce the topic. The first sentence is about the "tough" middle school years. The next two sentences point out that there are large differences between boys and girls of middle school age, and that these can cause a problem. The next sentence explains how the issue of single-sex classes has been changing. We don't, however, read about the author's position on the specific topic of single-sex classes until the introduction's final sentence. The final sentence is the essay's thesis statement.

> The middle school years (grades 6, 7, and 8) are known to be the "tough years." These are the years when the different rates of girls' and boys' physical, emotional, and cognitive development are most noticeable. Girls develop ahead of boys in every area, and both suffer. Educators debate whether separating boys and girls into single-sex classes might improve students' academic performance. Single-sex classes were against the law in public schools until several years ago, but now they have become more common (Bonner and Hollingsworth). Although some parents, educators, and civil liberties groups continue to oppose single-sex classes, there is some evidence that separating boys and girls in middle school produces positive results.

The thesis statement in the model is *specific:* It explains the author's point of view about single-sex education (in favor of separating boys and girls in middle school) and the reasoning that will be explored in the essay (positive results).

There are several different styles of introductory paragraphs. In this chapter, you'll learn about two of them: the funnel introduction and the attention-getting introduction.

Funnel Introduction

A funnel introduction is so called because it is shaped like a funnel—wide at the top and narrow at the bottom. It begins with one or two very general sentences about the topic. Each subsequent sentence becomes increasingly focused on the topic until the last sentence, which states very specifically what the essay will be about. Writing a funnel introduction is like focusing a camera with a telephoto lens. You start with a wide picture and gradually narrow the focus so that just one object appears in the camera's viewfinder: your thesis statement. The writing model has a funnel introduction.

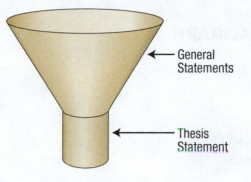

General Statements

Thesis Statement

Attention-Getting Introduction

Another kind of introduction is one that captures your reader's attention. Three of the most common attention-getting techniques are telling a dramatic or funny story, using surprising facts or statistics, and offering historical background.

PRACTICE 2   **Recognizing Introductory Techniques**

Work with a partner. Underline the thesis statement in each introductory paragraph. Then decide what kind of introduction each one is, funnel or attention-getting (dramatic story, surprising fact, or historical). Discuss which introduction captures the reader's interest the best and give reasons.

INTRODUCTORY PARAGRAPH 1

One day, a few miles off the southern coast of Iceland, the crew of a fishing boat noticed smoke on the horizon. Thinking that another fishing boat was on fire, they went to investigate. When they got closer, they discovered that the smoke was not from a boat on fire; rather, it was from an undersea volcano about to erupt. The next day, ash, cinders, and pumice were blown 1,000 feet into the air. The fishermen had witnessed a rare event—the violent birth of an island. The volcano continued to erupt for about four years, eventually creating an island about 1 square mile in area and 560 feet in height. The birth of Surtsey, as the island is named, offered scientists an extraordinary opportunity to learn how life takes hold on a sterile landmass.

INTRODUCTORY PARAGRAPH 2

Moving to a new country can be an exciting, even exhilarating experience. In a new environment, you somehow feel more alive. Seeing new sights, eating new food, hearing the foreign sounds of a new language, and feeling a different climate against your skin stimulate your senses as never before. Soon, however, this sensory bombardment becomes sensory overload. Suddenly, new experiences seem stressful rather than stimulating, and delight turns into discomfort. This is the phenomenon known as culture shock. Culture shock is more than jet lag or homesickness, and it affects nearly everyone who enters a new culture—tourists, business travelers, diplomats, and students alike. Although not everyone experiences culture shock in exactly the same way, many experts agree that it has roughly five stages.

INTRODUCTORY PARAGRAPH 3

The Pilgrims who arrived in Massachusetts in 1620 came to find religious freedom. In the 17th and 18th centuries, large numbers of African men and women were brought as slaves to work on large plantations in the South. Immigrants from northern and southern Europe came in the early 19th century to escape poor economic conditions at home. Later in the 19th century, the first immigrants from China came as contract laborers to build the railroads connecting East and West. In the 20th century, political and economic refugees arrived from Asia, Eastern Europe, and Latin America. Indeed, the United States has seen immigrants come from many different parts of the world, and they have come for many different reasons. Their ability to adjust to life in their adopted land has depended on several factors.

INTRODUCTORY PARAGRAPH 4

Got high blood pressure? Try a truffle. Worried about heart disease? Buy a bon-bon. It's the best news in years! Studies in two prestigious scientific journals say dark chocolate is good for you. It seems that eating a small piece of dark chocolate regularly can reduce the risk of heart disease because dark chocolate—but not milk chocolate or white chocolate—contains high amounts of flavenoids, powerful cholesterol-fighting compounds. What is the next health food going to be? Ice cream? Sugar cookies? There are so many conflicting news stories about which foods are good for you that it is often difficult to make the right choices at the supermarket.

Source: Paragraph 2 adapted from Hadley, Ryan. "Mr. Wygard's Story."

The sentences in each group are in the wrong order. On a separate sheet of paper, write the sentences in the correct order to form an introductory paragraph. Write the thesis statement last. Identify the type of introduction: funnel or attention-getting.

GROUP 1

1. If done properly, a handshake gives the impression of strength and honesty, and if done improperly, it conveys weakness and dishonesty.

2. In some cultures, people bow, and in others, they shake hands.

3. In English-speaking countries, shaking hands is the custom.

4. A proper handshake has four ingredients: pressure, pumps[1], eye contact, and verbal message.

5. The way people greet each other when they meet for the first time varies from culture to culture.

6. How one shakes hands sends an important message about one's character.

Type of introduction: _____

GROUP 2

1. To celebrate the occasion, Mr. X decided to throw a big party at the plant.

2. Mr. X went from his native land to a new country to manage a milk pasteurization plant.

3. Then one day an impressive new pasteurization unit arrived and was installed.

4. The employees did most of the planning and draped the new unit with garlands.

5. During the party one of Mr. X's supervisors took him aside and said, "Now we see what a good man you are; from now on I am sure everyone will really try to do their best for you."

6. And so it was—neither punctuality nor quality checks were any longer needed.

7. This story illustrates the need to understand that doing business in a different culture demands an understanding of the culture.

8. The party was a great success, and everybody had a good time.

9. For eight months, he tried every way possible to convince his workers of the importance of punctuality and of checking every detail of their work.

10. The response was always, "Yes, yes, we will do our best," but nothing ever changed.

Type of introduction: _____

----

[1] **pumps:** movements up and down

GROUP 3

Note: The order of sentences 2, 3, and 4 can vary.

1. Currently under study are four main methods for predicting when and where the next Big One will occur.

2. In 1976, an earthquake in Tangshan, China, killed over 250,000 people.

3. In an average year, earthquakes kill 10,000 people worldwide and cause millions of dollars worth of property damage.

4. Iran suffered more than 80,000 deaths in two massive quakes in 1990 and 2003.

5. Scientists keep trying to find ways to predict earthquakes—so far without much success.

Type of introduction: _____

The Thesis Statement

The thesis statement is the most important sentence in the introduction. It states the specific topic of the essay and often gives the writer's point of view.

> Although some parents and educators oppose same-sex classes, there is some evidence that separating boys and girls in middle school yields positive results.

> Young people in my culture have less freedom than young people in the United States.

> The large movement of people from rural to urban areas has major effects on cities.

Sometimes a thesis statement lists the subtopics that will be discussed in the body.

> Although some parents and educators oppose same-sex classes, there is some evidence that separating boys and girls in middle school yields positive results, particularly in improved learner self-confidence and decreased classroom discrimination.

> Young people in my culture have less freedom than young people in the United States in their choice of where they live, whom they marry, and what their job is.

PRACTICE 4 **Analyzing Thesis Statements**

Read each thesis statement. Draw a box around the topic. Underline the subtopics. Circle the words or punctuation marks that introduce the subtopics.

1. Capital punishment should be abolished not only because it deprives another person of life but also because it does not stop crime.

2. Women generally live longer than men for two main reasons: They tend to take better care of their health, and they have better resistance to stress.

3. Teenagers declare their separateness from their parents by the way they dress and talk.

(continued on next page)

4. In choosing a major, a student has to consider various factors, such as personal interests, job opportunities, and the availability of training institutions.

5. An architect should be both an artist and an engineer.

6. A healthy lifestyle involves eating a nutritious diet, exercising regularly, and getting enough sleep.

<table>
<tr><td>PRACTICE 5</td><td>**Adding Subtopics**</td></tr>
</table>

Complete the thesis statements by adding subtopics.

1. A computer is necessary for college students for three reasons:

   _____

   _____

2. Students have a difficult time taking notes in class due to

   _____

   _____

3. Successful politicians have the following qualities:

   _____

   _____

4. A generation gap[1] exists in my home because of

   _____

   _____

5. To survive a major disaster such as an earthquake requires

   _____

   _____

6. My two sisters are as different as day and night not only in

   _____

   but also in _____

_____

[1]**generation gap:** differences in attitudes and values between generations, especially between parents and children

7. Living in a large city has certain advantages over living in a small town:

_____

_____

8. Latino culture has enriched North American culture in several areas:

_____

_____

Thesis Statement Pitfalls

Because the thesis statement is so important, it must be written with special thought and care. Avoid these three common problems: The thesis is too general; the thesis makes a simple announcement; the thesis states an obvious fact.

Problem 1: The thesis is too general.

TOO GENERAL A college education is a good investment.

IMPROVED A college education is a good investment for four reasons.

TOO GENERAL Lasers are very useful.

IMPROVED Lasers have several applications in industry and medicine.

Problem 2: The thesis makes a simple announcement.

ANNOUNCEMENT I am going to write about sports injuries.

IMPROVED You can avoid sports injuries by taking a few simple precautions.

Problem 3: The thesis states an obvious fact.

OBVIOUS FACT The Internet is a communication superhighway.

IMPROVED The growth of the Internet has had both positive and negative consequences.

BODY PARAGRAPHS

The body paragraphs in an essay are like the supporting sentences in a paragraph. They are the place to develop your topic and prove your points. You can use facts, examples, and other details to support your points. Quotations and paraphrases can also help to develop the subtopics that you explore in the body paragraphs.

TRY IT OUT! Read these two essay "skeletons." Only the introductory paragraph and the topic sentences for the body paragraphs are given. For each essay, choose one topic sentence. On a separate sheet of paper, develop it into a full body paragraph. Remember that your points in the body paragraph must support the topic sentence.

Essay 1

Controlling Stress in Student Life

INTRODUCTORY PARAGRAPH   The busy schedules that most adults face every day have created a growing health problem in the modern world. Although we often think of stress affecting only highly pressured executives, in fact, it is one of the biggest health issues facing college students today. It can cause a variety of physical disorders ranging from headaches to stomach ulcers and even alcoholism. Stress, like the common cold, is a problem that cannot be cured; however, it can be controlled. Students can learn to control stress in four ways.

TOPIC SENTENCES FOR
BODY PARAGRAPHS

A. Set realistic goals.

B. Take up a hobby.

C. Exercise regularly.

D. Maintain close relationships with family and friends.

Essay 2

Studying in Great Britain

INTRODUCTORY PARAGRAPH   People come to Great Britain from all over the world to pursue an education. Some come for a year, while others may stay four years or longer to complete a program or earn a degree. Of course, the first few weeks in a new country are always a little stressful, but knowledge of a few British characteristics and customs can smooth the path for new arrivals. If you take into account these characteristics, students can understand how to adapt and what to do to have a positive experience studying in Great Britain.

TOPIC SENTENCES FOR
BODY PARAGRAPHS

A. British people are usually reserved[1].

B. The British are quite punctual.

C. In Great Britain, students are expected to speak up in class.

---

[1] **reserved:** quiet, restrained, undemonstrative in words and actions

THE CONCLUDING PARAGRAPH

The conclusion is the final paragraph in an essay. It has three purposes.

- It signals the end of the essay. To do so, begin your conclusion with a transition signal.
- It reminds your reader of your main points, which you can do by summarizing your subtopics and/or paraphrasing your thesis.
- It leaves your reader with your final thoughts on the topic. This is your opportunity to convey a strong, effective message that your reader will remember.

See Appendix B, pages 296–298, for more information about transition signals.

Techniques for Memorable Conclusions

Some techniques you can use to write a memorable conclusion include making a prediction, suggesting results or consequences, recommending a solution or call to action, or quoting an authority.

Make a prediction.

> We have seen how the costs of attending college have been rising while, at the same time, sources of financial aid for students have been disappearing. If this trend continues, fewer and fewer families will be able to send their children through four years of college.

Suggest results or consequences.

> To sum up, the costs of attending college are up and financial aid for students is down. Fewer and fewer future members of the workforce are able to educate themselves beyond high school. As a result, the nation will waste the intelligence, imagination, and energy of a large segment of the present college-age generation.

Recommend a solution or a call for action.

> It is clear that the U.S. system of higher education is in trouble. For many students, completing four years of college is no longer possible because of increasing costs and decreasing financial aid. To reverse this trend, we must demand that government increase its financial support of colleges and universities and restore financial aid programs. Our future depends on it.

Quote an authority on the topic.

> In conclusion, costs are rising and financial aid is declining, with the result that many can no longer afford to go to college. If our nation is to prosper, increased government funding for education is essential, even if it requires higher taxes. As Horace Mann[1] argued in his *Fifth Annual Report*, a nation's economic wealth will increase through an educated public. It is therefore in the self-interest of business to pay the taxation for public education.

---

[1] **Horace Mann:** public figure (1796–1859) considered the father of public education in the United States

Work with a partner. Read the essay and the two possible concluding paragraphs. Then answer the questions.

Student-Centered Teaching

For generations, students have complained that school is boring. A teaching approach called *student-centered teaching* aims to get learners more involved. With this approach, students do not simply listen to the teacher. Instead, they learn through group tasks or independent activities created by a teacher. These activities often require students to solve a problem, which exposes them to new information. As a result, students gain new understanding. Although there are many different ways to make a class student-centered, three approaches have become the most common: inquiry-based learning, problem-based learning, and project-based learning.

Inquiry learning is based on the writings of John Dewey. Inquiry learning starts with a question and then engages students in problem-solving activities. Students learn as they explore, gather data, and analyze their data. The teacher's role in inquiry learning is one of a facilitator[1] and provider of information (Savery). Ill-structured problems—ones with many different solutions and many paths to a solution (Jonassen)—are favored over well-structured problems. These are ones with a single correct answer.

Problem-based learning (PBL) was first used in medical education (Barrows) and then adopted by K–12[2] educators. Like inquiry learning, PBL encourages learning through exploration and experiments. Ill-structured problems are also typical of problem-based learning instruction. These problems provide the learner with a broad area of exploration[3]. However, the teacher's role in PBL differs from the role in inquiry learning. In PBL, the teacher acts as a facilitator, but does not provide information to the learner. Instead, the learners are expected to find the necessary information they need to solve the problem (Savery).

Project-based learning is also an active learning strategy. Similarly, it often focuses on a problem. However, the problem in project-based learning is well structured, and learners are told the goal of their project (Savery). Goals could be as diverse as determining the percentage of voters in a district or creating a bird-friendly area in the school yard. Project-based learning is focused on following a process described by the teacher. This process may involve arriving at a calculation or reading specific materials. In contrast to the first two methods, the teacher's role in project-based learning is more likely to be as a coach[4] who provides feedback and guidance (Savery).

One approach to education is called project-based learning.

Sources:
1. Article adapted from Morrison, G., and D. Lowther. *Integrating computer technology into the classroom: Skills for the 21st Century.*
2. Barrows, Howard S. *How to Design a Problem-based Curriculum for the Preclinical Years.*
3. Dewey, John. *Democracy and Education.*
4. Jonassen, David H. "Instructional Design Models for Well-structured and Ill-structured Problem-solving Learning Outcomes."
5. Savery, John R. "Overview of Problem-based Learning: Definitions and Distinctions."

---

[1] **facilitator:** someone who helps a group of people discuss things with each other or do something effectively

[2] **K–12:** from kindergarten to grade 12, the primary and secondary levels of education in the United States

[3] **exploration:** discovering more about something by discussing it, thinking about it, etc.

[4] **coach:** someone who helps a person or team improve, usually in a sport

Concluding Paragraph A

To sum up, student-centered teaching is very important to learning. Three kinds of student-centered approaches are inquiry-based learning, problem-based learning, and project-based learning. Of course, each individual teacher might use these approaches in different ways. In the end, however, student-centered methods will develop stronger critical thinking skills and better prepare students for future success.

Concluding Paragraph B

In conclusion, it is easy to see why these approaches are often used together. After all, each one focuses on problem solving, and the teacher's role in each approach is not limited to traditional lecturing. There are many approaches to making the learning environment more student-centered. Teachers must choose an approach that makes new information necessary and exciting.

Questions about the Essay

1. Which concluding paragraph provides a summary of the subtopics?

2. Which one paraphrases the thesis statement?

3. Which one presents a call to action?

4. Which one makes a prediction?

TRY IT OUT! Reread the two Try It Out! essays on page 86 along with the two body paragraphs you wrote. Then write a concluding paragraph for each.

PATTERNS OF ORGANIZATION

Like paragraphs, essays must be carefully organized. Remember that an essay has three parts: an introduction, a body, and a conclusion. However, the method that you choose for organizing the information and ideas in an essay can vary. In Chapter 2, you learned about three different patterns of order or organization: comparison / contrast, chronological order, and logical division of ideas. These and other organization patterns can be used to write an essay.

ORGANIZATION AND THESIS STATEMENTS

A thesis statement can indicate the pattern of organization that an essay will follow. Which of these thesis statements indicates chronological order? Logical division of ideas? Comparison / contrast?

When buying a used car, use these four strategies to get the best price.

There are several differences between a nurse practitioner and a physician's assistant.

My best friend and I spent an entire summer constructing a tree house in my grandmother's old apple tree.

A Study the thesis statements. Write the organization pattern used: comparison / contrast or time sequence (chronological order).

1. Beginning in World War II and continuing through the period of economic boom, the structure of education in Xanadu has changed remarkably.

    Pattern of organization: _____

2. Although higher education in Xanadu has improved remarkably in recent years, elementary and secondary schools lag far behind.

    Pattern of organization: _____

B Find the topic and subtopics of each paragraph. Then decide how many paragraphs will probably be in the body of each essay.

1. Beginning in World War II and continuing through the period of economic boom, the structure of education in Xanadu has changed remarkably due to an improved economy and efforts by the government to provide education in rural areas.

    Probable number of body paragraphs: _____

2. Education in Xanadu has improved remarkably in recent years in many areas of schooling, including liberal arts, medicine, law, and business.

    Probable number of body paragraphs: _____

ORGANIZATION AND BODY PARAGRAPHS

As you have learned, body paragraphs develop subtopics of an essay's main topic. The pattern of organization you choose will help determine the focus and order of your body paragraphs. Will the body paragraphs follow events in time order? Will they emphasize similarities and/or differences? Will they each discuss an important point related to the main topic? Sometimes, depending on your topic, you will need to use a combination of these patterns.

Logical Division of Ideas

As you read previously, a basic pattern for essays, like paragraphs, is the logical division of ideas. In this pattern, you divide your topic into subtopics, and each subtopic develops one important idea, category, or point related to the main topic. Each subtopic is discussed in a separate paragraph, and paragraphs are presented in an order that will make sense to your readers. Logical division is an appropriate pattern for explaining causes, reasons, types, kinds, qualities, methods, advantages, and disadvantages, as these typical college exam prompts ask you to do.

TYPICAL PROMPTS FOR COLLEGE EXAMS	
Subject	**Prompt**
Economics	Explain the three causes of inflation.
Agriculture / Landscape Design	Describe the basic types of soils and what additives are needed to prepare each type for planting.
U.S. History	Discuss the causes of the U.S. Civil War.
Business	Explain the three main forms of business organization.
Health sciences	Describe the various classes of drugs used to treat depression.

The writing model "Separating the Sexes" on page 75 and the essay "Student-Centered Teaching" on page 88 are both organized in a logical division of ideas pattern. There are three things to remember when you write a logical division essay.

- Divide your topic into subtopics and make sure your thesis statement indicates logical division.
- Discuss each subtopic in a separate paragraph.
- Use transitions between paragraphs to guide your reader from one subtopic to the next.

Thesis Statements for Logical Division of Ideas

As you learned on page 83, a thesis statement often indicates subtopics that will be discussed in the essay.

a. When the organization pattern is the logical division of ideas, the statement may list each subtopic:

> Native Americans have made many valuable contributions to U.S. culture, particularly in the areas of **language**, **art**, **food**, and **government**.

b. Sometimes the thesis statement of a logical division essay may simply indicate the number of subtopics:

> Native Americans have made valuable contributions to U.S. culture in **four** main areas.

c. When an essay has only two subtopics, paired conjunctions (*both . . . and, not only . . . but also*) may be an effective way to list them:

> Young people in my culture have very little freedom **not only** in their choice of lifestyle **but also** in their choice of careers.

d. A colon (:) is often useful before lists of two, three, or more subtopics in a thesis statement:

> The Father of Psychoanalysis, Sigmund Freud, believed that the human mind had three parts: the id, the ego, and the superego.

Notice that the subtopics of a logical division of ideas essay are in parallel form, which means that they have the same grammatical form: In the examples in *a* and *d*, all the words are nouns; in *c*, two prepositional phrases are linked by the paired conjunctions *not only . . . but also.*

See Parallel Structure in Sentences, pages 191–192, for information about parallel form.

Recognizing Thesis Statements for Logical Division

Check (✓) the thesis statements that suggest logical division as a method of organization.

☐ 1. Teenagers demonstrate their independence in several ways.

☐ 2. My 18th birthday was the most memorable day in my life so far.

☐ 3. On their 18th birthdays, U.S. citizens receive two important rights / responsibilities: They can vote, and they can sign legal contracts.

☐ 4. In most occupations, women are still unequal to men when careers are compared.

☐ 5. Living in a dormitory offers several advantages to first-year students.

☐ 6. Photosynthesis is the process by which plants manufacture their own food.

☐ 7. A college degree in international business requires (1) a knowledge of business procedures and (2) a knowledge of cultural differences.

☐ 8. A computer is usually faster and sometimes more accurate than a human.

☐ 9. Giving a surprise birthday party requires careful planning.

☐ 10. Being an only child is very different from having siblings.

TRY IT OUT! On a separate sheet of paper, write a thesis statement for a logical division essay on each topic. Use the suggested subtopics in parentheses or your own ideas.

TOPICS

- Strategies for succeeding in school (three strategies)
- Characteristics of effective classroom environments (three characteristics)
- Kinds of appeals television advertisers use to sell automobiles / cosmetics / any product or service (three kinds of appeals)
- Approaches to teaching young children, teenagers, and adults (three groups of learners)
- The advantages (or the disadvantages) of going to university in a large city / a small town / a rural area (three advantages or disadvantages)

Transition Signals for the Logical Division of Ideas

Transition signals are important to guide the reader through your essay. The ones you might use for a logical division essay include many that you already know. Review the chart for a list of common transition signals.

TRANSITION SIGNALS	
Words and Phrases	**Examples**
first, first of all, second, third, etc.	First, excessive government spending can lead to inflation.
also, in addition, moreover, furthermore	In addition, unrestrained consumer borrowing can cause inflationary tendencies.
next, last, finally	Finally, an increase in the supply of paper money gives rise to inflation.
Coordinators	**Examples**
and both . . . and not only . . . but also	Both an increase in the supply of paper money and unrestrained consumer borrowing can cause inflationary tendencies. To lose weight, one must not only exercise regularly but also eat wisely.
Others	**Examples**
the first cause, reason, factor, etc. the / a second problem, result, advantage, etc. one problem, reason, important factor, etc. another way, reason, disadvantage, etc. an additional problem, result, etc. in addition to math and science, . . .	A second cause is an increase in the supply of paper money. Regular exercise is one way to get fit and lose weight. In addition to government spending, unrestrained consumer borrowing can cause inflationary tendencies.

Transition Signals between Paragraphs

Linking paragraphs with transition signals helps your reader see how the subtopics are related. Link one paragraph to the next by adding a transition to the topic sentence of the second paragraph. This transition may be a single word, a phrase, or a dependent clause that repeats or summarizes the main idea in the preceding paragraph.

Study the essay "skeleton," and notice how the paragraphs are linked.

Aggressive Drivers

INTRODUCTORY PARAGRAPH   The number of vehicles on freeways and streets is growing at an alarming rate. This increase of motor vehicles is creating hazardous conditions. Moreover, drivers are in such a rush to get to their destinations that many become angry or impatient with other motorists who are too slow or who are in their way. Aggressive drivers react foolishly toward others in several dangerous ways.

TRANSITION WORDS

BODY PARAGRAPH 1   **One way** an angry driver may react is to cut off[1] another motorist. *(+ supporting sentences)* . . .

TRANSITION WORDS

BODY PARAGRAPH 2   **Another way** is to tailgate[2] the other car. *(+ supporting sentences)* . . .

TRANSITION PHRASE

BODY PARAGRAPH 3   **In addition to cutting off and tailgating other cars,** aggressive drivers often use rude language or gestures to show their anger. *(+ supporting sentences)* . . .

TRANSITION CLAUSE

BODY PARAGRAPH 4   **Although law enforcement authorities warn motorists against aggressive driving,** the number who act out their angry impulses has not declined. *(+ supporting sentences)* . . .

CONCLUDING PARAGRAPH   **To conclude,** aggressive drivers are endangering everyone because they create hazardous conditions by acting and driving foolishly. They should control their anger and learn to drive safely. After all, the lives they save could be their own.

[1] **cut off:** drive very quickly and closely in front of another car
[2] **tailgate:** drive too closely behind—or on the tail of—another car

PRACTICE 9   **Using Transitions between Paragraphs**

Connect the paragraphs in this essay by adding a transition to the topic sentences of each body paragraph. Vary the expressions you use. Rewrite the topic sentences as needed.

Medicine and Ethics[1]

1 Recent advances in the fields of medicine and biotechnology have brought about situations that could scarcely be imagined only a generation ago. Battery-operated plastic hearts can be implanted into[2] people. People can be kept alive indefinitely by machines. Exact duplicates of animals can be made. While such scientific achievements may ultimately benefit humankind, they have also created complex legal and ethical issues.

[1] **ethics:** the study of right and wrong
[2] **implanted into:** put into a person's body in a medical operation

2 _____ involves doctors' ability to intervene in human reproduction. A well-known example is the case of Baby M. A man paid a woman to bear a child for him and his wife, who could not have children. They signed a contract, but after the baby was born, the woman wanted to keep the baby. The father said the baby was his, but the woman said it was hers. It took the courts many months to decide who was right.

3 _____ another ethical dilemma[3] has arisen because doctors are now able to keep people who are in comas[4] alive for years by attaching their bodies to machines. This gives great power and great responsibility to the people who control the machines. As a result of this power, society has had to develop a new definition of death. How does a person decide whether another person whose heart cannot beat on its own and whose lungs are pumped by a machine is still alive or not?

4 _____ the ability of biotechnologists to produce new forms of life in their laboratories is another area with profound[5] ethical consequences. Isn't a scientist who creates, for example, a new bacterium "playing God"? Furthermore, is it even safe to introduce new life forms into Earth's atmosphere? Is there a risk that such life forms could get out of control? Some people fear so.

5 _____ scientists are now able to duplicate living organisms, cell by cell, through a process called cloning. Recently, the world was stunned by the successful cloning of a human embryo. Should biotechnologists be allowed to clone people? Who should control human cloning?

6 _____ revolutions—political or technological—cause upheaval[6] and force change. Our new ability to create and prolong life is raising questions and forcing changes in our very concept of life, an issue involving not only legal but also profound moral considerations.

---

[3] **dilemma:** difficult problem

[4] **comas:** states of unconsciousness (being unable to see, hear, or speak)

[5] **profound:** important; serious

[6] **upheaval:** social disturbance

OUTLINES OF ESSAYS

Because an essay is long, it is important to organize and plan before you begin to write. The best way to do this is to make an outline. An outline not only organizes your thoughts but also keeps you on track once you begin to write. Making an outline can help you organize both what you read and what you write.

A formal outline has a system of numbers and letters. Different fields of study may have different systems of outlining, but this one is the most common.

> Roman numerals (I, II, III) number the major sections of an essay (introduction, body, conclusion)
>> Capital letters (A, B, C, D) label the body paragraphs.
>>> Arabic numerals (1, 2, 3, 4) number the subpoints in each paragraph.
>>> Small letters (a, b, c, d) label the specific supporting details.

If another level is needed, use small Roman numbers (i, ii, iii).

PRACTICE 10 **Outlining an Essay**

Complete the outline of the writing model on pages 75–76.

Separating the Sexes, Just for the Tough Years

I. Introduction

Thesis statement: Although some parents, educators, and civil liberties groups oppose single-sex classes, there is some evidence that separating boys and girls in middle school yields positive results.

II. Body

  A. Although it is difficult to say conclusively whether single-sex education leads to higher test scores, in fact, it may make a difference in more important areas.
    1. Inconclusive information about test scores
      a. Some research does not show improved test scores
      b. Some research shows improvement
    2. Positive effect on student attitudes and motivations
      a. Girls: increased confidence and improved attitudes toward math and science ("Study")
      b. Girls: more likely to be "creative thinkers and risk-takers as adults if educated apart from boys in middle school" (Gross)
      c. Boys: gain confidence, no competition with girls
        i. Feel inferior when compared to girls
        ii. No girls = more at ease with themselves and more receptive to learning (Gross)

  B. _____
    1. Playing and squabbling with siblings
    2. Negotiating allowances, chores, and privileges with their opposite-sex parent

  C. _____
    1. Boys dominate discussions
    2. Boys receive more attention than girls

    3. _____

III. Conclusion

In my opinion, same-sex classes in public schools should be encouraged.

✎ Applying Vocabulary: Using Nouns and Noun Suffixes

In your writing, it is important to use the correct word form. Review the word forms you learned in Chapter 1 and at the beginning of this chapter. Practice using them correctly.

PRACTICE 11 **Using Correct Word Forms**

Ⓐ Correct the word forms. Cross out the incorrect form and write the correct form.

1. ~~Educate~~ is very important for every child. _____*Education*_____

2. If children are misbehaving in class, the teacher should separation them until they calm down. _____

3. When a teacher calls on some students more than others, it is a form of discriminate. _____

4. If the class is interesting, the students will be more attention.

   _____

5. The energetic teacher planned a very interaction lesson. _____

Ⓑ Complete the sentences with the correct form of the word in parentheses.

1. Children _____ (development) differently, so one four-year-old may be able to read while another is just learning the alphabet.

2. Often when a student misbehaves, he or she is trying to get the teacher's

   _____ (attend).

3. Over the course of a year, teachers can see great _____ (improve) in their students' work.

4. When students work on group projects, it may be more challenging to evaluate

   the _____ (perform) of each individual in the group.

5. However, this should not be used as an _____ (argue) against doing projects in the classroom.

WRITING ASSIGNMENT

Your assignment for this chapter is to write an essay of five or more paragraphs on a topic related to education. Choose one of the topics from the list to write about. Use the writing model on pages 75–76 to help you. To complete the assignment, follow the steps in the writing process.

TOPICS

- Criteria to consider when choosing a major
- Qualities of a successful student
- Factors that make a class productive and enjoyable

 STEP 1: Prewrite to get ideas.

- After selecting your topic, use a prewriting strategy such as listing (Chapter 1) or clustering (Chapter 2) to generate ideas.
- Look for related points in your list or cluster diagram. If you find anything that is completely off topic or repeated, cross it out.
- Group similar ideas together. These groups will become your body paragraphs.

 STEP 2: Organize your ideas.

- Decide how you want to organize your essay. Do you want to use a comparison / contrast pattern? A logical division of ideas?
- Write a thesis statement for your essay. Be sure it indicates the organization pattern you plan to use.
- Use ideas from your prewrite to make an outline as you did in Practice 10. Put your thesis statement at the top. Then, next to letters A, B, and C, write sentences that will form the topic sentences of your body paragraphs.
- In the spaces under A, B, and C, add details you will use in your body paragraphs.

 **STEP 3: Write the first draft.**

- Use your outline to write your first draft. Remember to include the three parts of the essay that you studied in this chapter: an introductory paragraph (including the thesis statement), body paragraphs, and a conclusion.
- Don't worry if you think of new ideas as you write. You can add or delete ideas later. Just be sure that your new ideas support your thesis.

 STEP 4: Revise the draft.

- Review the content and organization of your draft. Do not try to correct errors in format, mechanics (capitalization, punctuation, and spelling), grammar, and sentence structure at this stage. You will do this in Step 5.

- Begin by reading over your essay to get a general overview. As you read, make sure that
  - your essay has a thesis statement;
  - the thesis is developed with enough supporting information;
  - you support your opinions with facts and examples;
  - your conclusion supports your thesis statement.
- Make notes in the margin about anything you want to improve.
- Ask a classmate to read and give you feedback on your first draft using the Chapter 4 Peer Review on page 327.
- Discuss your classmate's suggestions and decide which ones to take.

 Proofread ➤ ### STEP 5: Edit and proofread the draft.

- Make sure that you have identified all of the changes you want to make in content and organization. Then review your essay for errors in format, mechanics, grammar, and sentence structure. Use the Chapter 4 Writer's Self-Check on page 328 to help you.
- When you find an error, make a note on your paper using the correction symbols from Appendix D on pages 309–311.

Write ➤ ### STEP 6: Write a new draft.

- In your new draft, include the changes you identified in Steps 4 and 5.
- Proofread your new draft again carefully. Make sure it is neat and error free.
- Hand in your essay to your teacher.

SELF-ASSESSMENT

In this chapter, you learned to:

○ Identify the parts of an essay

○ Analyze an essay's introduction and conclusion

○ Construct an appropriate thesis statement

○ Support the thesis statement with body paragraphs

○ Organize an essay, using transition signals as necessary

○ Write, revise, and edit an essay about education

Which ones can you do well? Mark them ✓

Which ones do you need to practice more? Mark them ✗

TIMED WRITING

In this expansion, you will write an essay in class. As you write, focus on using the techniques for logical division essays that you learned in this chapter. You will have 50 minutes. To complete the expansion in time, you will need to budget your time accordingly. Follow this procedure.

1. Read the writing prompt (or the prompt your teacher assigns) carefully. Choose one topic to write about. Make sure you understand the question or task. You may want to underline the key words in the prompt. (5 minutes)

2. Brainstorm to get ideas, write a thesis statement, and make a rough outline to organize your ideas. (10 minutes)

3. Write your essay. Be sure to include an introductory paragraph with your thesis statement, body paragraphs, and a concluding paragraph. (25 minutes)

4. Check your essay for errors. Correct any mistakes. (10 minutes)

5. Give your paper to your teacher.

Prompt: Write a logical division essay about one of these topics:

- Different kinds of teachers
- Benefits of learning a new language
- Three educational experiences that inspired you

USING QUOTES AND PARAPHRASES TO SUPPORT IDEAS

Write an essay about the challenges of education in a new culture. Use information given by students who have had this experience and experts in the field of international education. Quote, summarize, and paraphrase your outside sources as appropriate.

- If possible, interview individuals about the topic of your essay. Write down their answers. Then look at their answers to see which will help to explain and expand the ideas you are discussing in your essay.

- Use the Internet to find information about your topic. Find two or three websites with detailed information or expert opinions that you think will make your ideas clearer to the reader.

Remember to include in-text citations and a works-cited list to inform your readers about your sources. In doing so, you not only show your readers that you can speak authoritatively on the topic, but you also give them a chance to do further reading themselves.

CHAPTER 5

PROCESS ESSAYS

Nuclear power is a controversial source of energy.

In this chapter, you will learn about writing a **process essay**. This type of essay is written to explain processes and procedures, such as how something works or how to do something. In fact, a process essay is sometimes called a "how to" essay.

The information in a process essay is almost always presented in chronological order, or time sequence. For example, you would use chronological order to explain how to take a photograph, how to perform a chemistry experiment, or how to set up an accounting system. You would also use chronological order to explain processes such as how a snowflake forms, or how a piece of equipment operates. At the end of this chapter, you will write a process essay about a topic related to earth science.

ANALYZING THE MODEL

The writing model is a process essay. It explains two processes involving nuclear energy. As you read the model, look for the two processes. Before you read the model, look at this diagram.

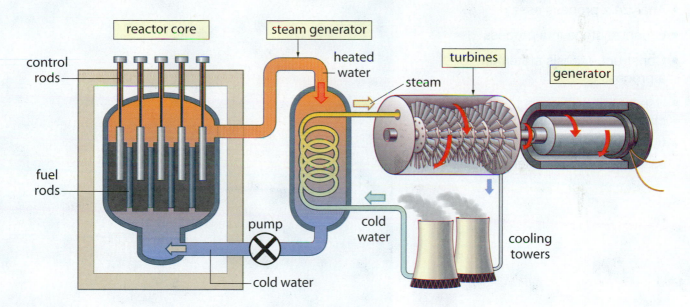

Read the model. Then answer the questions.

✎ **Writing Model**

Japan's Nuclear Crisis

1   Nuclear power is often used to generate electricity for twenty-first century needs. It is produced for this purpose by commercial nuclear reactors in nuclear power plants. In general, these reactors are reliable and efficient. Still, dangerous accidents or other serious problems can occur, so nuclear reactors must be built to withstand everything from hurricanes to terrorist attacks. Unfortunately, these safety measures are not always adequate. Shortly after an earthquake hit Japan on March 11, 2011, a chain of events led to explosions at the Fukushima Daiichi nuclear plant. To understand how the accident at Fukushima happened, it is necessary to understand how a nuclear reactor is constructed and operates.

2   A nuclear reactor produces energy through a nuclear reaction called fission, or the splitting of atoms. Reactors generally use uranium atoms for the fission process. First, small pieces of uranium are combined in metal tubes known as fuel rods. Many bundles of fuel rods form the reactor's core. As fission occurs, the uranium atoms in the fuel rods are split, and energy in the form of heat is generated.

3   However, too much heat can be dangerous. To regulate the heat generated by a reactor, fuel rods are interspersed with control rods. These are made of materials such as boron, which slow nuclear reactions. When the control rods are pushed into the reactor core, fission slows, and the reactor cools. When the control rods are pulled out, fission speeds up, and the reactor produces more heat.

4   The heat from the reactor is then channeled to a container of water called a steam generator. In a steam generator, heat is used to boil water and produce steam. Next, the steam turns a turbine, which powers a generator that creates electricity. Finally, the water is recirculated through the system with electric pumps to cool the reactor core. This cooling process is important because, if the fuel rods get too hot, the fuel can melt. A "meltdown" can destroy the walls of the reactor. It can allow nuclear radiation to escape and poison the surrounding area.

5   When the earthquake hit the Fukushima Daiichi nuclear power plant in Japan, there were many systems in place to prevent this kind of disaster. First, the reactor's control rods were fully inserted into the reactor core. This procedure automatically shut down the reactor. The shutdown helped to cool the reactor core, but of course it also made the nuclear power plant stop producing power. With no power, the electric pumps in the cooling system could not function. As a result, the core soon heated up again.

(continued on next page)

6   Once the plant itself stopped producing power, it began to draw power from the nation's power grid[1] to run the pumps. Other power plants around the country, nuclear and nonnuclear, were still producing electricity. Unfortunately, the earthquake had also damaged the power grid. It, too, soon stopped providing power to the Fukushima Daiichi pumps. At this point, there was still one more safety system that could prevent meltdown: backup diesel generators. These machines use diesel fuel, instead of nuclear power, to make electricity. The diesel generators had started to make electricity to run the plant's cooling pumps when another disaster occurred. Fukushima Daiichi was hit with a tsunami, or giant wave, caused by the earthquake. The tsunami flooded the generators. This left only batteries to operate the pumps. They lasted for just a few hours before they ran out of power.

7   After the batteries died, the pumps failed once and for all. They could no longer circulate water to cool the reactor. As a result, the water started boiling away, exposing the tops of the fuel rods. Then the metal tubes holding the uranium fuel overheated and split. The cracks allowed the remaining water to enter the tubes and interact with the fuel. This interaction began generating hydrogen gas. The hydrogen accumulated so quickly that it exploded inside the reactor building. To prevent disaster, operators decided to destroy the reactor in a flood of seawater mixed with boron. The seawater reduced the reactor's temperature while the boron stopped the process of nuclear fission. A meltdown was prevented.

8   As these events show, nuclear power is a resource with great potential, but in some circumstances it still can have serious risks. Prior to the earthquake and tsunami, Japan had planned to increase its use of nuclear power. It is now unlikely that a large increase can happen. It is also unclear how much of the country's nuclear infrastructure[2] will be rebuilt, and it is still unknown whether the Japanese people are open to continued reliance on nuclear fuel.

Sources:
  1. Brain, Marshall and Robert Lamb. "How Nuclear Power Works."
  2. "Explaining Nuclear Energy for Kids." *The Washington Post*.
  3. "Japan to Scrap Nuclear Energy in Favor of Renewables." *The Guardian*.
  4. Timmer, John. "Understanding Japan's Nuclear Crisis."
  5. "Uranium." *Energy Kids*. U.S. Energy Information Administration.

---

[1] **power grid:** the system for carrying electrical power around the country

[2] **infrastructure:** the basic systems and structures that a country or organization needs in order to work properly, for example roads, railways, and banks

Questions about the Model

1. What is the thesis statement? How does it indicate that at least part of this essay will use chronological organization?

2. What two processes are explained?

3. Which paragraphs explain the first process? Which paragraphs explain the second process?

4. What kind of introduction does this essay have—"funnel" or attention-getting?

5. What kind of conclusion does it have? Does it summarize the main points or paraphrase the thesis or is it a different kind? Does it give a final comment?

✏ Noticing Vocabulary: Word Parts and Word Families

In Chapters 1 and 4, you learned about word families and suffixes. You also learned that words in a word family often have similar meanings but are different parts of speech.

Words in the same word family are related because they share the same basic part, called a **base word** or **word root**. Base words—for example the verb *act*—can stand alone as words. (*Act* is the base of words like *action* and *actor*.) Word roots, however, cannot stand alone. For example, the root *struct*—the root of the word *structure*—is not a word.

Prefixes, like roots and suffixes, are word parts. Prefixes can be added to the beginning of a word's base or root to modify its meaning. For example, the prefixes *con* and *de* can be added to the root *struct* to create *construct* and *destruct*. *Construct* and *destruct* have different but related meanings.

Notice the words *reactor* and *constructed* in the model. These two words have both a prefix and a suffix added to the base or root. Understanding how words in word families are built from word parts can help you expand and enrich the vocabulary you use in your writing.

| PRACTICE 1 | Recognizing Word Parts |

Ⓐ Find words in the model that use one or more of the word parts in this chart. Write at least ten words.

PREFIX	BASE OR ROOT	SUFFIX
auto	act	ic
con	mat	ing
ex	pose	ly
re	source	or
	struct	

_____   _____

_____   _____

_____   _____

_____   _____

_____   _____

Ⓑ Now write a definition of each word. Use a dictionary as needed. Notice how the meanings of the words in a word family are related.

Like other essays, a process essay includes an introduction, a body, and a conclusion. What's different about a process essay is that it's usually organized into steps. You must discuss the steps in your process in the order in which they occur. Otherwise, readers will be confused.

It's usually a good idea to figure out what steps you want to include as soon as you decide on your topic. Then you'll be prepared to write your thesis statement and decide how many paragraphs to include in your essay's body. Here are three important points to remember in organizing a process essay:

- Write a thesis statement that names the process and indicates time order.
- Discuss the steps in your process in the order in which they occur.
- Use chronological order signal words and phrases to indicate the time sequence.

THESIS STATEMENTS FOR A PROCESS ESSAY

The thesis statement for a process essay indicates that chronological order will be used. Statements often use verbs like *plan*, *develop*, and *evolve* or expressions such as *the process of*, *the procedure for*, *five stages*, and *several steps*.

Follow these **steps** to make a beautiful ceramic vase for your home.

The field of genetic engineering has **developed** rapidly in the past ten years.

Heating water by solar radiation is **a simple process**.

Sometimes the thesis statement tells the number of steps in the process.

The process of heating water by solar radiation involves **three** main steps.

The thesis statement may even name the steps.

The main steps in the process of heating water by solar radiation are (1) trapping the sun's energy, (2) heating and storing the hot water, and (3) distributing the hot water to its points of use.

Creating Thesis Statements for Process Essays

Check (✓) the thesis statements that suggest the essay will describe a process or a procedure. Then, in the checked statements, circle the words that indicate chronological order.

☑ **1.** A child learns to handle responsibility in a series of small (steps).

☐ **2.** Both heredity[1] and environment contribute to a person's intelligence.

☐ **3.** There are two main reasons that governments should provide free higher education for their citizens.

☐ **4.** The procedure for submitting expense reports has recently changed.

☐ **5.** The tensions that led to last year's student riots had been developing for several years.

☐ **6.** Some cultures have very direct interaction styles, while other cultures are more indirect.

☐ **7.** Two of the busiest travel days in the United States are the Wednesday before and the Sunday after Thanksgiving.

☐ **8.** Cultures celebrate the end of winter and the arrival of spring in different ways.

☐ **9.** The preparation of the poisonous puffer fish for eating is a delicate process that is not for amateur chefs.

☐ **10.** The life cycle of the monarch butterfly is an interesting phenomenon.

TRY IT OUT! Choose five topics that you think would be interesting for a process essay. Write thesis statements for the five topics you choose on a separate sheet of paper. Remember to use words that suggest time order.

TOPICS

- How to take a good photograph
- How to research a topic for an essay
- How diamonds are processed from a diamond mine to a diamond ring
- How to perform a particular chemistry or physics experiment
- How to transplant a tree
- How a hybrid automobile works
- How to overcome a fear
- How to celebrate a special occasion (such as a favorite holiday, a birthday, a wedding, an anniversary)

---

[1] **heredity:** the process by which mental and physical qualities are passed from a parent to a child before the child is born

BODY PARAGRAPHS IN A PROCESS ESSAY

You discuss the steps in the process or procedure that you are writing about in your body paragraphs. You may want to discuss each step in a separate body paragraph, or you may want to group the steps. If you need to include a lot of information about a step, adding details that will help your readers understand how to do it or how it is done, you can present that step in a separate paragraph. On the other hand, you can discuss several steps in a single paragraph if doing so helps clarify the process.

To write about how to make a ceramic vase, you might divide the body into four paragraphs.

> **I.** Introductory paragraph
> **II.** Body
>   **A.** Shaping the vase
>   **B.** First (bisque) firing
>   **C.** Glazing
>   **D.** Second firing
> **III.** Concluding paragraph

In the paragraph on "shaping the vase," you might include details in time order such as placing the clay on the pottery wheel, shaping the form of the vase, hollowing out the center of the vase, and creating the rim of the vase.

PRACTICE 3   **Identifying and Organizing Steps**

A Choose the topic that interests you most. Then list five or more steps you might include to describe the process. Write the steps on a separate sheet of paper.
- Achieving a high grade in a class
- Setting up a wireless network of computers and printers
- Helping someone who is having a heart attack
- Organizing a community garden

B Look at the steps you listed in Part A and put them in chronological order. Decide which steps will require a separate paragraph and which can be grouped together.

C Choose one of the steps you listed. On the same paper, write a list of details you will include to explain the step.

Writing Tip

Make sure you use the right verb form for the type of process essay you are writing.
- Use the imperative form to tell how do to something
  First, place the clay on the pottery wheel.
- Use the simple present to say how something works.
  A GPS system receives signals from a satellite.
- Use the simple past to tell how something happened.
  The earthquake damaged the power grid.

TRANSITION SIGNALS FOR CHRONOLOGICAL ORDER

Chronological order signal words are especially important in a process essay. You have to be very clear about the sequence of steps: Does one step happen before, after, or at the same time as another step? Chronological order signals include all time expressions.

CHRONOLOGICAL ORDER SIGNAL WORDS AND PHRASES	EXAMPLES
first, first of all, second, third, etc.	First, choose a destination for your camping trip.
then, next, after that, soon, later, later on	
meanwhile, at the same time, now	Meanwhile, have a supply of clean rags ready.
gradually, eventually	Gradually increase your child's allowance.
finally, last, last of all	
SUBORDINATORS	**EXAMPLES**
after since as until as soon as when before while	After you have chosen a destination, make a list of equipment and supplies that you will need. Praise your child when he or she does something well.
OTHERS	**EXAMPLES**
the first (second, last, final) step	The last step is to decorate the cake.
on the third day	
later that morning	
for five minutes	Continue stirring the soup for five minutes.
in 2012	In 2012, scientists announced a major discovery.
several years ago	My parents emigrated to the United States several years ago.
a few weeks later	
in the next (past, last) 15 years	

See Chapter 12, page 224, to learn more about Time Clauses.

PRACTICE 4   **Identifying Chronological Order Signals**

Reread the writing model on pages 103–104. Find and circle all chronological order signals, including time words, time phrases, and time clauses.

Read "How to Make a Model Volcano." Complete the paragraph using chronological order signals from the box. Add commas where necessary.

after it erupts	once the paint has dried
after the outside of the volcano is complete	second
	then
finally	when the vinegar meets
first	the baking soda
next	

How to Make a Model Volcano

When a volcano erupts, gas from under the earth bubbles up to the surface and forces hot lava above the ground. It is an impressive sight, and there is much that volcanoes can teach us about physics and earth science.

To learn more about how volcanoes work, you can follow a process to make a model volcano out of a few common household materials. _____ take a jar or a bottle and cover it with clay or paper-maché. _____ mold the covering into the shape of a volcano and decorate it so that it resembles a volcanic mountain. _____ use small twigs to create miniature trees and pebbles to mimic boulders. You can use any leftover material to make other small hills surrounding the volcano. _____ spray or paint it with shellac or waterproof varnish. This will enable you to clean the volcano more effectively _____.

_____ fill the bottle most of the way with warm water. _____ add red food coloring to mimic the color of lava and dishwashing soap to create bubbles. _____ add baking soda. Baking soda contains sodium bicarbonate, which supplies the carbon for the carbon dioxide gas that will make the volcano erupt. When you are ready for the eruption, pour some vinegar into the bottle. _____ a chemical reaction happens, and carbon dioxide is released. The carbon dioxide gas bubbles up and pushes the liquid out of the bottle, causing the eruption.

✐ Applying Vocabulary: Using Word Parts and Word Familes

Understanding how words are built from word parts can help you expand your vocabulary and use words correctly in context. Of course, if you are unsure of a word's meaning or spelling, you should check the word in the dictionary before using it in your writing.

PRACTICE 6   **Using Word Parts and Word Families**

Ⓐ Combine the word parts to make at least five words. (Try not to repeat the words you wrote for Practice 1 on page 105.) Remember that word parts may slightly change in spelling when combined.

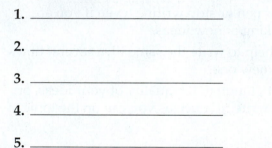

PREFIX	BASE OR ROOT	SUFFIX
auto	act	ic
con	mat	ing
ex	pose	ly
re	source	or
	struct	

1. _____

2. _____

3. _____

4. _____

5. _____

Ⓑ Choose five words from Practice 1 on page 105 and Part A above. Use each word in a sentence that you might use to describe a process.

1. _____

_____

2. _____

_____

_____

3. _____

_____

_____

4. _____

_____

_____

5. _____

_____

Your assignment for this chapter is to write an essay on a topic related to earth science. Choose one of the topics from the list. Use the writing model on pages 103–104 to help you. To complete the assignment, follow the steps in the writing process.

TOPICS

- What to do in case of an earthquake (or hurricane or other natural disaster)
- How to perform a particular science laboratory experiment
- How to conserve energy in your daily life

Prewrite ▶ **STEP 1: Prewrite to get ideas.**

- Use a prewriting strategy to generate ideas about your topic. One technique you can use is called **freewriting**. Freewriting is a brainstorming technique in which you write down all of your ideas without stopping.
  - Write your topic at the top of your page.
  - Place your pen on the first line of your paper and begin writing.
  - Do not pick up your pen or stop writing, even if you are having trouble thinking of new ideas.
  - Sometimes, it may help to write the same idea several times until you think of a new one.
  - Do not worry about grammar, the quality of your ideas, or anything else—just write as much as you can on the topic of your essay!

Omar did some freewriting to prepare for his essay about a science laboratory experiment. Here is the beginning of his freewriting.

> In chem class we sometimes did lot of experiment and I like them although sometime it is hard but you try and you do it ok so I need to write about how to do this so it is first you are reading the lab manual to understand then maybe I should think of an experiment to describe an experiment to describe an experiment to describe oh ok I will do the one from last week where we had to decide what is acid and what is base, so first we had to get some materials

Organize

STEP 2: Organize your ideas.

- Choose one main idea from the prewriting that you think will be a strong focus for your essay. This should be your thesis statement. Remember to use a thesis statement that indicates a process essay.
- Look for related ideas in the freewriting from Step 1. If you find anything that is completely off topic, or repeated, cross it out. Then rewrite your ideas so that they are grouped with similar ideas. These groups will become your body paragraphs.
- Next, make an outline as you learned to do in Chapter 4. Put your thesis statement at the top. Then, for letters A, B, and C, write the sentences that will form the topic sentences of your body paragraphs.

STEP 3: Write the first draft.

- Using your list, begin writing your first draft. Remember to use chronological order transitions in your body paragraphs.
- Describe the steps in your process or procedure in your body paragraphs.
- Don't worry if you think of new ideas as you write. You can add or delete ideas later. Just be sure that your new ideas support your thesis.

STEP 4: Revise the draft.

- Review the content and organization of your draft. Do not try to correct errors in format, mechanics (capitalization, punctuation, and spelling), grammar, and sentence structure at this stage. You will do this in Step 5.
- Begin by reading over your essay to get a general overview. As you read, make sure that
  - ○ your essay has a thesis statement that is appropriate for a process essay;
  - ○ you have organized the steps in the process clearly;
  - ○ you have used appropriate chronological order transition signals.
- Make notes in the margin about anything you want to improve.
- Ask a classmate to read and give you feedback on your first draft using the Chapter 5 Peer Review on page 329.
- Discuss your classmate's suggestions and decide which ones to take.

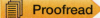 **Proofread** ▶ **STEP 5: Edit and proofread the draft.**

- Make sure that you have identified all of the changes you want to make in content and organization. Then review your essay for errors in format, mechanics, grammar, and sentence structure. Use the Chapter 5 Writer's Self-Check on page 330 to help you.
- When you find an error, make a note on your paper using the correction symbols from Appendix D on pages 309–311.

Write ▶ **STEP 6: Write a new draft.**

- In your new draft, include the changes you identified in Steps 4 and 5.
- Proofread your new draft again carefully. Make sure it is neat and error free.
- Hand in your essay to your teacher.

SELF-ASSESSMENT

In this chapter, you learned to:

○ Analyze a process essay

○ Organize steps in a process

○ Construct a thesis statement for a process essay

○ Use transition signals to show chronological order

○ Write, revise, and edit a process essay about earth science

Which ones can you do well? Mark them ✓

Which ones do you need to practice more? Mark them ⊗

EXPANSION

🕐 TIMED WRITING

In this expansion, you will write an essay in class. As you write, focus on using the techniques of process writing that you learned in this chapter. You will have 50 minutes. To complete the expansion in time, you will need to budget your time accordingly. Follow this procedure.

1. Read the writing prompt (or the prompt your teacher assigns) carefully. Choose one of the topics to write about. Make sure you understand the question or task. You may want to underline the key words in the prompt. (5 minutes)

2. Brainstorm to get ideas, choose a thesis and make a rough outline to organize your ideas. (10 minutes)

3. Write your essay. Be sure to include an introductory paragraph with your thesis, body paragraphs, and a concluding paragraph. (25 minutes)

4. Check your paragraph for errors. Correct any mistakes. (10 minutes)

5. Give your paper to your teacher.

Prompt: Write a process essay about one of these topics:
- How to cook a favorite food
- How to do a favorite hobby
- How to succeed in your major area or professional field
- How to accomplish an academic task (register for classes, apply for a scholarship, pass an exam, etc.)

WRITING FROM A DIAGRAM

Look at the diagram, which shows the process of generating energy from wind. Then write a paragraph that explains the process to someone who cannot see the diagram.

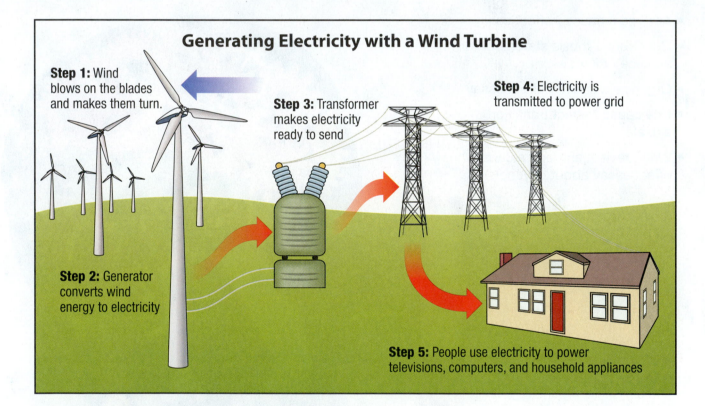

Generating Electricity with a Wind Turbine

Step 1: Wind blows on the blades and makes them turn.

Step 3: Transformer makes electricity ready to send

Step 4: Electricity is transmitted to power grid

Step 2: Generator converts wind energy to electricity

Step 5: People use electricity to power televisions, computers, and household appliances

CAUSE / EFFECT ESSAYS

OBJECTIVES

To write academic texts, you need to master certain skills.

In this chapter, you will learn to:

- Analyze a cause / effect essay

- Construct a thesis statement for a cause / effect essay

- Organize a cause / effect essay

- Use cause / effect transition signals

- Write, revise, and edit a cause / effect essay about psychology

Different parts of the brain are responsible for different kinds of thought and behavior.

INTRODUCTION

Another common type of essay examines cause and effect relationships. In a **cause / effect essay**, you discuss the causes (reasons) for something, the effects (results), or both causes and effects. You might use cause / effect organization to answer typical test questions such as these:

EDUCATION Explain reasons for the decline in reading ability among schoolchildren.

ENVIRONMENTAL STUDIES Discuss the effects of global warming on the environment.

BUSINESS, ECONOMICS Discuss the housing market and its effects on the U.S. economy.

HISTORY Discuss the causes of the U.S. Civil War.

PSYCHOLOGY Explain the causes and effects of depression.

At the end of this chapter, you will write a cause / effect essay on a topic related to psychology.

ANALYZING THE MODELS

In this chapter, you will read two cause / effect essays that look at psychological topics. Each model is organized differently: Writing Model 1 uses block organization, and Writing Model 2 uses chain organization.

Read the models. Then answer the questions.

✎ **Writing Model 1**

The Biological and Environmental Causes of Shyness

1   If you suffer from shyness, you are not alone, for shyness is a universal phenomenon[1]. According to recent research, "close to 50 percent of the general population report that they currently experience some degree of shyness in their lives. In addition, close to 80 percent report having felt shy at some point in their lives" (Payne). As shyness is so common, it is not surprising that social scientists are learning more about its causes. They have found that shyness can result from both biological and environmental factors.

2   Recent research shows that some individuals are born shy. Indeed, researchers say that between 15 and 20 percent of newborn babies have signs of shyness. These babies are quieter and more watchful. In fact, researchers have found differences between sociable and shy babies that show up as early as two months. In one study, two-month-olds later identified as shy reacted with signs of stress to moving mobiles[2] and tape recordings of human voices. These shy babies had increased heart rates as well as jumpy movements of arms and legs, and they cried

(continued on next page)

---

[1] **phenomenon:** something that happens or exists in society, science, or nature, especially something that is studied because it is difficult to understand (plural: *phenomena*)

[2] **mobiles:** a decoration made of small objects tied to wire or string which is hung up so that the objects move when air blows around them

a great deal. Furthermore, parents and grandparents of shy children often say that they were shy as children. They report childhood shyness more frequently than parents and grandparents of non-shy children (Henderson and Zimbardo).

3   However, environment can, at least in some cases, triumph over biology. On the one hand, a shy child may in time lose much of his or her shyness. On the other hand, many people who were not shy as children become shy as adults. Both facts point to environmental causes.

4   The first environmental cause of shyness may be a child's home and family life. Children who grew up with a difficult relationship with parents or older siblings are more likely to be inhibited[3] in social interactions. Another factor is that today's children are growing up in smaller families. They have fewer relatives living nearby. Also, more children are growing up in single-parent homes or in homes in which both parents work full time. These children may not have frequent visits by neighbors and friends. Because they have less interaction with relatives and other visitors, they may begin to feel shy when they start school (Henderson and Zimbardo).

5   A second environmental cause of shyness may be one's culture. In a large study conducted some years ago in several nations, 40 percent of participants in the United States rated themselves as shy. This percentage is compared to 57 percent of participants in Japan and 55 percent in Taiwan. Of the countries participating in the study, the lowest percentage of shyness was found in Israel. The rate there was 31 percent. Researchers Henderson and Zimbardo note that differences "in the way each culture deals with attributing credit for success and blame for failure" may account in part for the higher rate of shyness reported in Japan than in Israel. In Japan, failure is generally attributed to the individual but success is not, while the reverse is often true in Israel. Therefore, Israelis may be more likely to take risks than Japanese.

6   In addition to family and culture, technology may play a role. In the United States, the number of young people who report being shy has risen from 40 percent to 50 percent in recent years (Henderson and Zimbardo). The rising numbers may result in part from a growing dependence on technology (Payne). Watching television, playing video games, and surfing the Web have displaced activities that involve face-to-face social interaction for many young people. Adults, too, are becoming more isolated as a result of technology. Face-to-face interactions are no longer necessary in many situations. Instead, people can use machines to do their banking, fill their gas tanks, order merchandise, take college courses, and make friends. As a result, people have less opportunity to socialize in person. Therefore, they become more awkward at it. Eventually, they may start avoiding it altogether. In short, they become shy.

7   While being shy has some negative consequences, it has positive aspects, too. For example, shy people may be better listeners ("Shyness"). Furthermore, a university professor says, "Because of their tendency toward self-criticism, shy people are often high achievers, and not just in solitary activities like research and writing. Perhaps even more than the drive toward independent achievement, shy people long to make connections to others, often through altruistic behavior[4]" (Benton).

---

[3] **inhibited:** too embarrassed or nervous to do or say what you want

[4] **altruistic behavior:** altruistic behavior shows that you care about and will help other people, even though this brings no advantage for yourself

8   To sum up, shyness has both environmental and genetic causes. Some people come into the world shy. Others become shy as a result of their experiences in life. It appears that most people have experienced shyness at some time in their lives, and research indicates that the number of shy people is increasing. Therefore, if you are shy, you have lots of company.

Sources:
1. Benton, Thomas H. "Shyness and Academe."
2. Henderson, Lynne and Philip Zimbardo. "Shyness."
3. Payne, Karen S. "Understanding and Overcoming Shyness."
4. Wikipedia. "Shyness."

Questions about the Model

1. Is the topic of this essay primarily the causes or the effects of shyness?

2. Which paragraphs discuss the causes?

3. Which paragraph discusses the effects?

4. What two subtopics are named in the thesis statement?

5. Which paragraph discusses the first subtopic?

6. Which paragraphs discuss the second subtopic?

✎ Writing Model 2

SAD

1   Years ago, medical researchers identified a psychological disorder that they named Seasonal Affective Disorder, or SAD. People who suffer from SAD become very depressed during the winter months. Doctors now understand the causes of this condition, which affects millions of people. It is particularly common in areas of the far north where winter nights are long, and the hours of daylight are few.

2   SAD results from a decrease in the amount of sunlight sufferers receive. There are several reasons why decreased sunlight may have this impact on some people. Doctors know that decreased sunlight increases the production of melatonin. This sleep-related hormone is generated at increased levels in the dark. Therefore, when the days are shorter and darker, the level of melatonin rises. Shorter, darker days also decrease production of serotonin, a chemical that helps transmit nerve impulses. Lack of serotonin plays a role in causing depression in some people ("Seasonal Affective Disorder" HH). In others, who may not usually suffer from depression, winter depression may result from an imbalance of melatonin and serotonin in the body. Also, doctors believe that decreased sunlight may cause a disturbance in the body's natural clock ("Seasonal Affective Disorder" NMHA). The combination of chemical imbalance and biological clock disturbance, doctors say, results in characteristic symptoms. These can include lack of energy, oversleeping, weight gain, and anxiety. They are all signs of depression.

(continued on next page)

3   Since absence of light seems to be the cause of SAD, a daily dose of light appears to be the cure. Doctors advise patients to sit in front of a special light box that simulates natural light for a few hours every day. An hour's walk outside in winter sunlight may also help ("Seasonal Affective Disorder" NMHA).

4   In conclusion, the depressive effect of low sunlight levels may help explain why some people suffer feelings of tiredness and sadness in winter. The 19th-century American poet Emily Dickinson even wrote about the feelings of sadness she experienced during winter afternoons. But if low sunlight can produce such feelings, there is nevertheless hope for sufferers. In fact, the problem itself may suggest its own remedy! When the days grow short, turn on the lights.

Sources:
1. The Healthy House Ltd. "Seasonal Affective Disorder."
2. National Mental Health America. "Seasonal Affective Disorder."

Questions about the Model

1. What is the cause of increased melatonin and decreased serotonin in winter?

2. What effect do these seasonal changes in melatonin and serotonin have on some people?

3. What advice do doctors give people who suffer from SAD?

Noticing Vocabulary: Collocations 1

Collocations are words that are commonly found together. For example, in the model, the phrase *difficult relationship* is a collocation because the word *difficult* is frequently used with the word *relationship*. The word *hard*, on the other hand, does not collocate well with *relationship*. Being aware of collocations will make you a better writer. Try to notice collocations as you read or listen to people speaking English. Some dictionaries also list collocations.

PRACTICE 1   **Identifying and Using Collocations**

A   Writing Model 1 on pages 117–119 contains several adjective-noun collocations. Find the nouns in the model and write the adjectives.

_____ causes (*paragraph 3*)

_____ dependence (*paragraph 6*)

_____ consequences (*paragraph 7*)

_____ aspects (*paragraph 7*)

_____ causes (*paragraph 8*)

B Complete the sentences with the collocations from Part A.

1. It is not clear why some people are more likely to be optimistic than others, but it

   is likely that there are some _____ , or reasons related to
   the biological traits that people inherit from their parents.

2. One of the _____ of working as a teacher is the satisfaction
   of helping students learn.

3. Because of the _____ on cell phones, most people do not
   make clear plans far in advance; they assume that they will be able to get in touch
   whenever they want.

4. The _____ of lung disease include exposure to smoke, coal
   or asbestos dust, and certain chemicals.

5. One of the _____ of owning a car is decreased
   physical activity.

ORGANIZATION

You can organize a cause / effect essay in two main ways: "block" organization
and "chain" organization. You can write an effective essay using either type of
organization, but you should choose which one you will use before you start writing.
Knowing the type of organization will help you present information clearly.

BLOCK ORGANIZATION

In block organization, you first discuss all of the causes (in one, two, three, or more
paragraphs, depending on the number of causes). Then you discuss all of the effects.
You can discuss either causes or effects first. Of course, you can also discuss only
causes or only effects. Writing Model 1 on pages 117–119 is written using mostly
block organization.

In block organization, a short paragraph often separates one major section from
another major section. This paragraph is called a transition paragraph. Its purpose
is to conclude one section and introduce another section. You do not always have to
write a transition paragraph, but it is helpful when your topic is long and complex. For
example, an essay about global warming might include several paragraphs about the
causes and several paragraphs about the effects, with a transition paragraph between
the two blocks.

Essays that discuss mainly (or only) causes or mainly (or only) effects might have a
transition paragraph between blocks of different kinds of causes or between blocks
of different kinds of effects. For example, you might use a transition paragraph to
separate the personal effects of our increased life expectancy from its many effects on
the economy.

In short, a block-style cause / effect essay can have many different patterns. This chart shows some possibilities.

BLOCK ORGANIZATION

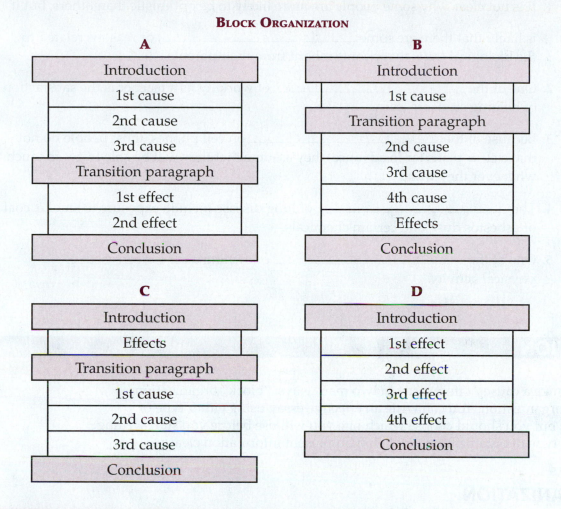

A

| Introduction |
| 1st cause |
| 2nd cause |
| 3rd cause |
| Transition paragraph |
| 1st effect |
| 2nd effect |
| Conclusion |

B

| Introduction |
| 1st cause |
| Transition paragraph |
| 2nd cause |
| 3rd cause |
| 4th cause |
| Effects |
| Conclusion |

C

| Introduction |
| Effects |
| Transition paragraph |
| 1st cause |
| 2nd cause |
| 3rd cause |
| Conclusion |

D

| Introduction |
| 1st effect |
| 2nd effect |
| 3rd effect |
| 4th effect |
| Conclusion |

PRACTICE 2   **Analyzing Block Organization**

Fill in the boxes to show the block organizational pattern of Writing Model 1 on pages 117–119. Write the topic of each paragraph and tell whether it is a cause or an effect.

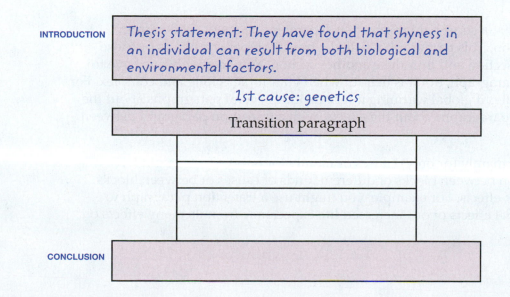

INTRODUCTION — Thesis statement: They have found that shyness in an individual can result from both biological and environmental factors.

1st cause: genetics

Transition paragraph

CONCLUSION

CHAIN ORGANIZATION

The other organizational pattern you can use to write about causes and effects is chain organization. Writing Model 2 on page 119 uses this organizational style.

In Writing Model 2, causes and effects are linked to each other in a continuous chain. One event (a change in seasons), causes another event (decreased sunlight), which causes a third event (disturbance in both hormonal balance and the body's natural clock), which in turn causes a fourth event (the development of depressive symptoms), and so on. Each new cause and its effect are links in a chain, with the effect of one event becoming the cause of the next event. Depending on the complexity of the ideas in each link, you can devote an entire paragraph to one link, or you may include several links in one paragraph, or you may describe the entire chain in one paragraph. Chain organization usually works better than block organization when the causes and effects are too closely linked to be separated. Notice the chain pattern in this diagram.

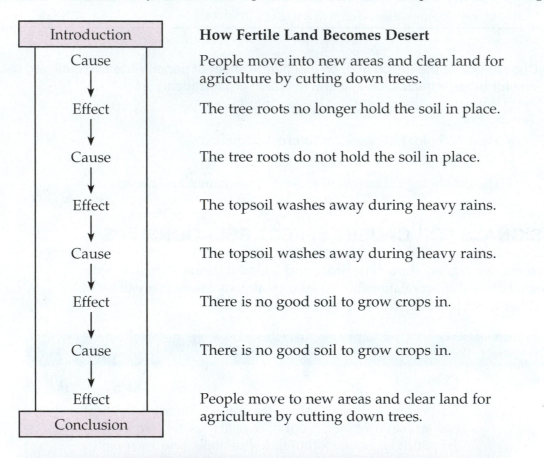

	How Fertile Land Becomes Desert
Introduction	
Cause	People move into new areas and clear land for agriculture by cutting down trees.
Effect	The tree roots no longer hold the soil in place.
Cause	The tree roots do not hold the soil in place.
Effect	The topsoil washes away during heavy rains.
Cause	The topsoil washes away during heavy rains.
Effect	There is no good soil to grow crops in.
Cause	There is no good soil to grow crops in.
Effect	People move to new areas and clear land for agriculture by cutting down trees.
Conclusion	

Writing Tip

The type of organization you choose depends on your topic.

- A chain pattern is usually easier if the causes and effects are very closely interrelated, as in an explanation of a natural phenomenon such as a thunderstorm.

- The block pattern is usually easier with larger, complex topics such as global warming or homelessness.

- Sometimes you will want to use a combination of block and chain organization. Writing Model 1 on pages 117–119 uses mostly block organization, but in paragraphs 4, 5, and 6, you will find chain organization.

Fill in the boxes to complete the flowchart, which illustrates the cause / effect chain described in Writing Model 2.

```
                    ┌─────────────────────┐
                    │    Less sunlight     │
                    └─────────────────────┘
                               │
                               ▼
┌────────────────────────────────────────────────────────────────────┐
│  Body produces                                                       │
│                                                                      │
│  more _____ and              +          _____  │
│                                                                      │
│  less _____                                               │
└────────────────────────────────────────────────────────────────────┘
                               │
                               ▼
┌────────────────────────────────────────────────────────────────────┐
│  Lack of energy, oversleeping, weight gain, anxiety                  │
└────────────────────────────────────────────────────────────────────┘
```

TRY IT OUT!   Choose one of the topics and, on a separate sheet of paper, write two outlines: one for block organization and one for chain organization.

TOPICS

- The psychological causes of Internet addiction
- The effect of job loss on mental health
- The psychological effects of violent video games and movies

TRANSITION SIGNALS FOR CAUSE / EFFECT RELATIONSHIPS

Just as certain transition signals show time order and logical division, certain words and phrases signal cause / effect relationships. You may already know many of them. This chart and the one on page 126 will help you review them.

CAUSE SIGNAL WORDS	
Coordinators	**Examples**
for	Bison were indispensable to the Native American tribes, for this one animal provided them with nearly everything they needed for survival: meat, clothing, shelter, tools, and weapons. (*Note:* When used in this way, *for* has the same meaning as *because*.) However, you must use a comma in front of *for*, and you must not use a comma in front of *because*.
Subordinators	**Examples**
because since as	Bison were indispensable to the Native American tribes as this one animal provided them with nearly everything they needed for survival: meat, clothing, shelter, tools, and weapons.

Others	Examples
to result from to be the result of	The bison's near extinction **resulted from** loss of habitat and overhunting.
due to because of	Bison nearly became extinct **because of** loss of habitat and overhunting.
the effect of the consequence of	One **consequence of** westward expansion was the destruction of habitat for the bison.
as a result of as a consequence of	The areas in which bison could roam freely shrank **as a result of** the westward expansion of the 1800s.

PRACTICE 4   **Recognizing Cause Signal Words**

 Underline the part of the sentence that states a cause. Circle the word or phrase that introduces the cause.

1. The computer is a learning tool (since) it helps children to master math and language skills. *(After* since, *we must use a clause with a subject and a verb.)*

2. Many department stores rely on computers due to their ability to keep records of sales and inventory.

3. A medical computer system is an aid to physicians because of its ability to interpret data from a patient's history and provide a diagnosis. *(How would you rewrite this sentence using* because *instead of* because of?)*

4. War, famine, and ethnic violence have caused a flood of refugees in the past 50 years.

5. Hollywood movies are known for their special effects because U.S. audiences seem to demand them.

6. Since European audiences seem to prefer movies that explore psychological or philosophical issues, European movies are generally quieter and more thought-provoking.

7. Smog results from chemical air pollutants being trapped under a layer of warm air.

8. John's promotion is the result of his brilliant management skills and company loyalty.

9. Little is known about life on the ocean floor, for scientists have only recently developed the technology to explore it.

10. Holes are created in the protective ozone layer of the stratosphere as a result of the burning of fossil fuels.

B Work with a partner or in a small group. Discuss the use of each word or phrase you circled. What kind of grammatical structure follows each one? Notice especially the difference between the use of *because* and *because of*.

EFFECT SIGNAL WORDS	
Transition Words and Phrases	**Examples**
as a result as a consequence therefore thus consequently hence	Workers building the new transcontinental railroad needed meat; as a result, hunters killed bison by the thousands. *Note:* Notice the difference between *as a result* and *as a result of*. *As a result* is followed by a full sentence (independent clause) and introduces an effect. *As a result of* is followed by a noun phrase and introduces a clause.
Coordinators	**Examples**
so	Native Americans began trading bison skins to the settlers for steel knives and guns, so they began killing bison in larger numbers.
Others	**Examples**
to result in to cause	Loss of habitat and overhunting resulted in the near extinction of bison.
to have an effect on to affect	The reduced numbers of bison had a terrible effect on the lives of the Native Americans who had depended on them for survival.
the cause of the reason for	Another cause of the problem was the loss of habitat as more farmers moved to the west.
thereby	The 85 bison that survived were given refuge in Yellowstone National Park in 1892, thereby saving this species from total extinction. *Note: Thereby* is most frequently used in front of *-ing* phrases.

PRACTICE 5 **Recognizing Effect Signal Words**

A Underline the part of the sentence that states an effect. Circle the word or phrase that introduces the effect.

1. The purchase price of electric cars is far greater than the price of cars with conventional internal combustion engines; consequently, the price must be lowered if they are to become popular.

2. However, electric cars are nonpolluting; therefore, the government offers cash incentives to people who purchase them.

3. In addition, electric cars use relatively inexpensive electricity for power; thus, they cost less to operate than cars that use gasoline.

4. Unfortunately, the operating cost of electric cars only begins to make up for the higher purchase price if a car owner keeps the car for more than eight years; as a result, most people still prefer gasoline-powered vehicles.

5. His patient diplomacy resulted in the successful negotiation of a peace treaty.

6. It has been documented that lack of sleep affects a person's ability to think clearly.

7. Cold water is denser than warm water and will therefore sink.

8. Freshwater is less dense than saltwater, so it tends to float on the surface of a body of saltwater.

9. Air pollution creates holes in the protective ozone layer of the stratosphere, thereby allowing harmful ultraviolet radiation to reach Earth's surface.

10. The cause of the patient's rapid recovery was the excellent care he received from his doctor.

B Work with a partner or in a small group. Discuss the use of each word or phrase that you circled. What kind of grammatical structure follows each one? How is the sentence punctuated?

PRACTICE 6   **Using Cause / Effect Signal Words**

Label the sentences in each item as either *C* (cause) or *E* (effect). Then combine the sentences to show a cause / effect relationship using the signal words in parentheses. Add, delete, or change words as needed.

1. __E__ There are fewer hours of daylight.

   __C__ In winter, the sun is lower in the sky.

   (thus) _In winter, the sun is lower in the sky; thus, there are fewer hours of daylight._

2. _____ Some breeds of dogs have a stronger desire to perform a service than other breeds.

   _____ They are more suitable as search-and-rescue animals.

   (since) _____

   _____

(continued on next page)

3. _____ Seals and other aquatic mammals can see when they are hunting for food in the dark ocean depths at night.

_____ They have very large eyes.

(due to) _____

4. _____ Metals have many free-moving electrons.

_____ Metals are good conductors of heat.

(consequently) _____

_____

5. _____ My company began offering employees flexible working hours.

_____ Productivity has increased.

_____ Absenteeism has declined.

(as a result) _____

_____

6. _____ The temperature of the reactor cooled down.

_____ The Fukushima nuclear reactor was flooded with cool seawater.

(hence) _____

_____

7. _____ The earthquake damaged the connection to the power grid.

_____ The pumps lost electricity and stopped working.

(because of) _____

_____

8. _____ Weather around the world changes.

_____ During an El Niño, the jet stream blows in a different pattern.

(therefore) _____

_____

9. _____ In some areas of the world, heavy rains fall.

_____ Devastating floods and mudslides happen.

(cause—verb) _____

_____

10. _____ In other parts of the world thousands of people suffer starvation.

_____ Drought happens.

(as a result of) _____

_____

11. _____ There was a dramatic rise in food prices in 2012.

_____ The Midwest of the United States suffered the worst drought in more than 60 years.

(the reason for) _____

_____

✏ Applying Vocabulary: Using Collocations 1

As you read earlier, collocations are certain words that are commonly found together. You will hear some collocations used casually in conversation, and you will come across others frequently in your reading. You will also use collocations in your academic writing as you become more familiar with them.

PRACTICE 7 **Using Collocations**

A Work with a partner. Answer the questions. Use the collocations in your answers.

1. What are some of the **negative consequences** of smoking?

2. What are some of the **positive aspects** of having a job?

3. Have you noticed a **growing dependence** on video games among teenagers?

4. What are some of the **environmental causes** of stress in college?

5. Do you think that the tendency to be violent has **genetic causes**?

B Write your own sentences using the collocations from the box.

environmental causes	negative consequences
genetic causes	positive aspects
growing dependence	

1. _____

2. _____

3. _____

4. _____

5. _____

WRITING ASSIGNMENT

Your assignment for this chapter is to write a cause / effect essay on a topic related to psychology. Choose one of the topics from the list to write about. You may notice that you read these topics previously in the Try It Out! on page 124. Use Writing Models 1 and 2 starting on page 117 to help you. To complete the assignment, follow the steps in the writing process.

Topics

- The psychological causes of Internet addiction
- The effect of job loss on mental health
- The psychological effects of violent video games and movies

 **Prewrite**

STEP 1: Prewrite to get ideas.

- Use a prewriting strategy, such as freewriting (Chapter 5), clustering (Chapter 2), or listing (Chapter 1), to generate ideas about your topic.

Organize

STEP 2: Organize your ideas.

- Look for related points from the prewriting you did in Step 1. If you find anything that is completely off topic, or repeated, cross it out.

- Then decide whether you will use chain or block organization, and re-group your ideas so that they follow the kind of organization you chose. These groups will become your body paragraphs.

- Make an outline as you learned to do in Chapter 4. At the start of the outline, after Roman numeral I, put a thesis that indicates a cause / effect essay. For letters A, B, and C in section II, write the sentences that will form the topic sentences of your body paragraphs.

Write

STEP 3: Write the first draft.

- Using your outline, begin writing your first draft. Remember to use cause / effect transitions in your body paragraphs.

- Don't worry if you think of new ideas that are not on your list as you write. You can add or delete ideas later. Just be sure that your new ideas support your thesis.

Revise

STEP 4: Revise the draft.

- Review the content and organization of your draft. Do not try to correct errors in format, mechanics (capitalization, punctuation, and spelling), grammar, and sentence structure at this stage. You will do this in Step 5.

- Begin by reading over your paragraph to get a general overview. As you read, check to make sure that
  - your essay has a thesis statement that is appropriate for a cause / effect essay;
  - you have organized the causes and effects clearly;
  - you have used appropriate cause / effect transition signals.
- Make notes in the margin about anything you want to improve.
- Ask a classmate to read and give you feedback on your first draft using the Chapter 6 Peer Review on page 331.
- Discuss your classmate's suggestions and decide which ones to take.

STEP 5: Edit and proofread the draft.

- Make sure that you have identified all of the changes you want to make in content and organization. Then review your essay for errors in format, mechanics, grammar, and sentence structure. Use the Chapter 6 Writer's Self-Check on page 332 to help you.
- When you find an error, make a note on your paper using the correction symbols from Appendix D on pages 309–311.

STEP 6: Write a new draft.

- In your new draft, include the changes you identified in Steps 4 and 5.
- Proofread your new draft again carefully. Make sure it is neat and error free.
- Hand in your essay to your teacher.

SELF-ASSESSMENT

In this chapter, you learned to:

○ Analyze a cause / effect essay

○ Construct a thesis statement for a cause / effect essay

○ Organize a cause / effect essay

○ Use cause / effect transition signals

○ Write, revise, and edit a cause / effect essay about psychology

Which ones can you do well? Mark them ✓

Which ones do you need to practice more? Mark them ✗

TIMED WRITING

In this expansion, you will write an essay in class. As you write, focus on using the writing process steps that you learned in this chapter. You will have 50 minutes. To complete the expansion in time, you will need to budget your time accordingly. Follow this procedure.

- Read the writing prompt (or the prompt your teacher assigns) carefully. Choose one topic to write about. Make sure you understand the question or task. You may want to underline the key words in the prompt. (5 minutes)
- Brainstorm to get ideas, choose a thesis and make a rough outline to organize your ideas. (10 minutes)
- Write your essay. Be sure to include an introductory paragraph with your thesis, body paragraphs, and a concluding paragraph. (25 minutes)
- Check your essay for errors. Correct any mistakes. (10 minutes)
- Give your paper to your teacher.

Prompt: Write a cause / effect essay of five or more paragraphs on one of these topics:

- The causes of obesity
- The effects of involvement in sports on young children
- The causes of stress in college students

WRITING A SUMMARY AND RESPONSE

In this assignment, you will write an essay in which you summarize and respond to an article called "Nice by Nature?" The topic of the article is helpful behavior in animals. Your response should focus on reasons why you think people help each other. Remember to include an in-text citation at the end of your summary with the name of the article's author.

Read the article "Nice by Nature?" on page 281 in Appendix A and answer the questions. Then following the steps in the writing process, write your summary essay.

CHAPTER 7

COMPARISON / CONTRAST ESSAYS

OBJECTIVES

To write academic texts, you need to master certain skills.

In this chapter, you will learn to:

- Analyze a comparison / contrast essay

- Construct a thesis statement for a comparison / contrast essay

- Organize a comparison / contrast essay

- Use comparison signals to connect similar ideas

- Use contrast signals to connect different ideas

- Write, revise, and edit a comparison / contrast essay about culture

The world is full of diverse cultures.

In a **comparison / contrast essay**, you explain the similarities and differences between two or more items. You can compare and contrast people, objects, ideas, countries, traditions, or just about anything else that makes sense. Comparison and contrast is a very common organizational pattern in most academic fields. It is also a common type of essay test prompt. You might encounter prompts such as these:

POLITICAL SCIENCE   Compare the forms of government of Great Britain and the United States.

AMERICAN LITERATURE   Compare the characters of Uncle Melik and his nephew in William Saroyan's short story "The Pomegranate Trees."

BUSINESS   Compare and contrast methods for promoting a new business, product, or service.

ANTHROPOLOGY   Compare the methods of childrearing in two different societies.

At the end of this chapter, you will write a comparison / contrast essay about a topic related to culture.

ANALYZING THE MODEL

The writing model is a comparison / contrast essay that describes some of the similarities and differences between Russia and the United States.

Read the model. Then answer the questions.

✎ Writing Model

Russia and the United States: Differences and Similarities

1   In a shrinking world, it has become vitally important to know and understand countries and cultures that were once seen as distant. Improvements in technology and long-distance transportation, along with the rise of a global economy, have created a need to identify how the society and circumstances of one country may be similar to or different from another's. In fact, although countries may differ significantly, usually enough similarities exist to enable each culture's representatives to find common ground. The United States and Russia provide a good example of two countries that are geographically distant and have fundamental differences but that still find commonalities.

2   As many people are aware, there are significant differences between Russia and the United States in their history and form of government. The United States is a young country with a long history of democratic government. Russia is a country with ancient roots that has experienced different kinds of government, including hundreds of years of monarchy, almost a century of communism, and, more recently, democracy. However, there are also many other areas in which the similarities and differences between these two countries can influence their relations.

3   A key difference between Russia and the United States is population growth. Russia's population has been shrinking because the birth rate is fairly low, although it has increased in recent years. In the United States, on the other hand, the fertility rate

has been consistently high: 2.06 children, compared to only 1.6 for Russia (CIA). There is comparatively little immigration to Russia, mostly from countries that were once part of the former Soviet Union. In the United States, on the other hand, immigration adds about 2.3 million people per year. The difference in population growth in Russia and the United States is also due in part to the fact that the death rate in Russia is second highest in the world. This is much higher than in the United States, which is 87th. The Russian population growth has increased with recent economic improvements, but the United States is likely to continue to grow at a faster pace.

4   Another important difference is in energy production and consumption. The U.S. population is much more reliant on energy than Russia, but the United States also produces more energy. While residents of the United States consume roughly 12,000 kilowatt-hours of electricity per capita, Russia uses only half that amount (The World Bank). Russians use even less oil compared to Americans, at a rate of 15 barrels per day per capita. This is about one-third of the American rate of 62 barrels per day (Indexmundi). At the same time, U.S. energy production is about 1.5 times that of Russia. However, Russia has large reserves of natural gas and does surpass the United States in the production of this energy source (U.S. Energy).

5   Despite the differences in population growth and energy use, there are still similarities between the two countries. One common factor is the relative diversity of the populations. The United States and Russia both have a majority racial group that constitutes about 80 percent of the population and several significant minority groups (CIA). Like the United States, Russia also has linguistic minorities, and there are parts of both countries in which it is common to see signs in two or more languages. The countries are also similar in their religious diversity. Although both countries' populations are largely Christian, they also both have significant numbers of religious minorities. Both countries have substantial populations of Muslims, Jews, and other small groups of religious minorities.

6   Not only do Russia and the United States have similarly diverse populations, but they have also both faced economic challenges in the recent past. Russia had a financial crisis in the late 1990s, and the United States followed almost ten years later. In both cases, the crises led to high unemployment, reduced social spending, and increased poverty (Perry). In Russia's case, the crisis was preceded by confused government policies regarding currency and privatization of industry (Stiglitz). Similarly, in the United States, inadequate government policies for regulating the financial industry were partly responsible for the recession. In both cases, the economic downturns had far-reaching global consequences.

7   In conclusion, there are many differences between Russia and the United States in areas as diverse as population growth and energy consumption. However, the similarities in other areas, such as diversity and recent economic challenges, cannot be ignored. Furthermore, their similarities and differences point to the need that these two countries have to cooperate in the international arena. It will be interesting to see how Russia and the United States work together in the future.

Sources:
1. CIA World Factbook.
2. Indexmundi.com.
3. Perry, Brian. *Credit Crises: Historical Crises*. Investopedia.com.
4. Stiglitz, Joseph. "The Ruin of Russia." The Guardian.
5. U.S. Energy Information Administration.
6. The World Bank.

Questions about the Model

1. What is the thesis statement of this article? Underline it.

2. What differences between the countries are discussed in paragraph 2?

3. What are two other differences between the countries? In which paragraphs are these differences discussed?

4. In which paragraph(s) are similarities discussed?

5. What is the function of the first sentence in paragraph 5?

Noticing Vocabulary: Antonyms

In Chapters 2 and 3, you learned about using synonyms, or words that mean the same thing. In this chapter, you will learn to enrich your vocabulary by using **antonyms**, or words that have opposite meanings. Just as synonyms can help connect similar ideas, antonyms are particularly useful when describing contrasting ideas. And just as a thesaurus is a useful tool for finding synonyms, it will also point you toward one or more antonyms for words you look up.

PRACTICE 1   **Noticing Antonyms**

A Find these words and their antonyms in the model. Write the antonyms.

1. differences *(paragraph 1)* _____

2. low *(paragraph 3)* _____

3. less *(paragraph 4)* _____

4. minority *(paragraph 5)* _____

5. reduced *(paragraph 6)*_____

B These words are also in the model. Write one or two antonyms for each word. Use a dictionary or thesaurus as needed.

1. distant *(paragraph 1)* _____

2. rise *(paragraph 1)* _____ _____

3. adds *(paragraph 3)* _____ _____

4. preceded *(paragraph 6)* _____

5. together *(paragraph 7)* _____

The first key to writing a successful comparison / contrast essay is to organize it carefully. In order to structure your essay, you need to select which things you are going to compare. Then you need to choose the specific points of comparison, or factors, that you will use to explain the similarities and differences you identify.

POINTS OF COMPARISON

Suppose, for example, that you want to compare family life in two cultures. There are many different aspects of this topic that you could examine. Which points of comparison will be your focus?

Before deciding how to organize your essay, you can list the points of comparison that you want to examine in each culture. After listing these points, you can make a chart that shows how they are similar or different in each culture.

Comparison / Contrast Chart

TOPIC: FAMILY LIFE IN CULTURE X AND Y			
Point of Comparison	**Culture X**	**Culture Y**	**Same or Different**
Number of children	1–2	5–6	Different
Living arrangements	Each set of parents and small children lives separately	Grandparents, aunts, uncles, cousins, children live in separate buildings on the same property	Different
Financial support	Both parents work outside the home	Both parents work outside the home	Same
Role of grandparents	Occasional visits	Primary childcare provider	Different
Age of adulthood	When they get married	When they get married	Same

Once you have decided on the particular points of comparison you want to use for your essay, you are ready to decide how you want to organize it. There are two methods for organizing a comparison / contrast essay: point-by-point and block.

POINT-BY-POINT ORGANIZATION

In point-by-point organization, each point of comparison becomes the topic of a paragraph. As you discuss individual points, you describe both similarities and differences. You can put the paragraphs in any order you wish—perhaps in order of importance.

Point-by-Point Outline

If you decided to use point-by-point organization for an essay based on the chart on page 137, your outline might look like this:

> I. **Introduction**
>   **Thesis statement:** It's possible to better understand Culture X and Culture Y by comparing several important aspects of family life in both cultures.
> II. **Body** (Points of Comparison)
>   A. Number of children
>   1. 1–2 in X
>   2. 5–6 in Y
>   B. Living arrangements
>   1. Separately in X
>   2. Extended families together in Y
>   C. Financial support
>   1. Parents work in both countries
>   2. Willing to work outside home
>   D. Role of grandparents
>   1. Occasional visits in X
>   2. Primary caregivers in Y
>   E. Age of adulthood
>   1. At marriage in both cultures
>   2. Specific ages
> III. **Conclusion**

BLOCK ORGANIZATION

The other way to organize a comparison / contrast essay is to arrange all the similarities together in one block and all the differences in another. The writing model on pages 134–135 uses this type of organization. In block organization, you can discuss either the similarities first or the differences first. Of course, you could discuss only similarities or only differences.

The number of paragraphs in each block depends on the topic. For some topics, you might write about all the similarities in a single paragraph; for other topics, you might need to discuss each similarity in a separate paragraph. The same is true of differences. Of course, some topics may have one paragraph of similarities and several paragraphs of differences, or vice versa.

Block Outline

If you decided to use block organization to write an essay based on the chart on page 137, your outline might look like this:

I. **Introduction**

   Thesis statement: Family life in Culture X and Culture Y is very similar in some ways, but it also shows several key differences.

II. **Body**

   A. Similarities

      1. Financial support

      2. Age of adulthood

   B. Differences

      1. Number of children

      2. Living arrangements

      3. Role of grandparents

III. **Conclusion**

Notice that the points of comparison in this outline are the same as the ones in the outline on page 138. However, each point in this outline is used to explain either similarities or differences, instead of being the topic of its own paragraph.

Writing Tip

Point-by-point is often the best choice when the two things you are comparing have both similarities and differences in all of the areas you are discussing. Block is better if there are only similarities in one area or only differences in another area.

Transitions in Block Organization

In block organization, you often insert a transition sentence or short transition paragraph between the two blocks. Its purpose is to conclude one section and introduce another section. You do not always have to write a whole transition paragraph, but it is helpful when your topic is long and complex.

Look at the writing model on pages 134–135. Then complete the outline.

I. **Introduction**

   Thesis statement: The United States and Russia provide a good example of two countries that are geographically distant and have fundamental differences but still find commonalities.

II. **Body**

   A. One key difference between Russia and the United States is population growth.

      1. The United States has higher fertility.

      2. _____

   B. _____

      1. _____

         a. _____

         b. _____

      2. Americans produce more energy than Russians.

   C. There are similarities between the two countries.

      1. Diverse populations

         a. _____

         b. _____

         c. _____

      2. _____

         a. Russian economic crisis in 1990s

         b. U.S. recession 10 years later

III. **Conclusion**

COMPARISON AND CONTRAST SIGNAL WORDS

If the first key element in writing a successful comparison / contrast essay is organization, the second key is the appropriate use of comparison and contrast signal words. These are words that introduce points of comparison and points of contrast. It is not sufficient simply to describe each item that you are comparing. You must refer back and forth to—for example, Culture X and Culture Y—and use comparison and contrast signal words to show what is the same and what is different about them. Of course, you should also use transition signals, such as *first, second, one. . . ., another. . . ., the final. . . ., for example,* and *in conclusion.*

Comparison Signal Words

The chart lists some of the words and phrases used to discuss similarities. Review the words and how they are used.

COMPARISON SIGNAL WORDS	
Transition Words and Phrases	**Examples**
similarly likewise	Human workers can detect malfunctions in machinery; similarly, a robot can be programmed to detect equipment malfunctions.
also	Human workers can detect malfunctions in machinery; a robot can also.
too	Human workers can detect malfunctions in machinery; a robot can, too.
Subordinators	**Examples**
as just as	Robots can detect malfunctions in machinery, just as human workers can. *Note:* Use a comma when *as* and *just as* show comparison even when the dependent clause follows the independent clause as in this example.
Coordinators	**Examples**
and	Robots and human workers can detect malfunctions in machinery.
both . . . and	Both robots and human workers can detect malfunctions in machinery.
not only . . . but also	Not only robots but also human workers can detect malfunctions in machinery.
neither . . . nor	Neither robots nor human workers are infallible[1].
Others	**Examples**
like (+ noun) just like (+ noun) similar to (+ noun)	Robots, like human workers, can detect malfunctions in machinery.
(be) like (be) similar (to) (be) the same as	Robots are similar to human workers in their ability to detect malfunctions in machinery.
(be) the same	In their ability to detect malfunctions in machinery, robots and human workers are the same.
(be) alike (be) similar	Robots and human workers are alike in their ability to detect malfunctions in machinery.
(be) compared (to / with)	Robots can be compared to human workers in their ability to detect malfunctions in machinery.

---

[1] **infallible:** always right and never making mistakes

Recognizing Signal Words

Look at the words in the chart on page 141 and then see how many of them you can find in the writing model on pages 134–135.

Using Comparison Signal Words

Write one new sentence to combine the information in each item below. Use a different comparison signal word in each sentence.

1. The United States has a democratic form of government. Great Britain has a democratic form of government.

   The United States has a democratic form of government, just as

   Great Britain does.

2. The United States operates under a two-party system. Great Britain operates under a two-party system.

   _____

   _____

3. The British Parliament has two separate houses, the House of Commons and the House of Lords. The United States Congress has two separate houses, the Senate and the House of Representatives.

   _____

   _____

4. The members of the U.S. House of Representatives are elected by district. The members of the British House of Commons are elected by district.

   _____

   _____

5. The method of choosing cabinet members in the United States = the method of choosing cabinet members in Great Britain. (*Use the comparison signal* the same.)

   _____

   _____

6. In Great Britain, the prime minister appoints the cabinet. The U.S. president appoints the cabinet.

   _____

   _____

7. The British monarch has the right to veto any law passed by Parliament. The U.S. president has the right to veto any law passed by Congress.

   _____

   _____

On a separate sheet of paper, write five sentences of your own, comparing two things you are familiar with. Use a different comparison signal word in each sentence, and remember to focus on the things that are the same. Some possible topics include:

- The culture of a local high school compared to that of a large university
- The culture of a small town compared to a big city
- Aspects of culture in two different societies

Contrast Signal Words

Contrast signal words fall into two main groups according to their meaning. The words in the first group show a relationship that is called concession. The words in the second group show an opposition relationship.

Concession (Unexpected Result)

Concession signal words indicate that the information in one clause is not the result you expect from the information given in the other clause.

┌ UNEXPECTED RESULT ┐
Although I studied all night, I failed the exam.

Failing the exam is not the result you might expect from the information in the first clause *I studied all night*.

See Contrast Clauses on pages 235–236 for additional examples of contrast subordinators.

CONCESSION SIGNAL WORDS	
Transition Words and Phrases	**Examples**
however nevertheless nonetheless still	Millions of people go on diets every year; however, very few succeed in losing weight.
Subordinators	**Examples**
although even though though	Although most dieters initially lose a few pounds, most gain them back again within a few weeks.
Coordinators	**Examples**
but yet	Doctors say that "fad" diets do not work, yet many people still try them.
Others	**Examples**
despite (+ noun) in spite of (+ noun)	Despite ten years of dieting, I am still overweight.

Look at the words in the chart on page 143 and then see how many of them you can find in the writing model on pages 134–135.

Direct Opposition

The second group of contrast signal words shows that two things are direct opposites. With direct opposites, the signal word can introduce either piece of information.

I am short, **whereas** my brother is tall.

My brother is tall, **whereas** I am short.

DIRECT OPPOSITION SIGNAL WORDS	
Transition Words and Phrases	**Examples**
however in contrast in (by) comparison on the other hand on the contrary	Rock music used to appeal primarily to younger listeners; however, some rock today has enthusiastic fans among senior citizens. Jazz is not just one style of music; on the contrary, jazz has many styles such as Chicago jazz, Dixieland, ragtime, swing, bebop, and cool jazz, to name just a few. *Note: On the contrary contrasts a truth and an untruth.*
Subordinators	**Examples**
while whereas	New Orleans-style jazz features brass marching-band instruments, while ragtime is played on a piano. *Note: Use a comma with while and whereas even when the dependent clause follows the independent clause.*
Coordinators	**Examples**
but	Jazz music was born in the southern part of the United States, but it now enjoys a worldwide audience.
Others	**Examples**
differ (from)	Present-day rock music differs from early rock music in several ways.
compared (to / with)	Present-day rock music has a harder sound compared with early rock.
(be) different (from) (be) dissimilar to (be) unlike	The punk, rap, grunge, and techno styles are very different from the rock music performed by Elvis Presley 50 years ago, but they have the same roots.

Look at the words in the chart on page 144 and then see how many of them you can find in the writing model on pages 134–135.

PRACTICE 7   **Using Contrast Signal Words**

Write one new sentence to combine the information in each item. Use a different comparison signal word in each sentence.

1. The chief executive in Great Britain is called the prime minister. The chief executive in the United States is called the president.

   While the chief executive in Great Britain is called the prime minister,

   the chief executive in the United States is called the president.

2. In the United States, the president fulfills the functions of both political leader and head of state. These two functions are separate in Great Britain.

   _____

   _____

3. In other words, Great Britain has both a monarch and a prime minister. The United States has only a president.

   _____

   _____

(continued on next page)

4. The president of the United States may be of a different political party than the majority of Congress. The British prime minister is the head of the political party that has the most seats in Parliament.

_____

_____

5. The United States has a written constitution. Great Britain has no written constitution.

_____

_____

6. In the United States, elections are held on a regular schedule, no matter how popular or unpopular the government is. In Great Britain, elections are held whenever the prime minister loses a vote of confidence.

_____

_____

7. The members of the U.S. Senate are elected. The members of the British House of Lords are appointed or inherit their positions.

_____

_____

8. As you can see, the two systems of government differ in several major aspects. They are both democracies.

_____

_____

TRY IT OUT! On a separate sheet of paper, write five sentences of your own, contrasting two cultures* you are familiar with. Use a different contrast signal in each sentence. Some possible topics include:

- The culture of a local high school compared to that of a large university
- The culture of a small town compared to a big city
- Aspects of culture in two different societies

* Culture often refers to the values and customs of a country or society, but it can also describe small units, such as a school or a smaller community.

✏ Applying Vocabulary: Using Antonyms

In your writing assignment for this chapter, you are going to write a paragraph about a topic related to culture. You will probably want to use antonyms to connect contrasting ideas.

PRACTICE 8   **Using Antonyms**

Ⓐ Write antonyms for the words. You may want to use some of these words and their antonyms in your writing assignment. Use a dictionary or a thesaurus as needed.

1. large _____

2. rural _____

3. respect _____

4. closeness _____

5. give _____

Ⓑ On a separate sheet of paper, write four pairs of sentences. Use the words from Part A in your sentences. Include one of the words in the first sentence of each pair and then use an antonym in the second sentence.

EXAMPLE

Classes at a university are often very large, with 100 or more students.

The classes at my high school were small, with only about 20 students.

WRITING ASSIGNMENT

Your assignment for this chapter is to write a comparison / contrast essay on a topic related to culture. Choose one of the topics from the list for your essay. (These are the same topics found in Try It Out! on pages 143 and 146. If you used one of these topics before, you may use the same topic again or choose a different one.) Use the writing model on pages 134–135 to help you. To complete the assignment, follow the steps in the writing process.

TOPICS
- The culture of a local high school compared to that of a large university
- The culture of a small town compared to a big city
- Aspects of culture in two different societies

STEP 1: Brainstorm about the topic.

- Collect information and generate ideas about your topic. One tool you can use is a **Venn diagram**. A Venn diagram is a brainstorming tool that uses overlapping circles to show the similarities and differences between two or more ideas.

  ○ Draw two circles that are partly overlapping.

  ○ Write one thing that you are comparing in one circle and the other thing in the other circle.

  ○ Then write the similarities between the two things in the overlapping part of the circle, and the differences between them in the separate areas of the circle. Brainstorm as many ideas as you can. You can decide which ideas to include later.

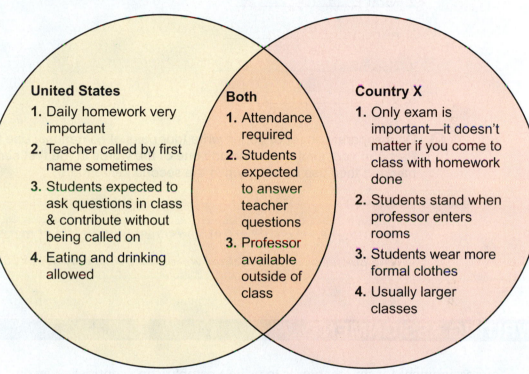

This Venn diagram could help generate and organize ideas for an essay comparing university culture in the United States with that of another country.

STEP 2: Organize your ideas.

- Review the comparison / contrast chart on page 137. Create your own chart, using the most important points from your Venn diagram. Which points of comparison will you examine in your essay? Once you have listed them on your chart, note whether there are more similarities or differences.

- Use your chart to decide whether you will use point-by-point or block organization. Write a preliminary thesis statement that indicates a comparison / contrast essay.

- You may want to make an outline based on your chart. Follow the type of organization you chose. Put your thesis at the top. Then for letters A, B, and C, write the sentences that will form the topic sentences of your body paragraphs.

STEP 3: Write the first draft.

- Begin writing your first draft. Remember to use comparison / contrast transitions in your body paragraphs.
- Don't worry if you think of new ideas that are not in your outline as you write. You can add or delete ideas later. Just be sure that your new ideas support your thesis.

STEP 4: Revise the draft.

- Review the content and organization of your draft. Do not try to correct errors in format, mechanics (capitalization, punctuation, and spelling), grammar, and sentence structure at this stage. You will do this in Step 5.
- Begin by reading over your paragraph to get a general overview. As you read, check to make sure that
  - your essay has a thesis statement that is appropriate for a comparison / contrast essay;
  - you have organized information clearly;
  - and you have used appropriate comparison / contrast transition signals.
- Make notes in the margin about anything you want to improve.
- Ask a classmate to read and give you feedback on your first draft using the Chapter 7 Peer Review on page 333.
- Discuss your classmate's suggestions and decide which ones to take.

STEP 5: Edit and proofread the draft.

- Make sure that you have identified all of the changes you want to make in content and organization. Then review your essay for errors in format, mechanics, grammar, and sentence structure. Use the Chapter 7 Writer's Self-Check on page 334 to help you.
- When you find an error, make a note on your paper using the correction symbols from Appendix D on pages 309–311.

STEP 6: Write a new draft.

- In your new draft, include the changes you identified in Steps 4 and 5.
- Proofread your new draft again carefully. Make sure it is neat and error free.
- Hand in your essay to your teacher.

EXPANSION

TIMED WRITING

In this expansion, you will write an essay in class. As you write, focus on using the writing process steps that you followed in this chapter. You will have 50 minutes. To complete the expansion in time, you will need to budget your time accordingly. Follow this procedure.

1. Read the writing prompt (or the prompt your teacher assigns) carefully. Make sure you understand the question or task. You may want to underline the key words in the prompt. (5 minutes)

2. Brainstorm to get ideas, choose a thesis and make a rough outline to organize your ideas. (10 minutes)

3. Write your essay. Be sure to include an introductory paragraph with your thesis, body paragraphs, and a concluding paragraph. (25 minutes)

4. Check your essay for errors. Correct any mistakes. (10 minutes)

5. Give your paper to your teacher.

Prompt: Compare and contrast the relationship between parents and children in two different cultures. You may include your own culture as one of the two you discuss. You may also write about two different subcultures within a larger cultural group. For example, you might look at the parent-child relationship in two different ethnic or religious groups in your local community.

In this assignment, you will write a four- to six-paragraph essay in which you summarize and respond to an article called "Marital Exchanges." The topic of the article is cultural differences in the custom of exchanging gifts at marriage. Your response should compare marital gift-giving in your culture to the examples given in the article.

Read the article "Marital Exchanges" on page 283 in Appendix A and answer the questions. Then following the steps in the writing process, write your summary essay.

CHAPTER 8

ARGUMENTATIVE ESSAYS

OBJECTIVES

To write academic texts, you need to master certain skills.

In this chapter, you will learn to:

- Analyze an argumentative essay
- Construct an introduction for an argumentative essay
- Use transitions of contrast
- Identify and rebut opposing arguments
- Support your ideas using statistics
- Write, revise, and edit an argumentative essay about space travel

Changes in technology have had a dramatic effect on many different areas of life, including the workplace.

INTRODUCTION

An **argumentative essay** is an essay in which you agree or disagree on an issue, using reasons to support your opinion. Your goal is to convince your reader that your opinion is right. Argumentation is a popular kind of essay question because it forces students to think on their own: They have to take a stand on an issue, support their stand with solid reasons, and support their reasons with solid evidence. At the end of this chapter, you will write an argumentative essay about whether it is wise or practical to attempt to send a human mission to Mars.

ANALYZING THE MODEL

The writing model is about the role of technology in the modern workplace.

Read the model. Then answer the questions.

✏ **Writing Model**

in class

REPLACED BY A ROBOT

1   Ever since the invention of computers, technology has done more and more of the job of the average worker. From mathematical calculations to mailing lists, computers have become more efficient, in more areas, than their human colleagues. Although some argue that computers will never replace people, others are concerned about the advanced robotic technology that computers make possible. Indeed, it is likely that the use of more and better robots will someday result in fewer jobs for humans. However, this should not be seen as a problem. Rather, as technology improves, employers in all fields should look to maximize their robotic workforce and minimize human error.

2   Until now, many have argued that robots can only replace humans in certain less-skilled jobs. They might, for example, be able to perform routine tasks on an assembly line. These opponents of a mechanized workforce may not be aware that technology has progressed in the areas of decision-making and creativity. Some robots' work in these areas is almost equal to that of humans. In fact, some interactive computers are so well-designed that it will soon be possible to talk with them almost endlessly before realizing that they are not human (Loftus). A computer even won the game show *Jeopardy* not long ago. These computers are clearly capable of more than simple tasks.

3   Others argue that, even though computers may someday be able to approximate human behavior, humans will always be able to do the job better. While that may be true for a general-purpose robot, highly-specialized machines can often do specific tasks better than a

(continued on next page)

human being, no matter how well-trained. For example, human lawyers may miss important evidence. This is particularly true when sifting through millions of emails to prosecute crime in so-called "white collar" jobs. Robots, on the other hand, can sort through this information quickly and accurately. In fact, there is now a software program that can detect not just obviously illegal proposals, but also changes in style that can point to suspicious activity. The computer searches for a switch from a formal to an informal tone, or particularly urgent wording. Within seconds, the program can identify the most questionable language and alert investigators (Murray). In this case, human legal experts cannot begin to compete with their electronic colleagues.

4   Finally, some say that it is morally wrong to replace human beings with robots. They argue that it is unethical to deprive real people of their jobs, merely for the sake of efficiency. If efficiency were the only concern, they might be correct. This argument, however, does not take into account the consequences of human failings in the workplace. In surgery, for example, a doctor's arm may shake. A minimally invasive surgical robot, on the other hand, will always make the right cut (Manjoo). It would be truly immoral for society to be concerned about the doctor's job at the expense of the patient's health.

5   Increasingly, employers will need to decide when and how to replace human workers with computers. This decision is not easy, and a robot will not always be the right answer. However, it is clear that as computers approach human ability to reason, as specialized programs develop, and as robots become more reliable, there will be more circumstances in which replacing a person with a robot is not just the most efficient choice, but the most ethical one.

Sources:
1. Loftus, Jack. "Computer Nearly Passes Turing Test for Artificial Intelligence."
2. Manjoo, Farhad. "Will Robots Steal Your Job?"
3. Murray, Peter. "Lawyers Object as Computer Program Does Job Better."

Questions about the Model

1. In which paragraph does the writer give background information to help readers understand the issue?

2. Does the thesis statement mention both sides of the issue, or does it give the writer's point of view only?

3. How many opposing arguments are given? Where are they given?

4. Where does the writer respond to the opposing arguments—in one paragraph or in separate paragraphs?

5. What is the function of the last paragraph?

Noticing Vocabulary: Collocations 2

In Chapter 6, you learned that collocations are words that are commonly found together, and that using collocations properly can improve your writing. You also learned to use noun-adjective collocations. In this chapter, you will learn to use other kinds of collocations, including adverb-adjective and verb-object collocations.

PRACTICE 1   **Identifying Collocations**

A These collocations are missing a word. Look back at the writing model, find the completed collocations, and use them to fill in the blanks. (*Note:* The part of speech of the missing word is in parentheses.)

1. _____ (v) tasks (*paragraph 2*)

2. _____ (adv) capable (*paragraph 2*)

3. _____ (adv) true (*paragraph 3*)

4. _____ (v) crime (*paragraph 3*)

5. _____ (adv) invasive (*paragraph 4*)

B Complete the sentences with the collocations from Part A.

1. The child said the work was too difficult for her, even though she was

   _____ _____ of doing it.

2. In order to succeed in the workplace, employees must _____

   _____ assigned by their supervisors.

3. Politicians often try to avoid stating a position on controversial measures; this is

   _____ _____ during an election year, when they do not
   want to do anything to anger voters.

4. The new mayor promised to aggressively _____ _____
   and make the community safe for law-abiding citizens.

5. With a laser, the doctor performed _____ _____
   surgery on the patient, who was able to go home the same day.

Organizing your arguments effectively will help you convince readers to agree with the ideas and opinions you present in your writing. In an argumentative essay, you do not just give reasons to support your point of view. You must also discuss the other side's reasons and then **rebut** them. *Rebut* means to point out problems with the other side's supporting reasons in order to prove that your opponent's opinion is not right. Rebuttals are one of the key elements that a writer needs to organize in an argumentative essay.

THE ELEMENTS OF AN ARGUMENTATIVE ESSAY

An argumentative essay contains five key elements:

- An explanation of the issue
- A clear thesis statement
- A summary of the opposing arguments
- Rebuttals to the opposing arguments
- Your own arguments

You can organize the elements of an argumentative essay in several ways. You can use a **block pattern** or a **point-by-point pattern**. The outlines in the chart show how these two patterns can be used to structure an argumentative essay.

BLOCK PATTERN	POINT-BY-POINT PATTERN
I. Introduction Explanation of the issue Thesis statement	I. Introduction Explanation of the issue, including a summary of the other side's arguments Thesis statement
II. Body **Block 1** A. Summary of the other side's arguments B. Rebuttal to the first argument C. Rebuttal to the second argument D. Rebuttal to the third argument **Block 2** E. Your first argument F. Your second argument G. Your third argument	II. Body A. Statement of the other side's first argument and rebuttal with your own counterargument B. Statement of the other side's second argument and rebuttal with your own counterargument C. Statement of the other side's third argument and rebuttal with your own counterargument
III. Conclusion	III. Conclusion—may include a summary of your point of view

There are many variations on these two patterns. Which pattern you use will depend on your topic. With some topics, one pattern works better than others. The important thing is to present your side and rebut the other side in a logical and organized way.

Complete the outline of the writing model on pages 153–154.

I. Introduction (explanation of the issue)

Thesis statement: _____

_____

II. Body

  A. Issue 1: Robot and human skills

    1. Opposing argument 1: Until now, many have argued that robots can only replace humans in certain, less-skilled jobs.

    2. Rebuttal to argument 1: Computer technology has now progressed in decision-making and creativity to be almost on a par with humans.

      a. Conversational ability

      b. _____

  B. Issue 2: Robot and human behavior

    1. Opposing argument 2:

    _____

    2. Rebuttal to argument 2:

    _____

      a. Specialized legal task—failings of human lawyers

      b. Specialized legal task—strengths of computer research

  C. Issue 3: Ethics of using robots

    1. Opposing argument 3:

    _____

    2. Rebuttal to argument 3:

    _____

      a. _____

      b. Patient's life is more important than doctor's job.

III. Conclusion

THE INTRODUCTORY PARAGRAPH

There are several ways to write an introductory paragraph for an argumentative essay. In the writing model on pages 153–154, the introductory paragraph contains an explanation of the issue, which is a necessary part of an argumentative essay. However, you may also begin an argumentative essay with a more engaging introduction—for example, with surprising statistics, a memorable quotation, or a dramatic story. For instance, the writer of the model could have opened with a dramatization of a worker being dismissed because he's been replaced by a computer.

If you write an attention-getting introduction, you may need to explain the issue in a second introductory paragraph and write your thesis statement at the end of this (the second) paragraph.

> This scene will become all too common in the near future. A highly educated employee walks into his office, ready to begin a new day at work. Instead of being given an interesting assignment, however, he is told that he is being dismissed—not because of economic problems or poor performance, but because he is being replaced by a robot. Computers taking over the workplace may seem like the plot of a melodramatic science fiction story, but in fact, it is quite real.
>
> In the last decade, technology has developed . . . .

Thesis Statement

The thesis statement in an argumentative essay states clearly which side you are for.

> Curfew laws are unfair and should be abolished.

> In my opinion, stem cell research should receive the full support of our government.

A thesis statement often mentions the opposing point of view. Notice that the writer's opinion is expressed in the independent clause, and the opposing point of view is normally put into a subordinate structure.

———— SUBORDINATE STRUCTURE ————
Despite the claims that curfew laws are necessary to control juvenile gangs,

——— INDEPENDENT CLAUSE ———
curfew laws are clearly unconstitutional.

———— SUBORDINATE STRUCTURE ————
Although there are reasons to be cautious with stem cell research,

——— INDEPENDENT CLAUSE ———
I believe that its potential benefits far outweigh its dangers.

The Opposing Point of View

Expressions such as these are often used to introduce opposing points of view:

> **Some people feel** that the United States should have a national health care plan like Canada's.

> **Many think** that genetically engineered crops are a grave danger to the environment.

> **It may be true** that the U.S. Constitution gives citizens the right to own weapons.

Transition Signals of Contrast

An opposing point of view can be connected to the writer's own point of view with transition signals of contrast.

Some people feel that the United States should have a national health care plan like Canada's; **however,** others feel that government should stay out of the health care business.

Although many think that genetically engineered crops are a grave danger to the environment, such crops can alleviate world hunger and malnutrition.

Supporters say that smokers should have a right to smoke **despite the fact that** smoking will most likely kill those who do it.

While it may be true that the U.S. Constitution gives citizens the right to own weapons, the men who wrote the Constitution lived in a different time.

PRACTICE 3 **Adding an Opposing Point of View**

A Rewrite the thesis statements to include an opposing point of view. Use expressions and transition signals of contrast.

1. Doctors or family members should never be allowed to "pull the plug[1]."

   Although some people believe that doctors and family members should never be allowed to "pull the plug," I believe that it is sometimes more humane to do so.

2. The sale of music containing lyrics that degrade women should be prohibited.

   _____

   _____

3. Television is the worst invention of modern times.

   _____

   _____

4. Environmental protection laws go too far.

   _____

   _____

5. The advertising industry performs many public services.

   _____

   _____

---

[1] **pull the plug:** let a person who is in an irreversible coma die by disconnecting him or her from life-sustaining machines

B Choose your own topic. Then write a thesis statement that expresses both sides of the issue.

_____

_____

TRY IT OUT!   Work with a partner. On a separate sheet of paper, write three supporting arguments for the writer's point of view in each thesis statement.

1. Censorship of the arts is always wrong.

   a. *Freedom to express oneself is a fundamental right stated in the U.S. Bill of Rights.*

   b. *Public morality is relative—what is objectionable in some cultures is acceptable in others.*

   c. *Many masterpieces—books, sculptures, and paintings—would be banned.*

2. Violence in video games, movies, and television programs should be censored.

3. Despite the fact that education's primary responsibility is to train minds, not bodies, I believe that schools should require students to practice a sport at least one hour each day.

4. Although some people think that curfew laws will help control teenage gangs, they are wrong for several reasons.

5. Engaged couples should be required to take marriage preparation classes for one full year before their wedding.

6. Your own topic:

STATISTICS AS SUPPORT

When you write an argumentative essay, you need to support your opinion with strong supporting details. In Chapter 3, you learned that quotes and examples can be effective support. Another kind of support that can be particularly helpful in argumentative writing is statistics, sets of numbers that show patterns of events or behaviors. Statistics are especially useful in argument because they are fact-based and hard to argue against.

ANALYZING THE MODEL

The writing model uses statistics from the graph "Internet users per 100 inhabitants, 1997–2007." As you read the model, notice the expression used to report the source of information. You must cite the source of any statistical data you use in your writing.

Study the graph and read the model. Then answer the questions.

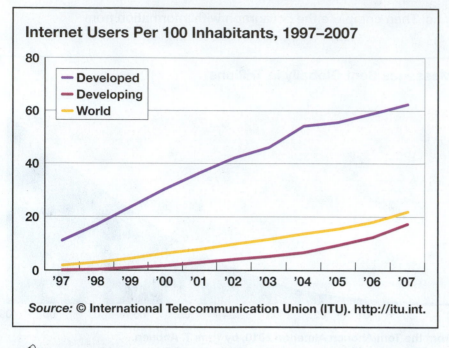

Internet Users Per 100 Inhabitants, 1997–2007

Source: © International Telecommunication Union (ITU). http://itu.int.

✎ Writing Model

The Digital Divide

According to statistics from the International Telecommunication Union, Internet use is increasing worldwide. Moreover, although a wide gap still exists between developed and developing countries, that gap may be closing. In 1997, developed countries had Internet access at a rate of 11 users per 100 inhabitants, whereas developing countries had zero users. By 2002, the developed world had 42 users for every 100 inhabitants, and the developing world had only four. By 2007, however, the increase in the developed world had slowed, adding only 20 users per 100 in five years, compared to the 31 added between 1997 and 2002. At the same time, the developing world was increasing in its rate of Internet spread, to 22 out of every 100 by 2007, an increase of 18 in five years, compared to four in the previous five years. While the digital divide is still certainly a reality, if the 1997–2007 trends continue, the developing world may soon catch up.

Source: Paragraph based on International Telecommunication Union (ITU). http://itu.int.

Questions about the Model

1. What is the topic sentence of the paragraph? Underline it.

2. What is the source of the statistics used to support this idea?

3. What reporting expression is used to identify this source?

4. What is the graph measuring?

Using Statistics

Study the graphs. Then complete the paragraph with information from the graphs.

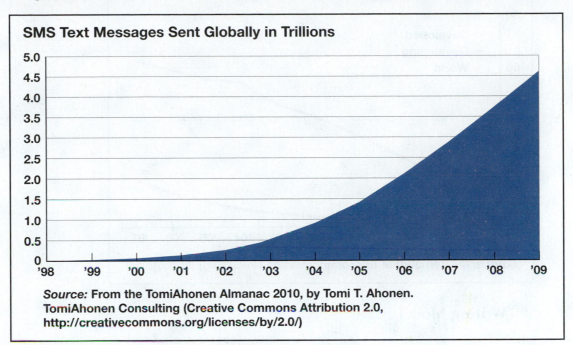

SMS Text Messages Sent Globally in Trillions

Source: From the TomiAhonen Almanac 2010, by Tomi T. Ahonen. TomiAhonen Consulting (Creative Commons Attribution 2.0, http://creativecommons.org/licenses/by/2.0/)

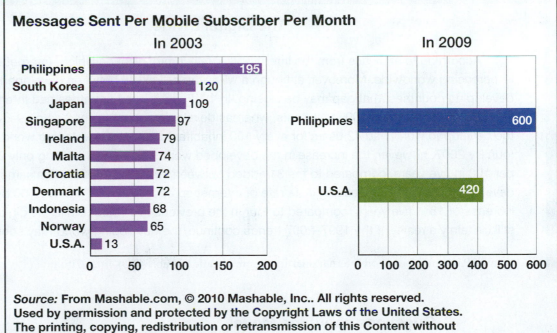

Messages Sent Per Mobile Subscriber Per Month

In 2003

Philippines	195
South Korea	120
Japan	109
Singapore	97
Ireland	79
Malta	74
Croatia	72
Denmark	72
Indonesia	68
Norway	65
U.S.A.	13

In 2009

Philippines	600
U.S.A.	420

Source: From Mashable.com, © 2010 Mashable, Inc.. All rights reserved. Used by permission and protected by the Copyright Laws of the United States. The printing, copying, redistribution or retransmission of this Content without express written permission is prohibited.

Text Message Use

According to _____ , global text messaging

1.

has _____ since 1998. Each year brings

2.

dramatic change. In 2007, the nations of the world sent just under

_____ text messages, whereas in 2008, they sent

3.

almost _____ . The distribution of text messages is

4.

also changing. Although _____ has led the world

5.

in text messages since 2003 and remains on top, it has only increased its

usage from _____ messages per subscriber in

6.

2003 to _____ messages in 2009 (Dimacali). The

7.

United States, on the other hand, is quickly catching up, moving from

_____ messages per mobile subscriber in 2003 to

8.

_____ messages per mobile subscriber in 2009. If

9.

this trend continues, the United States may soon lead the world in text

messages sent.

Choose a graph and, on a separate sheet of paper, write a paragraph explaining its significance. Follow the instructions.

1. Decide what main idea the graph illustrates, and write this idea as a topic sentence.

2. Write five to ten supporting statements, using the statistical information shown in the graphs.

3. Use a reporting verb or phrase to identify the source of your statistics.

4. Write an in-text citation in the proper form at the end of your paragraph.

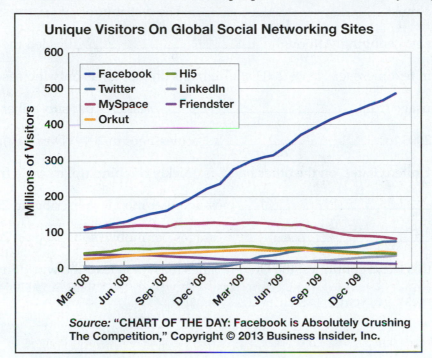

Unique Visitors On Global Social Networking Sites

Source: "CHART OF THE DAY: Facebook is Absolutely Crushing The Competition," Copyright © 2013 Business Insider, Inc.

U.S., Non-U.S., and Worldwide Online Advertising Spending on MySpace and Facebook, 2009 and 2010 (millions and percent change)

	2009	2010	Percent change
MySpace			
U.S.	$465	$360	–23%
Non-U.S.	$25	$25	3%
Worldwide	**$490**	**$385**	**–21%**
Facebook			
U.S.	$335	$450	34%
Non-U.S.	$100	$155	65%
Worldwide	**$435**	**$605**	**39%**

Note: Percent change based on unrounded figures
Source: Courtesy of eMarketer.com.

In academic writing, argument requires evidence researched from outside sources, such as books, scholarly journals, personal interviews and experiments, and the Internet. Learning to do research and evaluate sources is an important academic skill.

See Appendix E, pages 312–319, for information on doing research and evaluating sources.

✍ Applying Vocabulary: Using Collocations 2

Before you begin your writing assignment, review what you learned about collocations on page 155.

PRACTICE 5   **Using Collocations**

A Work with a partner. Answer the questions. Use the collocations in your answers.

1. What types of **crime** do you think should be **prosecuted** most aggressively?

2. Have you (or anyone you know) ever had **minimally invasive** surgery? What kind?

3. Some people believe that technology makes people stupid, and that this is **particularly true** of text messaging. Do you agree or disagree?

4. Most people have household tasks that they enjoy and others that they hate. Which household **tasks** do you most (or least) like to **perform**?

5. Some people think that technology is already as advanced as it can get, while others believe that we do not yet know what computers are **clearly capable** of. What do you think?

B Write your own sentences using the collocations from the box.

clearly capable	perform tasks
minimally invasive	prosecute crime
particularly true	

1. _____

2. _____

3. _____

4. _____

5. _____

Your assignment for this chapter is to write an argumentative essay in response to this question: Is it worth the expense and risk to make a human flight to Mars? Use the writing model on pages 153–154 to help you. You can also use the model on page 161 if you are planning to include statistics in your argument.

Before you begin this writing assignment, research the topic to get ideas and supporting reasons for both sides of the argument. The readings for this chapter on pages 286 and 288 of Appendix A provide information you will need to write your essay. Read the two articles, "Why We Should Send a Manned Mission to Mars" on page 286 and "Let's Not Go to Mars: Why a Staffed Mission Is Impractical" on page 288. Then answer the questions. When you have read both articles and answered the questions, follow the steps in the writing process.

 Prewrite

STEP 1: Prewrite to get ideas.

- After you have finished the readings and their exercises, you will need to decide which side of the argument you agree with. Use freewriting to help you clarify your thoughts on the topic.
- Write as much as you can on the topic. Include any facts, details, statistics, and examples that you researched or that come to your mind.
- Read your freewrite and circle the ideas you would like to develop.

Organize

STEP 2: Organize your ideas.

- Decide whether you will use block or point-by-point organization.
- Write your thesis statement. Your thesis statement can state either just your point of view or both points of view. If it states both points of view, connect them by using transition signals of contrast.
- Develop an outline. Write your thesis statement at the beginning of your outline.

 Write

STEP 3: Write the first draft.

- Before you start writing, decide on the best type of introductory paragraph for your topic: an explanatory paragraph or an attention-getting introduction.
- Using your outline, write the first draft.

Revise

STEP 4: Revise the draft.

- Review the content and organization of your draft. Do not try to correct errors in format, mechanics (capitalization, punctuation, and spelling), grammar, and sentence structure at this stage. You will do this in Step 5.

- Begin by reading over your paragraph to get a general overview. As you read, check to make sure that
  - your essay has a thesis statement that is appropriate for an argumentative essay;
  - you have supported your arguments with facts, quotations, statistics, or examples;
  - you have summarized the opposing viewpoints;
  - you have rebutted the opposing viewpoints.
- Make notes in the margin about anything you want to improve.
- Ask a classmate to read and give you feedback on your first draft using the Chapter 8 Peer Review on page 335.
- Discuss your classmate's suggestions and decide which ones to take.

Proofread

STEP 5: Edit and proofread the draft.

- Make sure that you have identified all of the corrections you want to make in content and organization. Then review your essay for errors in format, mechanics, grammar, and sentence structure. Use the Chapter 8 Writer's Self-Check on page 336 to help you.
- When you find an error, make a note on your paper using the correction symbols from Appendix D on pages 309–311.

Write

STEP 6: Write a new draft.

- In your new draft, include the changes you identified in Steps 4 and 5.
- Proofread your new draft again carefully. Make sure it is neat and error free.
- Hand in your essay to your teacher.

SELF-ASSESSMENT

In this chapter, you learned to:

○ Analyze an argumentative essay

○ Construct an introduction for an argumentative essay

○ Use transitions of contrast

○ Identify and rebut opposing arguments

○ Support your ideas using statistics

○ Write, revise, and edit an argumentative essay about space travel

Which ones can you do well? Mark them ✓

Which ones do you need to practice more? Mark them ✗

TIMED WRITING

In this expansion, you will write an argumentative essay in class. As you write, focus on using the writing process steps that you learned in this chapter. You will have 50 minutes. To complete the expansion in time, you will need to budget your time accordingly. Follow this procedure.

1. Read the writing prompt (or the prompt your teacher assigns) carefully. Make sure you understand the question or task. You may want to underline the key words in the prompt. (5 minutes)

2. Brainstorm to get ideas, choose a thesis and make a rough outline to organize your ideas. (10 minutes)

3. Write your essay. Be sure to include an introductory paragraph with your thesis statement, body paragraphs, and a concluding paragraph. (25 minutes)

4. Check your paragraph for errors. Correct any mistakes. (10 minutes)

5. Give your paper to your teacher.

Prompt: Write an argumentative essay on this topic:

- What is the most important technology in society today?

REBUTTING AN ARGUMENT

Look back at the writing model "Replaced by a Robot" on pages 153–154. Think about the topic of replacing workers with robots. Why might someone disagree with the author's opinion? Write a short essay in which you oppose the arguments made in the model. Summarize the model briefly. Then make sure to clearly disagree in your response to the model. Support your position with examples and ideas both from the model and from supporting strategies you learned in this chapter.

PART III

SENTENCE STRUCTURE

TYPES OF SENTENCES

To write academic texts, you need to master certain skills.

In this chapter, you will learn to:

- Recognize independent and dependent clauses

- Analyze different types of sentences

- Use coordinators, conjunctive adverbs, and semicolons to create compound sentences

- Use adverb clauses to create complex sentences

- Combine different types of clauses to create compound-complex sentences

- Write a paragraph that uses a variety of sentence types

New medical research is helping scientists identify the causes and cures of some allergies.

In the first two parts of this book, you learned to organize, write, revise, and edit paragraphs and essays. In this third part, you will focus on better understanding sentence structure and on improving your skills in crafting sentences. When you know how to vary the kinds of sentences you write, you can express your thoughts in the clearest and most interesting way possible. In this chapter, you will learn to use **clauses** to develop varied types of well-structured sentences.

Clauses are the building blocks of sentences. A clause is a group of words that contains a subject and a verb.

CLAUSES	NOT CLAUSES
SUBJECT VERB ecology is a science	to protect the environment
SUBJECT VERB because pollution causes cancer	after surviving a long illness

At the end of the chapter, you will write a paragraph using various types of well-structured sentences.

ANALYZING THE MODEL

You are going to read two drafts of a writing model about an allergy. As you read, try to identify the improvements that the author made between the first draft and the second draft.

Work with a partner or in a small group. Read the models. Then answer the questions.

✏ **Writing Model**

Dangerous Allergies (First Draft)

1 Most people do not think of peanuts when they think of poisons. **2** Serious peanut allergies are putting an increasing number of individuals at risk for death. **3** Between 1997 and 2008, the peanut allergy rate among children in the United States nearly tripled. **4** The problem is causing great concern. **5** There are no signs that the allergy rate will decrease. **6** No one knows for certain why this increase is happening. **7** There are several theories. **8** Some believe that children are becoming more sensitive to allergens. **9** Cleaning products and antibiotic medicines have made our environment too sanitary. **10** This level of cleanliness, some say, leads to underdeveloped immune systems. **11** Another group of theorists believes that the problem lies in the way peanuts are prepared. **12** This argument blames the roasting process for making peanuts more allergenic. **13** Severe allergies have risen at such an alarming rate. **14** It is likely that research into the causes of these allergies will grow. **15** Science may soon be able to explain why more and more children are threatened by such a simple food.

Dangerous Allergies (Second Draft)

1 Most people do not think of peanuts when they think of poisons, but serious peanut allergies are putting a growing number of individuals at risk for death. **2** Between 1997 and 2008, the peanut allergy rate among children in the United States nearly tripled. **3** The problem is causing great concern, for there are no signs that the allergy rate will decrease. **4** Although no one knows for certain why this increase is happening, several theories have been proposed. **5** Some believe that children are becoming more sensitive to allergens because cleaning products and antibiotic medicines have made our environment too sanitary. **6** This level of cleanliness, some say, leads to underdeveloped immune systems. **7** On the other hand, another group of theorists believes that the problem lies in the way peanuts are prepared. **8** This argument blames the roasting process for making peanuts more allergenic. **9** Because severe allergies have risen at such an alarming rate, it is likely that research into the causes of these allergies will grow. **10** Thus, science may soon be able to explain why more and more children are threatened by such a simple food.

Questions about the Model

1. What differences do you notice between sentences 1–7 of the first draft and sentences 1–4 of the second draft? Underline sentences 1–7 of the first draft. Underline sentences 1–4 of the second draft.

2. When the author combined sentences, what words were added in sentences 1–4 of the second draft? Circle the added words.

3. Why do you think the author made these revisions?

4. What is the total number of sentences in the first draft? How many sentences are in the second draft?

5. What other revisions do you notice in the second draft?

6. Which draft is easier to read? Why?

INDEPENDENT AND DEPENDENT CLAUSES

There are two kinds of clauses: independent and dependent. Academic writers combine these kinds of clauses to write a variety of sentence types.

INDEPENDENT CLAUSES

An **independent clause** contains a subject and a verb, and often a complement. It expresses a complete thought and can stand alone as a sentence.

SUBJECT	VERB	(COMPLEMENT)
The sun	rose.	
Water	evaporates	rapidly in warm climate zones.

DEPENDENT CLAUSES

A **dependent clause** is formed with a subordinator, such as *when*, *if*, *that*, or *who*. It also has a subject, a verb, and sometimes a complement. A dependent clause does not express a complete thought and cannot stand alone as a sentence. Using a dependent clause as a complete sentence is an error, referred to as a *sentence fragment*.

SUBORDINATOR	SUBJECT	VERB	(COMPLEMENT)
. . . when	the sun	rose . . .	
. . . because	water	evaporates	rapidly in warm climate zones . . .
. . . whom	the voters	elected . . .	
. . . if	the drought	continues	for another year . . .

A few of the most common subordinators follow.

SUBORDINATORS				
after	before	that	when	which
although	even though	though	whenever	while
as, just as	how	unless	where	who
as if	if	until	wherever	whom
as soon as	since	what	whether	whose
because	so that			

See Appendix B, pages 292–294, for a complete list of subordinators.

Identifying Independent and Dependent Clauses

Read and label each sentence *Indep.* (independent clause) or *Dep.* (dependent)
Add periods to the independent clauses. (*Hint:* An independent clause by itself
is a complete sentence, but a dependent clause is not.)

Indep. 1. Globalization means more travel for businessmen and women.

Dep. 2. As business executives fly around the globe to sell their companies'
products and services

_____ 3. Jet lag affects most long-distance travelers

_____ 4. Which is simply the urge to sleep at inappropriate times

_____ 5. During long journeys through several time zones, the body's inner
clock is disrupted

_____ 6. For some reason, travel from west to east causes greater jet lag than
travel from east to west

_____ 7. Also, changes in work schedules can disrupt the body's inner clock

_____ 8. When hospital nurses change from a day shift to a night shift,
for example

_____ 9. Although there is no sure way to prevent jet lag

_____ 10. There are some ways to minimize it

KINDS OF SENTENCES

A **sentence** is a group of words that you use to communicate your ideas. Every
sentence is formed from one or more clauses and expresses a complete thought.

The four basic kinds of sentences in English are **simple**, **compound**, **complex**, and
compound-complex. The kind of sentence is determined by the kind of clauses used to
form it.

SIMPLE SENTENCES

A **simple sentence** is one independent clause.

   s   v
Freshwater boils at 100 degrees Celsius at sea level.

   s   v   v
Freshwater boils at 100 degrees Celsius and freezes at 0 degrees Celsius.

   s   s   v   v
Freshwater and saltwater do not boil and do not freeze at the same temperatures.

Notice that the second sentence has two verbs, *boils* and *freezes*. This is called a
compound verb. The third sentence has both a **compound subject** and a compound
verb. All three examples are simple sentences because they have only one clause.

Although simple sentences have only one independent clause, they can still vary greatly. Write sentences following these instructions.

1. Write two simple sentences with one subject and one verb.

_____

_____

2. Write two simple sentences with one subject and two verbs.

_____

_____

3. Write two simple sentences with two subjects and one verb.

_____

_____

4. Write two simple sentences with two subjects and two verbs.

_____

_____

COMPOUND SENTENCES

A **compound sentence** is two or more independent clauses joined together. There are three ways to join the clauses:

- With a coordinator

    Saltwater boils at a higher temperature than freshwater, **so** food cooks faster in saltwater.

- With a conjunctive adverb

    Saltwater boils at a higher temperature than freshwater; **therefore,** food cooks faster in saltwater.

- With a semicolon

    Saltwater boils at a higher temperature than freshwater; food cooks faster in saltwater.

Study each type of compound sentence in more detail on the following pages.

Compound Sentences with Coordinators

A compound sentence can be formed as follows:

INDEPENDENT CLAUSE —— COORDINATOR —— INDEPENDENT CLAUSE

Saltwater boils at a lower temperature than freshwater, so food cooks faster in saltwater.

There are seven **coordinators**, which are also called coordinating conjunctions. You can remember them by the phrase *FAN BOYS* (*For, And, Nor, But, Or, Yet, So*). The examples in the chart illustrate the meanings of the seven FAN BOYS coordinators. (*Punctuation note:* Use a comma after the first independent clause.)

COORDINATORS (COORDINATING CONJUNCTIONS)		
Coordinator	**Meaning / Use**	**Examples**
for	To add a reason	Japanese people live longer than many other nationalities, for they eat healthful diets.
and	To add a similar, equal idea	They eat a lot of fish and vegetables, and they eat lightly.
nor	To add a negative, equal idea	They do not eat a lot of red meat, nor do they eat many dairy products.
but	To add an opposite idea	Diet is one factor in how long people live, but it is not the only factor.
or	To add an alternative possibility	However, people should limit the amount of animal fat in their diets, or they risk getting heart disease.
yet	To add an unexpected or surprising continuation	Cigarette smoking is a factor in longevity, yet some smokers live long lives.
so	To add an expected result	Doctors say that stress is another longevity factor, so try to avoid stress if you wish to live a longer life.

Notes

- *Nor* means "and not." It joins two negative independent clauses. Notice that question word order is used after *nor*.
- *But* and *yet* have similar meanings: They both signal that an opposite idea is coming. *But* is preferred when the two clauses are direct opposites. When the second clause is an unexpected or surprising continuation because of information given in the first clause, *yet* is preferred. (*But* is acceptable for both meanings; *yet* for only one meaning.) Compare these examples:

  I want to study art, **but** my parents want me to study engineering. (direct opposite)

  I am very bad at math, **yet** my parents want me to study engineering. (surprising continuation after "I am very bad at math")

Choosing *But* vs. *Yet*

Which coordinator would you use to connect the two clauses in these sentences? Write either *but* or *yet* on the line.

1. **a.** Too much sun damages the skin, _____ many people still do not use sunscreen.

   b. Too much sun damages the skin, _____ too little sun also causes health problems.

2. **a.** The company's sales increased last year, _____ its profits declined.

   b. The company moved its marketing division to Phoenix, _____ the operations division stayed in Boston.

3. **a.** Population growth has slowed in most developing countries, _____ it has not slowed enough to avoid serious problems.

   b. The fertility rate in India has decreased from 6 to 2.58 births per female,

   _____ India's population is expanding at the rate of 17.5 million per year.

Forming Compound Sentences with Coordinators

A Form compound sentences by adding another independent clause. Be sure to write a complete clause containing a subject and a verb. Circle the coordinator and add punctuation as needed.

1. The college campus is located in the center of the city, (so) *it is very easy to get*

   there by public transportation.

2. According to the Big Bang Theory, the universe began expanding about _____

   13.7 billion years ago and _____

   _____.

3. Does the universe have an outer edge or _____

   _____.

4. Scientists predict that intelligent life exists somewhere in the universe but _____

   _____

   _____.

5. Mars probes have photographed rocks with water markings on them yet _____

   _____

   _____.

(continued on next page)

6. We may not be able to communicate with other life forms for _____

_____.

7. Instead of taking the psychology final exam, we can write a ten-page research

paper or _____

_____.

8. I want to write a research paper yet _____

_____.

9. Three weeks before the end of the term, I had not started my paper nor _____

_____

_____.

10. I needed help choosing a topic so _____

_____.

B **For each pair of sentences, form a compound sentence by joining the two independent clauses with a coordinator that best fits the meaning. Use each FAN BOYS coordinator once. Write your new sentences on a separate sheet of paper and punctuate them correctly.**

1. Nuclear accidents can happen. Nuclear power plants must have strict safety controls.

  Nuclear accidents can happen, so nuclear power plants must have strict

  safety controls.

2. The accidents at nuclear power plants in the United States and the former Soviet Union in the 1980s created fears about the safety of this energy source. The disaster at Fukushima in Japan in 2011 reinforced them.

3. Solar heating systems are economical to operate. The cost of installation is very high.

4. Energy needs are not going to decrease. Energy sources are not going to increase. (*Note: Use* nor *and question word order in the second clause, deleting the word* not).

5. Burning fossil fuels causes serious damage to our planet. We need to develop other sources of energy.

6. Ecologists know that burning fossil fuels causes holes in the ozone layer. People continue to do it.

7. Developed nations especially will continue this harmful practice. They require more energy to fuel cars, air-conditioning, and other modern luxuries.

8. All nations of the world must take action. Our children and grandchildren will suffer the consequences.

TRY IT OUT! On a separate sheet of paper, write seven compound sentences of your own, using each FAN BOYS coordinator once.

Compound Sentences with Conjunctive Adverbs

A second way to form a compound sentence is like this:

```
|————————— INDEPENDENT CLAUSE —————————|  |—— COORDINATOR ——|  |—— INDEPENDENT CLAUSE ——|
Saltwater boils at a higher temperature than freshwater; therefore, food cooks faster in saltwater.
```

Punctuation note: Put a semicolon before and a comma after the conjunctive adverb.

Several transition signals, such as *on the other hand*, *as a result*, and *for example*, act like conjunctive adverbs; they can also connect independent clauses with a semicolon and a comma. The chart lists common conjunctive adverbs and a few transition signals that can be used in this way.

CONJUNCTIVE ADVERBS		
Conjunctive Adverb	Meaning / Use	Examples
also besides furthermore in addition moreover	To add a similar, equal idea	Community colleges offer preparation for many jobs; moreover, they prepare students to transfer to a four-year college or university.
as well		Community colleges offer preparation for many jobs; they prepare students to transfer to a four-year college or university as well.
too		Community colleges offer preparation for many jobs; they prepare students to transfer to a four-year college or university, too.
however nevertheless nonetheless still	To add an unexpected or surprising continuation	The cost of attending a community college is low; still, many students need financial aid.
on the other hand in contrast	To add a complete contrast	Tuition at a community college is low; on the other hand, tuition at private schools is high.
otherwise	To give an alternative possibility, often negative	Students must take final exams; otherwise, they will receive a grade of Incomplete.
accordingly as a result consequently hence therefore thus	To add an expected result	Native and nonnative English speakers have different needs; thus, most schools provide separate English classes for each group.
for example for instance	To add an example	Most colleges now have a writing requirement for graduation; for instance, students at my college must pass a writing test before they register for their final semester.

Forming Compound Sentences with Conjunctive Adverbs

Form compound sentences by adding a second independent clause. Circle the conjunctive adverb and add punctuation. Some of these sentences are from Practice 3A on pages 177–178.

1. The college campus is located in the center of the city; (therefore) _it is very easy_ _to get there by public transportation_.

2. According to the Big Bang Theory, the universe began expanding about 13.7 billion years ago moreover _____ _____ .

3. Students must pay their tuition and fees before they register for classes otherwise _____ _____ .

4. Scientists predict that intelligent life exists somewhere in the universe however _____ _____ .

5. Mars probes have photographed rocks with water markings on them nevertheless _____ _____ .

6. My roommate scored high on the English placement test as a result _____ _____ .

7. Tuition and fees increase every year for example _____ _____ .

8. The class thought the teacher would give a test last Friday instead _____ _____ .

TRY IT OUT!

On a separate sheet of paper, write five compound sentences, using each of these conjunctive adverbs once: *in addition*, *nevertheless*, *on the other hand*, *therefore*, and *for instance*.

Compound Sentences with Semicolons

A third way to form a compound sentence is to connect the two independent clauses with a semicolon alone.

INDEPENDENT CLAUSE

Poland was the first Eastern European country to turn away from communism;

INDEPENDENT CLAUSE

others soon followed.

This kind of compound sentence is possible only when the two independent clauses are closely related in meaning. If they are not closely related, they should be written as two simple sentences, each ending with a period.

PRACTICE 5 **Forming Compound Sentences with Semicolons**

Place a semicolon between the two independent clauses in the compound sentences.

1. The practice of yoga strengthens the body and promotes flexibility it also strengthens the mind and refreshes the soul.

2. Motherhood causes some women to quit their jobs others continue working despite having young children to care for.

3. Three hundred guests attended his wedding two attended his funeral.

TRY IT OUT! On a separate sheet of paper, write three compound sentences of your own, using a semicolon to join the independent clauses.

PRACTICE 6 **Editing to Form Compound Sentences**

On a separate sheet of paper, rewrite the paragraphs, creating compound sentences wherever possible. Try to use each of the three methods of forming a compound sentence at least once. There are many possible ways to combine sentences.

Robots

1 A robot is a mechanical device that can perform boring, dangerous, and difficult tasks. 2 First of all, robots can perform repetitive tasks without becoming tired or bored. 3 They are used in automobile factories to weld and paint. 4 Robots can also function in hostile environments. 5 They are useful for exploring the ocean bottom as well as deep outer space. 6 Finally, robots can perform tasks requiring pinpoint accuracy. 7 In the operating room, robotic equipment can assist the surgeon. 8 For instance, a robot can kill a brain tumor. 9 It can operate on a fetus with great precision.

10 The field of artificial intelligence is giving robots a limited ability to think and to make decisions. 11 However, robots cannot think conceptually. 12 Robots cannot function independently. 13 Humans have to program them. 14 They are useless. 15 Therefore, humans should not worry that robots will take over the world—at least not yet. (*Note:* Use *otherwise* to combine sentences 13 and 14.)

COMPLEX SENTENCES

A **complex sentence** contains one independent clause and one (or more) dependent clause(s). In a complex sentence, one idea is generally more important than the other. We place the more important idea in the independent clause and the less important idea in the dependent clause.

There are three kinds of dependent clauses: noun, adverb, and adjective. You will study all of these kinds of clauses in greater detail in Chapters 11, 12, and 13.

Complex Sentences with Adverb Clauses

An **adverb clause** acts like an adverb; that is, it tells where, when, why, and how. An adverb clause begins with a subordinator, such as *when, while, because, although, if, so,* or *that*. It can come before or after an independent clause.

| ——————— DEPENDENT ADVERB CLAUSE ——————— | —— INDEPENDENT CLAUSE —— |

Although women in the United States could own property, they could not vote until 1920.

| —— INDEPENDENT CLAUSE —— | —— DEPENDENT ADVERB CLAUSE —— |

A citizen can vote in the United States when he or she is 18 years old.

Complex Sentences with Adjective Clauses

An **adjective clause** acts like an adjective; that is, it describes a noun or pronoun. An adjective clause begins with a relative pronoun, such as *who, whom, which, whose,* or *that*, or with a relative adverb, such as *where* or *when*. It follows the noun or pronoun it describes.

DEPENDENT
ADJECTIVE CLAUSE

Men who are not married are called bachelors.

—— DEPENDENT ADJECTIVE CLAUSE ——

Last year we vacationed in Cozumel, which features excellent scuba diving.

Complex Sentences with Noun Clauses

A **noun clause** begins with a *wh-* question word, *that, whether,* and sometimes *if*. A noun clause acts like a noun; it can be either the subject or an object of the independent clause.

——————— DEPENDENT NOUN CLAUSE ———————

That there is a hole in the ozone layer of Earth's atmosphere is well known.

DEPENDENT
NOUN CLAUSE

Scientists know what caused it.

In the first example, *That there is a hole in the ozone layer of Earth's atmosphere* is the subject of the verb *is*. In the second example, *what caused it* is the object of the verb *know*.

Analyzing Complex Sentences

A Underline the independent clauses and double underline the dependent clauses. Label the subordinators as *Sub*. (*Note: Refer to the list of subordinators on page 173.*)

      Sub.

1. Because the cost of education is rising, many students must work part-time.

2. When students from other countries come to the United States, they often suffer from culture shock.

3. Because financial aid is difficult to obtain, many students have to work part-time.

4. Please tell me where the student union is.

5. Engineers, who have an aptitude for drafting and mechanics, must also be artistic and imaginative.

6. While the contractor follows the blueprint, the engineer checks the construction in progress.

7. Since the blueprint presents the details of the engineer's plans, it must be interpreted accurately by the contractor.

8. Students should declare a major by their junior year unless they have not made up their minds.

9. Even though students declare a major now, they can change it later.

10. The government says that inflation is holding steady.

B Add a logical independent clause to each of the dependent clauses. Make sure you punctuate each sentence correctly.

1. _I cannot register for classes_____ until I pay my tuition.

2. Unless I take 12 units each term _____.

3. _____ that computer engineering is a popular major.

4. _____ who taught this course last term?

5. Because I had to look for a part-time job _____.

6. _____ if I want to get to school on time.

7. _____ whether I should take advanced calculus.

8. _____ whom I met at the math club meeting last week.

9. When I left my country _____.

10. _____ that my college adviser recommends.

COMPOUND-COMPLEX SENTENCES

A **compound-complex sentence** has at least three clauses— two are always independent and one dependent. You can use almost any combination of dependent and independent clauses. Just be sure that there is at least one dependent clause.

In these sentences, independent clauses are underlined once and the dependent clauses twice.

1. I wanted to travel after I graduated from college; however, I had to go to work immediately.

2. After I graduated from college, I wanted to travel, but I had to go to work immediately.

3. I wanted to travel after I graduated from college, but I had to go to work immediately because I had to support my family.

4. I could not decide where I should work or what I should do, so at first I did nothing.

Punctuate the compound part of a compound-complex sentence like a compound sentence; that is, use a semicolon / comma combination (sentence 1), or put a comma before a coordinator joining two independent clauses (sentences 2, 3, and 4).

Punctuate the complex part like a complex sentence. With adverb clauses, put a comma after a dependent adverb clause (sentence 2) but not before it (sentence 3). With noun clauses (sentence 4), use no commas.

PRACTICE 8 **Punctuating Sentences**

Read each sentence. Underline the independent clauses. Double underline the dependent clauses. Then add commas and / or semicolons as needed.

1. Information and communication technology is reaching out to help people in the poorest countries improve their lives for example fishermen on the Bay of Bengal can now receive online weather reports that tell them when it is safe to go out.

2. Furthermore, when the fishermen bring in a boatload of fish they can find out the current market prices for their fish, which will help them bargain with the middlemen to whom they sell their catch.

3. The cost of the cheapest computer is at least $200 and since this is more than an individual fisherman can afford several fishing villages together can pool their money and buy one to share.

4. When you call your U.S. bank you may find yourself speaking to a customer service representative who is located in the Philippines or Puerto Rico and when you need technical support for your home computer you may get help from a programmer in India.

SENTENCE TYPES AND WRITING STYLE

Now that you know the basic kinds of sentences in English, you can develop a good writing style. Writing that uses only one kind of sentence is boring and may not convey the message that you intend.

As you read the two drafts of this essay, notice the kinds of sentences. The first draft has some sentence problems.

- Paragraphs 1 and 4 have too many compound sentences. This style is boring because so many sentences use *and* as the connector.
- Paragraph 2 has too many simple sentences. This style sounds choppy.
- Paragraph 3 uses a good mixture of sentence types.

FIRST DRAFT

Rosa Parks

1. Rosa Parks is a famous African-American woman, **and** she is often called "the mother of the civil rights movement." She was born into a poor but hardworking African-American family in Alabama, **and** no one suspected that she would become the spark that ignited the civil rights movement in the United States. This movement changed U.S. society forever, **and** it helped African-Americans attain equal rights under the law.

2. Parks became famous quite by accident. One day in 1955, she was on her way home from her job in a Montgomery, Alabama, department store. She boarded a city bus with three other African-Americans. They sat in the fifth row. The fifth row was the first row African-Americans were allowed to sit in. A few stops later, the front four rows filled up. A white man was left standing.

3. According to the laws of that time, African-Americans had to give up their seats to whites, so the bus driver asked Parks and the three other African-Americans to get up and move. Although the others complied, Parks refused. She later said she was not tired from work, but tired of being treated like a second-class citizen. The bus driver called the police, who arrested Parks and took her away in handcuffs.

4. Over the weekend, a protest was organized, **and** on the following Monday, African-American people in Montgomery began a boycott of the public buses, **and** the boycott was tremendously successful, **and** it lasted more than a year. The Supreme Court of the United States finally ruled that segregation on public transportation was unconstitutional. African-Americans had won a huge victory, **and** they realized their power to change the system.

Now read the same essay with the sentence structure revised.

REVISED DRAFT

Rosa Parks

1   Rosa Parks is a famous African-American woman who is often called "the mother of the civil rights movement." When she was born into a poor but hardworking African-American family in Alabama, no one suspected that she would become the spark that ignited the civil rights movement in the United States. This movement changed U.S. society forever by helping African-American people attain equal rights under the law.

2   Parks became famous quite by accident. One day in 1955, on her way home from her job in a Montgomery, Alabama, department store, she boarded a city bus with three other African-Americans. They sat in the fifth row, which was the first row African-Americans were allowed to sit in. A few stops later, the front four rows filled up, and a white man was left standing.

3   According to the laws of that time, African-Americans had to give up their seats to whites, so the bus driver asked Parks and the three other African-Americans to get up and move. Although the others complied, Parks refused. She later said she was not tired from work, but tired of being treated like a second-class citizen. The bus driver called the police, who arrested Parks and took her away in handcuffs.

4   Over the weekend, a protest was organized, and on the following Monday, African-American people in Montgomery began a boycott of the public buses. The boycott was tremendously successful, lasting for more than a year. The Supreme Court of the United States finally ruled that segregation on public transportation was unconstitutional. Because they had won a huge victory, African-Americans realized their power to change the system.

PRACTICE 9   **Combining Sentences in Different Ways**

On a separate sheet of paper, rewrite and improve this paragraph, which contains too many compound sentences. Change compound sentences into complex sentences, using the subordinators from the box.

after	as soon as	since
although	because	when

Equal Rights for Women

Russian women started to gain equality earlier than women in the United States. In the former Soviet Union, men and women had access to equal education and job opportunities, and that reflected the Soviet philosophy. The 1937 Soviet constitution declared that women and men had equal rights and responsibilities, and women joined the workforce. Also, millions of Russian men were away in the military during World War II, so Russian women filled their places at work. Russian women worked full time at their jobs, but they also had the primary responsibility for taking care of the family. They finished their work, and they had to shop, cook the evening meal, and perhaps wash, iron, or mend the family's clothes. U.S. women started to demonstrate that they could do the work of men during World War II.

On a separate sheet of paper, rewrite and improve the essay, which contains too many simple sentences. Use different methods of combining the sentences.

Nonverbal Communication

1   Nonverbal communication, or body language, is used everywhere in the world. It is a very powerful means of communication. It communicates much more than spoken words.

2   One example of nonverbal communication is what occurs between parents and child. Parents smile at their child. They communicate love, acceptance, and reassurance. The child feels comfortable and safe. The smile signifies approval. The child is happy and well adjusted.

3   Another example of nonverbal communication is the image a person shows in public. A woman is walking alone on an unfamiliar and possibly dangerous street. She wants to appear confident. She walks quickly. She may be tired. She walks with her shoulders straight and her head held high. Her eyes are focused straight ahead. Someone is looking at her. She returns the glance without hesitation. In contrast, a nervous woman appears afraid. She walks slowly with her shoulders and eyes down.

4   Indeed, body language can express more than spoken language. Merely by raising an eyebrow, clenching a jaw, or softening the eyes, a person can express disapproval, anger, or love. It is a very strong method of communication.

WRITING PRACTICE

On a separate sheet of paper, write a paragraph that uses a variety of types of well-structured sentences. Use the second draft of the writing model on page 172 to help you. Choose one of the prompts to write about.

Prompts
- Preventive health care
- The energy source of the future
- Changes in men's and women's roles

After you have written a draft of your paragraph, look carefully at each sentence and consider these questions:
- Does your paragraph have a strong topic sentence?
- Do all the other sentences relate to the topic sentence?
- Have you used a variety of sentence types, including simple, compound, complex, and compound-complex?
- Have you punctuated each kind of sentence correctly?
- Do your sentences flow smoothly from one sentence to the next?

Edit your paragraph as needed to improve it.

SELF-ASSESSMENT

In this chapter, you learned to:

○ Recognize independent and dependent clauses

○ Analyze different types of sentences

○ Use coordinators, conjunctive adverbs, and semicolons to create compound sentences

○ Use adverb clauses to create complex sentences

○ Combine different types of clauses to create compound-complex sentences

○ Write a paragraph that uses a variety of sentence types

Which ones can you do well? Mark them ✓

Which ones do you need to practice more? Mark them ✗

PARALLELISM AND SENTENCE PROBLEMS

OBJECTIVES

To write academic texts, you need to master certain skills.

In this chapter, you will learn to:

- Analyze and use parallel structure

- Identify and correct choppy writing

- Identify and correct sentence fragments

- Identify and correct run-on sentences and comma splices

- Identify and correct stringy sentences

- Write a paragraph that uses parallel structure

Some of the ways we use computers today include writing, researching, taking pictures, listening to music, and staying in touch with friends.

INTRODUCTION

In this chapter, you will learn to use parallel structure to add symmetry and style to your sentences. **Parallelism** is an important element in English writing, especially when you are listing or comparing and contrasting items or ideas. Parallelism means that each item in a list or in a comparison follows the same grammatical pattern. For example, if you are writing a list and the first item in your list is a noun, you write all the other items as nouns also. Or if the first item is an *-ing* word, you make all the others *-ing* words.

You will also learn to recognize and repair common sentence problems: fragments, run-ons, comma splices, and choppy or stringy sentences. At the end of this chapter, you will write a paragraph that uses parallelism and avoids these common sentence problems.

ANALYZING THE MODEL

The writing model is about Steve Jobs, the founder of Apple Computer. The model contains several examples of parallelism.

Read the model. Then answer the questions.

✎ **Writing Model**

Steve Jobs

Steve Jobs, the founder of Apple Computer, was (1) *both a brilliant computer specialist and a savvy businessman*. His company has been responsible for a number of popular products, including (2) *the iPod, the iPhone, and the iPad*. These products (3) *not only have sold well, but also have changed the way people think about computers*. In part because of the influence of Apple and Jobs, people began to (4) *listen to computerized music files, carry phones that could play songs while sending email, and access the Internet from almost anywhere*. A few decades ago, individuals worked on desktop computers, but they did not play games or chat with friends on them. Nowadays, it is hard to imagine a time when computers were not part of our daily lives. However, many people believe that, without Steve Jobs, personal computing might not have become so ingrained in everything we do.

Questions about the Model

1. Which number identifies two different types of individual?
2. Which number identifies two different types of accomplishment?
3. Which number identifies a list of products?
4. Which number identifies a list of activities that people can do?

PARALLEL STRUCTURE IN SENTENCES

In order to make your writing easier to read, you need to follow certain rules. One of these rules is called *parallelism*. In these examples, the sentences in the column on the right follow the rule of parallelism.

NOT PARALLEL	PARALLEL
My English conversation class is made up of Chinese, Spaniards, and Bosnian students.	My English conversation class is made up of **Chinese, Spanish**, and **Bosnian** students. *(The items are all adjectives.)*
The students who do well attend class, they do their homework, and practice speaking in English.	The students who do well **attend class, do their homework**, and **practice speaking in English**. *(The items are all verbs + complements.)*
The teacher wanted to know which country we came from and our future goals.	The teacher wanted to know **which country we were from** and **what our future goals were**. *(The items are both noun clauses.)*
The language skills of the students in the evening classes are the same as the day classes.	**The language skills of the students in the evening classes** are the same as **the language skills of the students in the day classes**. *(The items are both noun phrases.)*

Notes

- You may substitute a pronoun for the second "the language skills" here:

    The language skills of the students in the evening classes are the same as those of the students in the day classes.

- All the words in the first item do not always have to be repeated in the second. You may repeat all or some of the words, depending on what you wish to emphasize. Both sentences are correct.

    Before you write a paper or **before you take a test**, you must organize your thoughts.

    Before you **write a paper** or **take a test**, you must organize your thoughts.

PARALLELISM WITH COORDINATORS: *AND, OR, BUT*

Words, phrases, and clauses that are joined by *and*, *or*, and *but* are written in parallel form. Notice the parallel structures joined by coordinators in the sentences.

The Federal Air Pollution Control Administration regulates automobile exhausts, **and** the Federal Aviation Administration makes similar regulations for aircraft.

States regulate the noise created by motor vehicles **but** not by commercial aircraft.

Pesticides cannot be sold if they have a harmful effect on humans, on animal life, **or** on the environment.

PARALLELISM WITH CORRELATIVE (PAIRED) CONJUNCTIONS

Use parallel forms with the paired conjunctions *both . . . and, either . . . or, neither . . . nor,* and *not only . . . but also.*

Paired conjunctions are placed directly before the elements they join in the sentence. Notice the parallel structures in these clauses joined by paired conjunctions:

A new law provides for **both** regulating pesticides **and** ordering their removal.

Air pollutants may come **either** from the ocean as contaminants given off by sea life **or** from the engines of automobiles.

If **neither** industry **nor** the public works toward reducing pollution problems, future generations will suffer.

Many people are **neither** concerned about pollutants **nor** worried about their future impact.

At this time, air pollution is controlled by laws passed **not only** to reduce pollutants at the source, **but also** to set standards of air quality.

PRACTICE 1   **Identifying and Creating Parallelism**

A Underline the items or ideas in each sentence that are in parallel form. Circle the word(s) that connect the parallel structures.

1. An ideal environment for studying includes good lighting, a spacious desk, and a comfortable chair.

2. You know you are truly fluent in another language when you can calculate in it and when you begin to dream in it.

3. People often spend as much time worrying about the future as planning for it.

4. You can learn a second language in the classroom, at home, or in a country where the language is spoken.

5. My new personal computer is both fast and reliable.

6. My mother's old typewriter is neither fast nor reliable.

7. Ann is growing older but unfortunately not wiser.

8. Young people buy computers not only to do schoolwork but also to play games.

9. If industrial nations continue to burn fossil fuels and if developing nations continue to burn their rain forests, the level of CO_2 in the atmosphere will continue to increase.

10. Before the judge announced the punishment, he asked the murderer if he wanted to speak either to the victim's family or to the jury.

B Underline the part of each sentence that is not parallel. Then rewrite the sentence in parallel form. (There may be more than one possible answer.)

1. You do not need to risk carrying cash or <u>to risk to miss</u> a sale.

   You do not need to risk carrying cash or missing a sale.

2. Credit cards are accepted by department stores, airlines, and they can be used in some gas stations.

   _____

3. The disadvantages of using a credit card are overspending and you pay high interest rates.

   _____

4. With credit cards, you can either pay your bill with one check, or you can stretch out your payments.

   _____

5. You can charge both at restaurants and when you stay at hotels.

   _____

6. Many people carry not only credit cards but they also carry cash.

   _____

7. Many people want neither to pay off their balance monthly nor do they like paying interest.

   _____

8. Not making any payment or to send in only the minimum payment every month is poor money management.

   _____

TRY IT OUT! On a separate sheet of paper, write seven original sentences in parallel form. Use the conjunction or paired conjunctions listed with each topic.

CONJUNCTIONS	TOPICS
and	two weekend activities you enjoy
or	two foods you would not eat / give to a baby
but	one school subject that you excel at and one that you struggle with
both . . . and	two advantages of being bilingual
either . . . or	two places you might spend a month's vacation or a honeymoon
neither . . . nor	two places you would never spend a month's vacation or a honeymoon
not only . . . but also	two reasons to get a college degree

SENTENCE PROBLEMS

In this section, you will learn to recognize and correct some common errors in sentence structure: sentence fragments, and choppy, run-on, and "stringy" sentences.

SENTENCE FRAGMENTS

Sentence fragments are incomplete sentences or parts of sentences. Remember that a complete sentence must contain at least one independent clause. Study the sentence fragments and the suggested methods for correcting them.

Problem A

FRAGMENT Because some students work part-time while taking a full load of classes.

This is a dependent clause. It begins with a subordinator (*because*). It does not express a complete thought because there is no independent clause. There are two possible ways to correct this problem: add an independent clause, or delete the subordinator.

CORRECT Because some students work part-time while taking a full load of courses, they have very little free time.

CORRECT Some students work part-time while taking a full load of classes.

Problem B

FRAGMENT For example, the increase in the cost of renting an apartment.

FRAGMENT To live and work for at least a year in a foreign country.

The problem with these is that neither sentence has a verb and therefore they are not independent clauses. This can be corrected by adding a verb.

CORRECT For example, the increase in the cost of renting an apartment is one reason for more people being homeless.

CORRECT To live and work for at least a year in a foreign country has always been my dream.

Problem C

FRAGMENT Teachers who give too much homework.

Teachers is a noun followed by an adjective clause (*who give too much homework*). The noun is the beginning of an independent clause that is incomplete. To correct this problem, simply complete the independent clause by adding a subject complement.

CORRECT Teachers who give too much homework are unpopular.

Always check your own writing for sentence fragments. Pay particular attention to sentences beginning with subordinators (*although, since, because, if, before,* and so on). These can be dangerous words because they can introduce the problems described above. Make sure that every clause beginning with these words is attached to an independent clause.

PRACTICE 2   **Rewriting Sentence Fragments**

A Label each sentence *Frag.* (sentence fragment) or *Comp.* (complete sentence). Then, on a separate sheet of paper, rewrite each fragment to make a complete sentence.

_____ 1. The desire of all humankind to live in peace and freedom, for example.

_____ 2. Second, a fact that men are physically stronger than women.

_____ 3. The best movie I saw last year.

_____ 4. *Titanic* was one of the most financially successful movies ever made, worldwide.

_____ 5. For example, many students have part-time jobs.

_____ 6. Although people want to believe that all men are created equal.

_____ 7. Finding a suitable marriage partner is a challenging task.

_____ 8. Many of my friends who did not have the opportunity to go to college.

_____ 9. A tsunami that occurred in the Indian Ocean in December 2004, killing more than 200,000 people.

_____ 10. Despite a lag of up to several hours between the earthquake and tsunami, nearly all of the victims were taken completely by surprise.

B Find the sentence fragments in the essay. Put brackets [ ] around them and label them *Frag*. Rewrite the fragments on a separate sheet of paper, making corrections.

Teenage Drivers

1   Teenagers are often seen as irresponsible and overly confident. These attitudes can even be seen in the driver's seat. *Frag* [Believing that they are far better drivers than they are.] Teenagers can be incompetent, inattentive, and even dangerous behind the wheel.

2   Indeed, statistics prove that teenagers are, in fact, the most dangerous drivers on the road. For example, insurance rates for teenagers can be as much as twice the rate for adult drivers. Another proof is that the traffic accident rate for teenagers is higher than for any other group. Also, in the United States, traffic accidents are the number one cause of death for teenagers.

3   The reasons for teenage drivers' dangerous driving habits can perhaps be found in the tension between the biological phases of brain development and teenagers' role in society. On the one hand, the frontal cortex, or decision-making area, of a teenager's brain which is still developing. So they take risks because they literally do not understand the danger. On the other hand, teenagers want to be treated like adults. Using cars to show their maturity. Or using them as status symbols to gain popularity.

4   All in all, teenagers are not safe drivers. Because of their attitude. Teenagers will learn to become safe drivers. As they get older and their brains, and decision-making capacities, mature.

CHOPPY SENTENCES

Choppy sentences are sentences that are too short. Short sentences can be effective in certain situations. For instance, when you want to make an impact, use a short sentence.

In this example, a sentence of 25 words is followed by a sentence of 6 words. The second sentence has greater impact because it is so short.

> Despite countless doctors' warnings, news stories, and magazine articles about the importance of eating a nutritious, balanced diet, many people resist developing healthy eating habits. Some people just like junk food.

However, overuse of short sentences is considered poor style in academic writing.

Choppy sentences are easy to correct. Just combine two or three short sentences to make one compound or complex sentence. Your decision to make a compound or a complex sentence should be based on whether the ideas in the short sentences are equal or whether one idea is dependent on the other.

- If the sentences express equal ideas, use coordination to combine them.

  CHOPPY Wind is an enduring source of power. Water is also an unlimited energy source. Dams produce hydraulic power. They have existed for a long time. Windmills are relatively new.

  CORRECT Both wind and water are enduring sources of power. Dams have produced hydraulic power for a long time, but windmills are relatively new.

- If the sentences express unequal ideas, that is, if one sentence expresses a less important idea than the other, use subordination to combine them.

  CHOPPY We must find new sources of energy. Natural sources of energy are decreasing. Solar energy is a promising new source of energy. Solar energy is energy from the sun.

  CORRECT We must find new sources of energy because natural sources of energy are dwindling. Solar energy, which is energy from the sun, is a promising new source.

See Appendix B, pages 291–294, for complete lists of coordinating and subordinating conjunctions with notes about their usage.

PRACTICE 3 **Rewriting Choppy Sentences** X

Combine the choppy sentences. Decide whether the ideas are equal or unequal and what the relationship is between the ideas. Then rewrite the sentences as one sentence using appropriate conjunctions.

1. (a) Gasoline became expensive. (b) Automobile manufacturers began to produce smaller cars. (c) Smaller cars use less gasoline.

   Equal / (Not equal?)

   Main idea? _Sentence (b)_____

   Relationships: _Sentence (a) could be time (when)_____

   _Sentence (c) could be reason (because)._____

   Combined sentence: _When gasoline became more expensive, automobile_

   manufacturers began to produce smaller cars because

   _they use less gasoline._____

   (continued on next page)

2. (a) Electric cars are powered solely by batteries. (b) The new hybrid vehicles switch between electricity and gasoline.

Equal / Not equal?

Main idea?   _____

Relationship: _____

Combined sentence: _____

_____

_____

3. (a) Government and private agencies have spent billions of dollars advertising the dangers of smoking. (b) Many people still smoke cigarettes.

Equal / Not equal?

Main idea?   _____

Relationship: _____

Combined sentence: _____

_____

_____

_____

4. (a) Some students go to a vocational school to learn a trade or profession. (b) Some students go to a university to study an academic field.

Equal / Not equal?

Main idea?   _____

Relationships: _____

Combined sentence: _____

_____

_____

5. (a) The grading system at our college should be abolished. (b) The students do not like getting grades. (c) The instructors do not enjoy giving grades.

Equal / Not equal?

Main idea?   _____

Relationships: _____

Combined sentence: _____

_____

_____

RUN-ON SENTENCES AND COMMA SPLICES

A **run-on sentence** is a sentence in which two or more independent clauses are written one after another with no punctuation. A similar error happens when two independent clauses are incorrectly joined by a comma without a coordinating conjunction. This kind of error is called a **comma splice**.

RUN-ON My family went to Australia then they emigrated to Canada.

COMMA SPLICE My family went to Australia, then they emigrated to Canada.

The ways to correct these two sentence errors are the same.
- Add a period:

    My family went to Australia. Then they emigrated to Canada.

- Add a semicolon:

    My family went to Australia; then they emigrated to Canada.

- Add a coordinator:

    My family went to Australia, **and** then they emigrated to Canada.

- Add a subordinator:

    My family went to Australia **before** they emigrated to Canada.

    After my family went to Australia, they emigrated to Canada.

PRACTICE 4 Correcting Run-On / Comma Splice Sentences

Ⓐ Correct the run-on / comma splice sentences using the methods indicated.

1. New York City is very cosmopolitan, people from many cultures and ethnic groups live there.

    a. Add a period: _____

    _____

    b. Add a semicolon: _____

    _____

    c. Add a subordinator: _____

    _____

    d. Add a coordinator: _____

    _____

(continued on next page)

2. A newly arrived international student faces several challenges, for example, he or she has to cope with a new culture.

a. Add a period: _____

_____

b. Add a semicolon: _____

_____

3. Learning a new language is like learning to swim it takes a lot of practice.

Add a coordinator: _____

_____

4. Ask for assistance at the reference desk in the library, a librarian is always on duty.

Add a semicolon: _____

_____

B Label each sentence as *C* (correct), *RO* (run-on), or *CS* (comma splice). Then, on a separate sheet of paper, correct the incorrect sentences.

___RO___ 1. Two emails from Jane came on Monday a third one came on Wednesday.

Two emails from Jane came on Monday; a third one came on Wednesday.

_____ 2. An encyclopedia is a valuable source of information it contains summaries of every area of knowledge.

_____ 3. Because of the rapid expansion of human knowledge, it is difficult to keep printed encyclopedias current.

_____ 4. A printed encyclopedia may quickly go out of date also it is quite expensive to purchase.

_____ 5. Online encyclopedias are available to everyone with access to the Internet.

_____ 6. Articles in most encyclopedias are written by experts in each subject, who are often university professors.

_____ 7. An editor of an encyclopedia does not write articles he or she only collects and edits articles.

_____ 8. To find a book on a certain subject, you used to look in a card catalog, to find a magazine article on a subject, you used to look in a periodical index.

_____ 9. If you cannot find any information on a subject, you can always ask a librarian to help you, they are paid to assist students.

C Find run-ons and comma splices in the essay. Label them *RO* or *CS*. Then rewrite the paragraphs on a separate sheet of paper, making corrections. There are four errors.

Question of Grades

1 Teachers at Stone Mountain State College give higher grades than teachers at 12 of the 19 other colleges in the state college system, according to a recent report from the State Institutional Research Committee. **2** This report showed that more than one-third of the undergraduate grades awarded in the spring semester 2005 were As only 1.1 percent were Fs. **3** The percentage of As awarded to graduate students was even higher, almost two-thirds were As.

4 While students may be happy to receive high grades, evidence suggests that this trend is having negative consequences. **5** Investigation of the admissions criteria[1] of some graduate and professional schools indicates that the admissions offices of these schools are discounting high grades on the transcripts of SMSC students, this means that an A from SMSC is not equal to an A from other universities. **6** Grade inflation may, therefore, hurt a student from SMSC who intends to apply to a graduate or professional school he or she may not be accepted despite a high grade point average.

---

[1] **criteria:** standards by which a judgment is made

STRINGY SENTENCES

A **stringy sentence** is a sentence with too many clauses, usually connected with *and*, *but*, *so*, and sometimes *because*. It often results from writing the way you speak, going on and on like a string without an end.

To correct a stringy sentence, divide it and / or recombine the clauses, remembering to subordinate when appropriate.

STRINGY Many students attend classes all morning, and then they work all afternoon, and they also have to study at night, so they are usually exhausted by the weekend.

CORRECT Many students attend classes all morning and work all afternoon. Since they also have to study at night, they are usually exhausted by the weekend.

OR

Because many students attend classes all morning, work all afternoon, and study at night, they are usually exhausted by the weekend.

Correcting Stringy Sentences

Improve these stringy sentences.

1. He enrolled in an intermediate calculus class, but he found it too easy, so he dropped it, and he signed up for the advanced class.

_____

_____

_____

2. First-born children in a family often have more responsibility than their younger siblings, and they feel pressure to set a good example, so they often become superachievers.

_____

_____

_____

3. Last-born children, on the other hand, often have little responsibility, and they may be pampered as the "baby" of the family, but they are the smallest, and they have to get people to like them, so they often develop superior social skills.

_____

_____

_____

4. The students in my engineering class could not do the homework, so we got together and worked for several hours, and we finally solved all the problems.

_____

_____

_____

5. The lack of rainfall has caused a severe water shortage, so people have to conserve water every day, and they also have to think of new ways to reuse water, but the situation is improving.

_____

_____

_____

Read the paragraphs and then find, underline, and label examples of these sentence errors: lack of parallel structure, fragments, comma splices, and choppy or stringy sentences. Rewrite the corrected paragraphs on a separate sheet of paper.

The United States: Melting Pot or Salad Bowl?

stringy sentence

1 The United States counts its population every ten years, and each census[1] reveals that the country's racial and ethnic mix is changing dramatically, so by the year 2050, the "average" person in the United States will not be descended from Europeans, but the majority of U.S. residents will trace their ancestry[2] to Africa, Asia, the Hispanic world, the Pacific Islands, or the Middle East. 2 Once the United States was a microcosm[3] of European nationalities, today the United States is a microcosm of the world. 3 The United States is no longer considered a "melting pot" society by many of its residents. 4 Instead, many people prefer the term "salad bowl." 5 They use this term to describe U.S. society. 6 U.S. society will soon be predominantly nonwhite. 7 "Melting pot" implies that the different ethnic groups blend together into one homogeneous mixture, "salad bowl" implies that nationalities, like the ingredients in a mixed green salad, retain their cultural identities.

8 Earlier generations of immigrants believed that they had to learn English quickly not only to survive but also for success. 9 Now, many immigrant groups do not feel the same need. 10 Because there are some places in the United States where you can work, shop, get medical care, marry, divorce, and die without knowing English. 11 For example, Chinatown in many large cities. 12 In addition, many immigrant groups want their children to know their own culture. 13 Many Hispanics, for instance, want their children to learn both English and study the Spanish language in school. 14 They are fighting for the right to bilingual education in many communities. 15 In many communities they are in the majority.

---

[1] **census:** population count

[2] **ancestry:** a person's family origins

[3] **microcosm:** small community representing a large one

On a separate sheet of paper, write a paragraph that uses parallel structure and a variety of sentence types. Use the writing model on page 190 to help you. Choose one of the prompts to write about.

Prompts

- Two inventions that changed society
- Traditions of three different holidays
- The most effective parenting strategies
- Characteristics of an excellent leader

After you have written a draft of your paragraph, look carefully at each sentence and consider these questions:

- Does your paragraph have a strong topic sentence?
- Do all your other sentences relate to the topic sentence?
- Have you used parallel structure as appropriate with *and, but, or* and the structures *both / and, neither / nor, either / or* and *not only / but also*?
- Can you improve choppy sentences by combining them with other sentences?
- Have you corrected any run-on sentences, stringy sentences, or sentence fragments?
- Do your sentences flow smoothly from one sentence to the next?

Edit your paragraph as needed to improve it.

SELF-ASSESSMENT

In this chapter you learned to:

- ○ Analyze and use parallel structure
- ○ Identify and correct choppy writing
- ○ Identify and correct sentence fragments
- ○ Identify and correct run-on sentences and comma splices
- ○ Identify and correct stringy sentences
- ○ Write a paragraph that uses parallel structure

Which ones can you do well? Mark them ✓

Which ones do you need to practice more? Mark them ✗

CHAPTER 11

NOUN CLAUSES

OBJECTIVES

To write academic texts, you need to master certain skills.

In this chapter, you will learn to:

- Form noun clauses beginning with the word *that*

- Form sentences beginning with *it*

- Use special verb tenses in *that* clauses

- Form noun clauses beginning with the words *if / whether*

- Form question clauses

- Write a letter that includes sentences with noun clauses

The qualities and virtues that are admired in a role model can vary from culture to culture.

In Chapters 9 and 10, you learned how to vary your types of sentences, use parallelism, and repair common sentence problems. In the next three chapters, you will learn more about using clauses correctly to create clear, interesting sentences. In this chapter, you will study different methods for forming noun clauses. A **noun clause** is a dependent clause that functions as a noun. A noun clause is often part of an independent clause, where it can be a subject or an object.

SUBJECT — VERB
What the newspaper reported was incorrect.

VERB — OBJECT
People once believed **that the world was flat**.

A noun clause can also follow certain adjectives and nouns.

ADJECTIVE
We were happy **that the semester was over**.

NOUN
Who first challenged the belief **that the world was flat**?

There are three kinds of noun clauses:

1. *That* clauses, which begin with the word *that*

2. *If / Whether* clauses, which begin with the words *whether* or *if*

3. Question clauses, which begin with a question word, such as *who*, *what*, *where*, *when*, or *how*

Punctuating Noun Clauses

- NEVER use a comma to separate a noun clause from the independent clause.

  I am sure X that the address is correct.

- If the independent clause is a statement, put a period at the end of the entire sentence. If the independent clause is a question, put a question mark at the end of the entire sentence.

  INDEPENDENT CLAUSE — NOUN CLAUSE
  I am sure   that the address is correct**.**

  Are you sure   that the address is correct**?**

You will study each kind of noun clause in this chapter. At the end of the chapter, you will write a letter that includes sentences with noun clauses.

ANALYZING THE MODEL

The writing model is about the characteristics of role models. The paragraph contains a number of noun clauses. As you read, try to identify them. Remember that there are three kinds of noun clauses.

Read the model. Then answer the questions.

✏️ **Writing Model**

Characteristics of a Role Model

Many people believe that sports stars and entertainers are role models in our society. However, before deciding if someone is a role model, it should first be determined whether he or she fits certain criteria. Role models should be ethical, selfless, and determined. For example, they should care about what the morally right choice is in any situation, and they should consistently try to avoid making unethical decisions. In addition, role models should focus on who might need their help, rather than on where they can find personal gain. Finally, role models should know how to keep working to achieve their goals, even though the road may be difficult. Using these three criteria can help us figure out who is truly a good candidate to be a role model.

Questions about the Model

1. Which clause begins with *that*? Underline it.
2. Which clauses begin with *if* or *whether*? Double underline them.
3. Which clauses begin with *who, what, where* or *how*? Triple underline them.
4. What do you think it means when we say a noun clause "functions as a noun"? To answer this question, look at the words that come before the underlined clauses.

THAT CLAUSES

A *that* **clause** is a dependent noun clause that begins with the word *that*.

The young filmmaker hopes **that** his film will be a financial success.

You can sometimes omit *that* if the meaning is clear without it. However, you can never omit *that* when it is the first word in a sentence.

CORRECT The young filmmaker hopes **that** his film will be a financial success.

CORRECT The young filmmaker hopes his film will be a financial success.

CORRECT **That** his film is a critical success is beyond doubt.

INCORRECT His film is a critical success is beyond doubt.

A *that* clause can appear in different locations.

- **After the independent clause verb.** The most common position of a noun clause is after the verb of the independent clause, where it functions as the object of that verb.

  ┌─ INDEPENDENT CLAUSE ─┐┌──────────── NOUN CLAUSE (OBJECT) ────────────┐
       S   V

  The catalog states that science courses require a laboratory period.

- **After certain adjectives.** A *that* clause can also follow certain adjectives such as *happy, glad, proud, pleased, sad, upset, worried, sorry, certain, surprised,* and *sure*. These adjectives describe emotions.

  ┌──── INDEPENDENT CLAUSE ────┐┌──────────── NOUN CLAUSE ────────────┐
            ADJECTIVE

  The class was surprised that the instructor canceled the final exam.

- **After certain nouns.** A *that* clause can follow certain nouns such as *idea, theory, thought, claim, assertion, statement, belief, notion,* and *opinion*.

  ┌──── INDEPENDENT CLAUSE ────┐┌──────────── NOUN CLAUSE ────────────┐
            NOUN

  No one believed Galileo's theory that Earth revolves around the sun.

- **At the beginning of a sentence.** A *that* clause at the beginning of a sentence functions as the subject of the independent clause verb.

  ┌──────── INDEPENDENT CLAUSE ────────┐
  ┌──── NOUN CLAUSE (SUBJECT) ────┐ V

  That Earth is getting warmer is certain.

SENTENCES BEGINNING WITH *IT*

Starting a sentence with a noun clause seems awkward to many English speakers, so they often rewrite such sentences by putting *It* at the beginning and moving the noun clause to the end.

AWKWARD **That Earth is getting warmer** is certain.

BETTER **It** is certain **that Earth is getting warmer**.

In addition, the verb following *It* (except *be* or any intransitive verb like *seem* or *appear*) is often written in the passive voice, especially in academic writing.

It is believed that carbon dioxide is responsible for global warming.

It was agreed that the meeting would be postponed until next week.

It has been proven that the world's deserts are expanding.

You can also write these sentences in the active voice:

Many scientists believe that carbon dioxide is responsible for global warming.

The participants agreed that the meeting would be postponed until next week.

Measurements have proven that the world's deserts are expanding.

Active and Passive Voice

In general, English writers prefer the active voice because it is more direct. However, the passive voice is preferred in five specific situations. Review the situations in the chart.

RULES	EXAMPLES
1. The emphasis is on what happened, not who did it.	Jack was promoted last month.
2. The performer of the action is unknown.	The wheel was invented during the Bronze Age.
3. The performer of the action is unimportant.	Smoking is prohibited on airplanes.
4. Content is objective, as in a scientific or technical report.	Three ml of HCl were added to the test tube.
5. Statement is diplomatic; it does not say who did something wrong or made an error.	I believe a mistake has been made on our bill.

PRACTICE 1   **Using *That* Clauses**

A Complete each sentence with a *that* clause.

1. A comparison of the size of glaciers and icebergs over the past hundred years

   reveals _that they are shrinking in size._

2. Scientists believe _____ .

3. Environmentalists warn _____ .

4. People living near seacoasts and on low-lying islands are worried _____

   _____ .

5. _____ has been proven.

6. The idea _____ is controversial.

7. The author was very concerned _____ .

B On a separate sheet of paper, rewrite each sentence so that it begins with *It* and ends with a *that* clause.

1. That air temperatures are rising is significant.

   It is significant that air temperatures are rising.

2. That ocean levels are rising is undeniable.

3. That burning fossil fuels is a cause of global warming has been well documented.

4. That winters in the Northeast are getting warmer has been proven.

SPECIAL VERB TENSES IN *THAT* CLAUSES

Some kinds of *that* clauses require special verb tenses. These kinds of *that* clauses are called reported speech and subjunctive noun clauses.

Reported Speech

One of the most common uses of noun clauses in academic writing is to report what someone else has said or written. This kind of noun clause is called **reported speech**. Sometimes it is also called indirect speech or indirect quotation. Verb tenses in reported speech follow special rules.

- If the independent clause verb is in the simple present, present perfect, or future, the verb in the noun clause is in the tense that expresses the meaning that the independent clause intends.

   The prime ministers **agree** that global warming **is** a serious world problem.

   They **hope** that all nations **will be** responsible for solving this problem.

   Scientists **report** that atmospheric warming **has** already **begun**.

   Measurements **have indicated** that the average temperature of Earth **was** lower 100 years ago.

   Further research **will prove** that carbon dioxide **is** largely responsible.

- If the independent clause verb is in the past tense, the verb in the noun clause is usually in a past form.

   The prime ministers **agreed** that global warming **was** a serious world problem.

   They **hoped** that all nations **would be** responsible for finding a solution.

   An international group of scientists **reported** that Earth's temperature **had risen** 1.1 degrees Fahrenheit (0.6°C) in the last century.

   Their report **stated** that carbon dioxide **was** largely responsible.

Exception: The verb in the noun clause stays in the present tense when it reports a fact or a general truth:

   Researchers in the field **verified** that icebergs and glaciers **are** melting.

See also Indirect Quotations and Sequence of Tenses Rules in Chapter 3, page 56, for more examples and practice.

Read the article. Then use the prompts and information from the article to write sentences with *that* clauses.

- When the prompt begins with *it*, use the passive voice in the independent clause.
- Use an appropriate verb tense in both clauses.

Men and Women *Are* Different

Family, environment, and temperament—an individual's unique identity and abilities are influenced by many different factors. One of these factors is biology, and research suggests that there are some biological differences between men's and women's brains. Neither sex is more intelligent than the other; their brains are just different. For example, a certain area of the brain controls language, and women have more brain cells in that area than men do. Therefore, women generally learn language more easily than men do. However, women's superior language skills certainly do not mean that women are more intelligent than men. Indeed, men often show superior ability at math and reasoning.

Another difference between the sexes involves spatial tasks. Men tend to be better at reading maps, but women tend to be better at remembering the location of objects. Perhaps men's and women's brains developed different spatial skills because of the different tasks it is thought that they performed in prehistoric times. In those days, according to researchers, men were the hunters. They had to be able to track prey, make a kill, and then find their way back to the camp. Women, on the other hand, were the gatherers. They were responsible for finding edible leaves, roots, and berries, so they had to remember the location of particular trees and plants. Thus, men's brains were programmed to follow routes and women's to remember locations.

1. Experts / agree

   Experts agree that neither sex is more intelligent than the other.

2. It / know / for a long time

   It has been known for a long time that women generally learn languages more easily than men do.

3. Research / indicate / a long time ago

   _____

4. Scientists / reassure / men

   _____

5. It / often observe

   _____

6. It / think / by many scientists

   _____

Subjunctive Noun Clauses

After certain verbs and adjectives in independent clauses, you must use the **subjunctive form** of the verb in the noun clause that follows. The subjunctive form of a verb is the same as the base form—for example, *be, go, come, do.*

VERBS			ADJECTIVES	
advise	insist	request	advisable	mandatory
ask	order	require	desirable	necessary
command	prefer	suggest	essential	urgent
demand	propose	urge	important	vital
direct	recommend			

The verbs and adjectives that require the subjunctive form in the noun clauses that follow indicate urgency, advisability, necessity, and desirability.

The company president **urged** that the marketing department **be** more aggressive.

It is **necessary** that each salesperson **work** longer hours.

Make a subjunctive verb negative by putting the word *not* in front of it.

She **insisted** that the company **not lose** any more customers to its competitors.

The subjunctive also occurs when the independent clause verb is in the passive voice.

It **was recommended** that the department **not hire** new staff at this time.

PRACTICE 3	**Writing Subjunctive Noun Clauses**

Read the Background Information. Then answer the questions using subjunctive noun clauses. (*Hint:* The answer to each question is contained in the corresponding lettered item on the list of restrictions: for example, 1 = a, 2 = b.)

Background Information

A three-year drought has caused a serious water shortage in the fictitious country of Sunnyland. As a result, Sunnyland's water department has recommended restrictions on water use.

Due to the recent drought in our region, the County of Sunnyland is imposing restrictions on water use, effective immediately. Violators will be subject to penalties.

Restrictions on Water Use

a. All citizens must conserve water wherever possible.
b. Every individual must decrease water use.
c. Every family must reduce its water use by 40 percent.
d. In the cities, everyone must limit showers to 5 minutes.
e. In the countryside, farmers must cut their water use by 25 percent.
f. Every farmer should install a drip irrigation system.
g. People in the suburbs must not use water to wash cars, sidewalks, or streets.

1. What does the water department recommend?

   The water department recommends that all citizens conserve water wherever possible.

2. What will the water department demand?

   _____

3. What is necessary?

   _____

4. What does the water department propose for city dwellers?

   _____

5. What is required of farmers?

   _____

6. What is suggested for farmers?

   _____

7. What does the water department urge for people living in suburban areas?

   _____

TRY IT OUT! On a separate sheet of paper, write three sentences of your own using a different verb or adjective from the charts on page 212 in each independent clause.

IF / WHETHER CLAUSES

An *if* / *whether* clause is a dependent noun clause that begins with the subordinator *if* or *whether*. *Whether* is more formal than *if*. The optional phrase *or not* may be added in two places with *whether* and in one place with *if*. Therefore, there are five possible patterns:

The patient wants to know **whether Dr. Chen practices acupuncture**.

The patient wants to know **whether or not Dr. Chen practices acupuncture**.

The patient wants to know **whether Dr. Chen practices acupuncture or not**.

The patient wants to know **if Dr. Chen practices acupuncture**.

The patient wants to know **if Dr. Chen practices acupuncture or not**.

Notice that *if* / *whether* clauses are statements, not questions, even though they are made from *yes* / *no* questions (questions that can be answered *yes* or *no*). *If* / *Whether* clauses use statement word order (subject-verb) and do not contain *do*, *does*, or *did*.

To change a question into an *if* / *whether* clause, add a subordinator (*if* or *whether*), change the word order to statement word order, and delete *do*, *does*, and *did* if necessary.

QUESTION	SENTENCE WITH *IF* / *WHETHER* CLAUSE
Is the test easy?	The students want to know if ~~is~~ the test easy.
Does he know the answer?	I want to know whether ~~does~~ he knows the answer.

Follow the sequence of tenses rules if necessary. (If the independent clause verb is in a past tense, the verb in the noun clause should also be in a past tense.)

was
John asked if the test ~~is~~ hard.

| PRACTICE 4 | Using *If* / *Whether* Clauses |

A Imagine that you are doing research on acupuncture. In addition to getting information from the library and the Internet, you have decided to write to Dr. Robert Hsu, a leading authority in the field, to ask for further information. Here are the questions you wish to ask Dr. Hsu:

1. Is acupuncture a risky medical procedure?

2. Are the needles made of stainless steel or of some other metal?

3. Do the needles hurt when they are inserted?

4. Has the effectiveness of acupuncture in relieving back pain ever been documented?

5. Can acupuncture strengthen the immune system?

6. Does acupuncture use the body's energy to promote healing?

7. Did you study acupuncture in China or in the United States?

8. Have you ever used acupuncture during an operation?

Add one questions of your own.

9. _____

_____

B Complete the letter to Dr. Hsu. Change the questions into *if / whether* clauses. Add an *if / whether* clause to each incomplete sentence.

415 Burleigh Avenue
Norfolk, VA 23505
July 8, 2014

Robert Hsu, M.D.
1200 South Eliseo Drive
Los Angeles, CA 90034

Dear Dr. Hsu:

I am a prenursing student at a community college in Norfolk, Virginia. I am doing research about the practice of acupuncture in China and the United States. I hope you will be kind enough to answer a few questions.

The first thing I would like to know is (1) _whether or not acupuncture is a risky_ _medical procedure_. Also, can you please tell me (2) _____ _____?

People who have never had acupuncture are curious to find out (3) _____ _____. Since I have frequent backaches, I am personally interested in learning (4) _____ _____.

I also have two questions about the way acupuncture works in the body. Can you say for certain (5) _____? I also wonder (6) _____.

About your own background, I would like to ask (7) _____ _____.

Finally, I have heard that acupuncture is used as an anesthetic during surgery in China, and I am wondering (8) _____ _____.

(9) _____

_____

Thank you sincerely for your time.

Very truly yours,

Marvin Lemos
Marvin Lemos

QUESTION CLAUSES

A question clause is a dependent noun clause that begins with a subordinator such as *who, what, when, where, why, how, how much, how long*, and so on. There are two possible patterns. In the first pattern, the subordinator is the subject of the clause.

                                    SUBJECT / SUBORD. V
    The police do not know **who** committed the robbery.

In the second pattern, the subordinator is not the subject of the clause.

                          SUBORD.   SUBJECT   V
    The police do not know **when** the robbery happened.

Notice that the word order in question clauses is statement order (subject + verb), not question order (verb + subject). Also, question clauses do not contain *do, does,* or *did* because they are not questions even though they begin with a question word.

To change a question into a question clause, change the word order to statement word order and delete *do, does,* and *did* if necessary.

QUESTION	SENTENCE WITH QUESTION CLAUSE
What time is it?	Please tell me what time ~~is it~~.
How did the robbers enter the apartment?	The police want to know how ~~did~~ the robbers enter^ed the apartment.

Follow the sequence of tenses rules if necessary.

    The victims **did not know** how the robbers **had entered** the apartment.

PRACTICE 5   **Using Question Clauses**

Ⓐ Imagine that you are working as a summer intern at your local newspaper, the *Fog City News*. A well-known rock group, Marble Pelicans, is in town to give a concert. Your boss, the editor of the newspaper's Sunday entertainment section, has asked you to write an article about the group for the newspaper's entertainment blog. However, when you try to interview the group, they are not very helpful.

Here is a list of questions that you have prepared for the interview.

1. When and where will the concert take place?

2. When did you last perform in Fog City?

3. How many years have you been together as a group?

4. Who writes your songs?

5. Where do you practice on the road?

6. How many songs have you recorded?

Add two questions of your own.

7. _____

8. _____

B Complete the email memo. Change the questions into question clauses. Add a question clause to each incomplete sentence.

- Change the word order of the questions to SV statement order.
- Delete *do, does,* and *did* from the questions, if necessary.
- Follow the sequence of tenses rules.

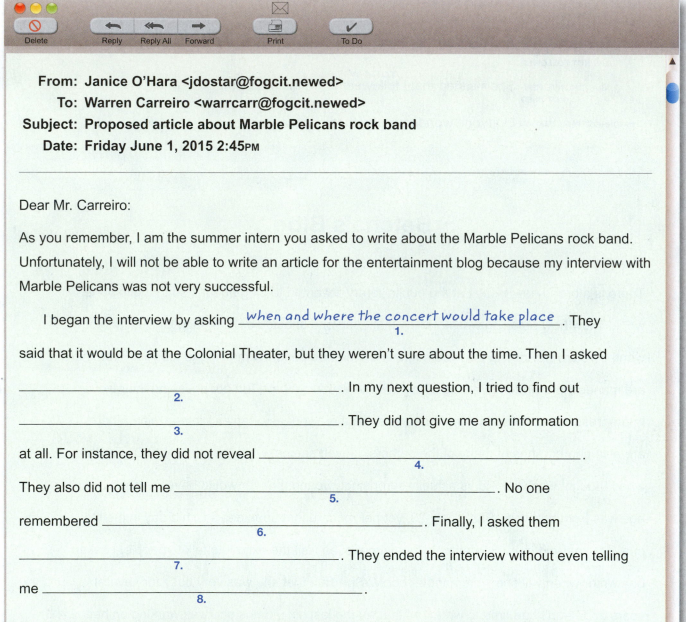

From: Janice O'Hara <jdostar@fogcit.newed>
To: Warren Carreiro <warrcarr@fogcit.newed>
Subject: Proposed article about Marble Pelicans rock band
Date: Friday June 1, 2015 2:45PM

Dear Mr. Carreiro:

As you remember, I am the summer intern you asked to write about the Marble Pelicans rock band. Unfortunately, I will not be able to write an article for the entertainment blog because my interview with Marble Pelicans was not very successful.

I began the interview by asking *when and where the concert would take place*. They

1.

said that it would be at the Colonial Theater, but they weren't sure about the time. Then I asked

_____. In my next question, I tried to find out
2.

_____. They did not give me any information
3.

at all. For instance, they did not reveal _____.

4.

They also did not tell me _____. No one

5.

remembered _____. Finally, I asked them

6.

_____. They ended the interview without even telling

7.

me _____.

8.

Again, I am very sorry that I was not able to complete this assignment for the *Fog City News.* However, I am eager to accept another assignment, and I hope that I will be assigned one.

Very truly yours,
Janice O'Hara
Summer Intern

Edit the blog for nine more errors in noun clauses. Look for these kinds of errors:

INCORRECT WORD ORDER	We do not know when ~~is it.~~ *it is*
MISSING OR WRONG SUBORDINATOR	She asks ^*whether* the time is noon. Then she asks ~~that~~ *what* I am doing.
SEQUENCE OF TENSES RULES NOT FOLLOWED	I saw that the exhibit's hours ^*had* changed.
SUBJUNCTIVE VERB NOT USED	She insisted that I ~~followed~~ *follow* her to the museum.
INCORRECT PUNCTUATION	Everyone wondered why the time changed~~?~~ ^.

www.myblog.com

Betcha's Blog

Hi there,

There is a brand new exhibit at the public library. I wanted to blog about it so that everyone would know how amazing ~~was it~~ *it was*. I think that everyone should see it. In fact, I insist that you went! If you're wondering that you might find there, be patient! I'm going to tell you. First, there are manuscripts written by some of my favorite writers. What's fun about seeing their work-in-progress is that these famous authors revise their work as often as I revise mine. There are also photographs of many of the authors. I loved seeing, what they look like. One author, who I thought was very old, is actually surprisingly young. I never would have guessed her age was from her work. She's only 23, yet her most recent book deals with a day in the life of a 100-year-old man. Sometimes, the writers even visit the exhibit to talk to people. I asked one writer when will she write another book? She said that she was very busy for several years and hadn't had time to write, but that for the last six months she was working on her next book. I can't wait till it is published! Anyway, if you want to know when should you go to the exhibit, I suggest that you are there early in the morning. That's when the exhibit is less crowded.

On a separate sheet of paper, write a letter of inquiry in response to a job listing. Use noun clauses in your letter. Before starting to write, read the background information in the box. Then read the remainder of the writing prompt and complete the writing practice.

Background Information

Imagine that you are going to graduate from the university a year from now, and you want to write to potential employers to learn more about what kinds of positions employers are offering to graduates in your field (business, engineering, teaching, and so on). You could start by looking in your local newspaper or online to see what job opportunities are available. You might find ads such as these:

College Grad

Do you have a B.A. or B.S. degree in accounting or business?
No experience necessary. Training program in national firm. Inquiries welcomed.
Write: Billings, Goodwill, and Rush Accountants, Inc., 354 Waterfront Center,
Suite 3790, New York, New York, 10017. Affirmative Action Employer.
Email: jobs@acmesacct.com

Engineering Graduates

Must possess degree in electrical / chemical / industrial engineering. Company is expanding. Job opportunities on U.S. West and East Coasts and in Middle East.
No phone calls, please. Direct all inquiries to Frank Memry, MHC Engineering, Inc., 475 Evanston Drive, Santa Clara, CA 94301. Equal Opportunity Employer.
Call for details: (555) 111-2222

If you are planning to become an accountant or an engineer, you might answer one of these ads. If you have a different career preference, look online or in your local newspaper for an ad that fits your needs, and attach the ad to your letter of inquiry.

Remember to use noun clauses in your letter of inquiry. Use *that* clauses to state information that you already know ("Your ad stated that your company was seeking . . . "). Use *wh-* word clauses and *if / whether* clauses to ask for information. You might want to inquire about the size of the company, travel requirements, salary, benefits, number of employees, advancement opportunities, support for further education, and so on.

Use the letter in Practice 4 on page 215 as a model for the format of your letter. Notice the punctuation in the greeting and closing. Also note the capitalization of proper nouns, of the word *Dear*, and of the first word of the closing. Study the line spacing between different parts of the letter. When you write your own letter, follow this format.

Also notice that both of the sample job advertisements in the box allow inquiries to be sent either through the postal service or by email. If your teacher asks you to write an email rather than a letter, you can use the email in Practice 5 on page 217 as a model or follow the format suggested by your teacher.

After you have written a draft of your letter of inquiry, look carefully at each sentence and consider these questions:

1. Have you clearly stated your reasons for writing the letter?

2. Have you asked any questions you had about the job?

   ○ Have you used noun clauses correctly?

   ○ Does each noun clause use appropriate word order, verb tense, and punctuation?

   ○ Have you used the correct format for your letter?

Edit your letter as needed to improve it.

SELF-ASSESSMENT

In this chapter, you learned to:

○ Form noun clauses beginning with the word *that*

○ Form sentences beginning with *it*

○ Use special verb tenses in *that* clauses

○ Form noun clauses beginning with the words *if / whether*

○ Form question clauses

○ Write a letter that includes sentences with noun clauses

Which ones can you do well? Mark them ☑

Which ones do you need to practice more? Mark them ☒

CHAPTER 12

ADVERB CLAUSES

OBJECTIVES

To write academic texts, you need to master certain skills.

In this chapter, you will learn to:

- Recognize kinds of adverb clauses

- Punctuate sentences with adverb clauses

- Use adverb clauses to express concepts such as time, place, manner, reason, result, purpose, and contrast

- Write a paragraph that includes sentences with adverb clauses

Some individuals who are not usually shy may feel uncomfortable when they speak in public.

INTRODUCTION

In this chapter you will learn to form many different kinds of adverb clauses. An **adverb clause** is a dependent clause that functions as an adverb. It can tell *when, where, why, how, how long, how far, how often*, and *for what purpose* something happened. An adverb clause can also express a contrast.

An adverb clause always begins with a subordinator that expresses the relationship between the adverb clause and the independent clause.

RELATIONSHIP	ADVERB CLAUSE	INDEPENDENT CLAUSE
Time	SUBORDINATOR **As soon as** a baby opens its eyes,	it begins to observe its surroundings.
Contrast	SUBORDINATOR **Although** some people are more productive in the morning,	others work better at night.

You will study each kind of adverb clause in this chapter. At the end of the chapter, you will write a paragraph with a variety of well-structured sentences that include adverb clauses.

ANALYZING THE MODEL

The writing model is about the fear of public speaking. As you read, notice the clauses that begin with the words *whenever, everywhere, since, so that,* and *even though*. These are adverb clauses.

Read the model. Then answer the questions.

✏ **Writing Model**

Fear of Public Speaking

1 Fear of public speaking is very common. 2 Indeed, many individuals fear speaking in public more than anything else. 3 Whenever they have to speak in front of others, they become paralyzed by feelings that range from extreme discomfort to absolute terror. 4 They see unfriendly, critical faces everywhere they look. 5 Sometimes they even experience physical symptoms of terror such as breaking out in a sweat, having heart palpitations, or developing shaky hands or a quivering voice. 6 Of course, this type of situation can become very embarrassing! 7 Since people often need to make speeches for career advancement, those who suffer from this extreme fear, or phobia, sometimes enroll in speech classes. 8 They take these classes so that they can overcome their phobia about facing an audience. 9 Even though someone may have achieved success in business, he or she may continue to feel uncomfortable speaking in public.

Questions about the Model

1. When do people with a fear of public speaking become paralyzed? Underline the adverb clause in sentence 3 that provides this information. What word introduces this clause?

2. Why do individuals with this fear sometimes take classes? Double underline the adverb clauses in sentences 7 and 8 that provide this information. What words introduce each clause?

3. Where do these individuals see unfriendly faces? Triple underline the clause in sentence 4 that provides this information. What word introduces this clause?

4. What contrast is established by the adverb clause in sentence 9? What words introduce this clause?

KINDS OF ADVERB CLAUSES

These are the various kinds of adverb clauses. In the pages that follow, you will study and practice each kind.

- **Time clauses** answer the question "When?"
- **Place clauses** answer the question "Where?"
- **Clauses of manner** answer the question "How?"
- **Distance clauses** answer the question "How far?"
- **Frequency clauses** answer the question "How often?"
- **Purpose clauses** answer the question "For what intention?"
- **Result clauses** answer the question "For what effect?"
- **Conditional clauses** answer the question "Under what circumstance?"
- **Contrast clauses of direct opposition** show how one thing differs from another.
- **Contrast clauses of concession** show an unexpected result.

Punctuation of Adverb Clauses

The punctuation of an adverb clause depends on the order of the clauses. When an adverb clause comes first in a sentence, put a comma after it. When an adverb clause follows an independent clause, do not separate the clauses with a comma.

ADVERB CLAUSE
Because humans are curious animals,

INDEPENDENT CLAUSE
they constantly explore their world.

INDEPENDENT CLAUSE
Humans constantly explore their world

ADVERB CLAUSE
because they are curious animals.

TIME CLAUSES

An **adverb time clause** tells when the action described in the independent clause took place. The action in a time clause can occur at the same time or at a different time. Be aware that verbs in time clauses often take forms that you do not expect. For example, the verb in a future time clause uses a present form, not a future form. A time clause can come before or after an independent clause. A time clause is introduced by one of the subordinators in the chart.

TIME SUBORDINATORS	EXAMPLES
when: a specific time	**When people had to hunt for food,** they moved from place to place.
whenever: at any time	**Whenever food became scarce in one area,** they moved to another area.
while: at the same time	The men hunted game **while the women gathered plants**.
as soon as: soon after	Eating habits changed **as soon as people stopped moving from place to place in search of food**.
after: later	**After people learned how to grow their own food,** they settled in villages.
since: from that time	**Since the United States changed from an agricultural to an industrial society,** eating habits there have changed.
as: at the same time	People in the United States started eating more processed convenience foods **as their lives became busier**.
before: earlier	**Before people in the United States moved to cities,** they grew most of their own food.
until: up to the time	Women had time to cook meals "from scratch"[1] **until they went to work in factories and offices**.

PRACTICE 1   **Using Adverb Time Clauses**

Combine each pair of sentences by using an adverb time clause. Add a comma if necessary. Write your sentences in paragraph form on a separate sheet of paper. Circle the subordinators.

1. Everyone should know what to do. An earthquake strikes.

   Everyone should know what to do (when) an earthquake strikes.

2. If you are inside, move away from windows, and get under a desk or table, or stand in a doorway. You feel the floor begin to shake.

3. Try to stay calm. The earthquake is happening.

4. Do not move. The floor stops shaking.

5. You are sure the earthquake is over. You may begin to move around.

6. You have checked carefully for fallen power lines. You may go outside.

---

[1] **from scratch:** not using convenience foods (such as cake mixes) that have been previously prepared

Choose a topic and write an original paragraph on a separate sheet of paper. Use adverb time clauses in your paragraph. Use a variety of time subordinators and circle them.

TOPICS

1. Tell someone what to do in the event of a house fire, an auto accident, a boat sinking, or any other dramatic event.

2. Tell a story (real or imaginary) about a dramatic event that happened to you in the past.

PLACE CLAUSES

An **adverb place clause** tells where the action described by the main verb took place. The subordinators *wherever*, *everywhere*, and *anywhere* are similar in meaning and are interchangeable. You can begin a sentence with *wherever*, *everywhere*, and *anywhere* clauses, but usually not with a *where* clause. (Expressions such as these are exceptions: *Where there is lightning, there is thunder. Where there is smoke, there is fire.*)

PLACE SUBORDINATORS	EXAMPLES
where: a specific place	Most people shop **where they get the lowest prices**.
wherever: any place	I pay by credit card **wherever I can**.
everywhere: every place	Can you use an ATM card **everywhere you shop**?
anywhere: any place	**Anywhere you go,** you hear people talking on their cell phones.

PRACTICE 2   **Using Place Clauses**

Combine each pair of sentences by using an adverb place clause. Use each place subordinator once. Add a comma if necessary. Circle the subordinators. (*Hint:* Do not use the word *there* in the new sentence.)

1. People prefer to shop / credit cards are accepted there

   People prefer to shop (where) credit cards are accepted.

2. Consumers tend to buy more / credit cards are accepted for payment of merchandise there.

   _____

3. Consumers cannot use credit cards / they shop there.

   _____

4. There are a few places of business / a credit card is not accepted there.

   _____

5. Travelers can use credit cards in foreign countries / they are accepted there.

   _____

Think of something that did not exist 50 years ago but that is everywhere today. For example, ATM machines and cell phones are two common objects invented within the last 50 years.

Write a short paragraph on your topic. Use at least two adverb place clauses. Circle the subordinators. (If you cannot write a whole paragraph on one topic, write at least four sentences on different topics.)

Suggested topics: cell phones, personal computers, E-readers, digital cameras, flat screen TVs, ATM machines, mp3 players, video chat, GPS

DISTANCE, FREQUENCY, AND MANNER CLAUSES

Adverb clauses of distance answer the question "How far?" **Adverb clauses of frequency** answer the question "How often?" **Adverb clauses of manner** answer the question "How?" Distance, frequency, and most (but not all) manner clauses follow the independent clause.

DISTANCE, FREQUENCY, AND MANNER SUBORDINATORS	EXAMPLES
as + (adverb) + as: distance	Fire had destroyed the trees in the forest **as far as the eye could see**.
as + (adverb) + as: frequency	I do not visit my parents **as often as they would like me to**.
as: manner	We mixed the chemicals exactly **as the lab instructor had told us to**.
as + (adverb) + as: manner	Our instructor asked us to fill out the questionnaire **as carefully as we could**.
as if, as though: manner	The bus's engine sounds **as if / as though it is going to stall at any moment**.

Notes

- In informal spoken English, people often use *like* in place of *as if* and *as though*. *Like* is not correct in formal written English, so use only *as if* and *as though* in your writing.

  FORMAL It looks **as if** it is going to rain.

  INFORMAL It looks **like** it is going to rain.

- In very formal written English, the verb takes the same form as it does in conditional clauses when the information in the *as if / as though* clause is untrue (or probably untrue). However, many English speakers use normal verb forms in this situation.

  FORMAL John acts as if he **were** the Prince of Wales.

  INFORMAL John acts as if he **is** the Prince of Wales.

Using Distance, Frequency, and Manner Clauses

A Complete the sentences by adding a distance, frequency, or manner clause. Use your own ideas. Use each subordinator at least once.

1. People should try to recycle ____*as often as they can*____. (frequency)

2. Most people want to move _____. (distance)

3. We should not consume our natural resources _____. (manner)

4. Should teenagers have the right to dress _____? (manner)

5. No nation in the world can afford to act _____. (manner—use *as if* or *as though*)

B Answer the questions with sentences containing a clause of distance, frequency, or manner. Make sure that your answer contains two complete clauses: an independent clause and an adverb clause. (*Hint:* A phrase such as *as fast as possible* is not a clause.)

1. How does your writing instructor want you to write your essays?

   *Our writing instructor wants us to write our essays as thoughtfully as we can.*

2. How should you act when you see an enraged elephant running toward you?

   _____

3. How can you overcome stage fright[1]? (*Use* as if *or* as though *in your sentence.*)

   _____

4. How can you perfect your pronunciation of a foreign language?

   _____

5. When the teacher catches you sleeping in class, how can you avoid embarrassment? (*Use* as if *or* as though *in your sentence.*)

   _____

---

[1] **stage fright:** fear of performing on a stage

REASON CLAUSES

An **adverb reason clause** answers the question "Why?" A reason clause can come before or after the independent clause in a sentence.

REASON SUBORDINATORS	EXAMPLES
because	Europeans are in some ways better environmentalists than North Americans **because** **they are more used to conserving energy**.
since	**Since** **many Europeans live, work, and shop in the same locale,** they are quite accustomed to riding bicycles, trains, and streetcars to get around.
as	**As** **the price of gasoline has always been quite high in Europe,** most Europeans drive high-mileage automobiles that use less fuel.

PRACTICE 4   **Using Adverb Reason Clauses**

Ⓐ Combine each pair of sentences using an adverb reason clause. Do not change the order of the clauses. Add a comma if necessary. Circle the subordinator.

1. Electricity is expensive. Europeans buy energy-saving household appliances such as washing machines that use less water.

   (Since) electricity is expensive, Europeans buy energy-saving household

   appliances such as washing machines that use less water.

2. Europeans experienced hardship and deprivation[1] during and after World War II. They are used to conserving.

   _____

   _____

3. Coal pollutes the air and gives off a lot of carbon dioxide. Many European nations switched to natural gas or nuclear power to produce electricity.

   _____

   _____

4. In the United States, 42 percent of the nation's electricity is generated by burning coal. Coal is cheap and plentiful.

   _____

   _____

5. European heads of government have more power than the U.S. president. They may be able to force industry to make environmentally responsible changes.

   _____

   _____

---
[1]**deprivation:** lack of necessities for living

B Complete the first sentence of each letter. Use the clause in parentheses and add a reason clause. Use each subordinator at least once and vary the order of the clauses. Use your own ideas for the reason clause.

Imagine that you have a summer job as an administrative assistant to a company manager. You have to write letters for the manager, some with good news and some with bad news.

GOOD NEWS LETTERS

Dear _____:

I am pleased to inform you that . . .

1. (you have won the salesperson of the year award)

   Because your sales have shown such outstanding growth over the past

   12 months, you have won the salesperson of the year award.

2. (we are increasing the limit on your credit card to $5,000)

   _____

   _____

3. (the company has decided to offer you a raise)

   _____

   _____

4. (we have decided to extend the time limit for repayment of your loan)

   _____

   _____

(continued on next page)

Dear _____:

I regret to inform you that . . .

5. (the company has decided not to renew your car insurance policy)

_____

_____

6. (we are unable to offer you employment at this time)

_____

_____

7. (we have decided not to extend the time limit for repayment of your loan)

_____

_____

RESULT CLAUSES

An **adverb result clause** expresses the effect or consequence of the information in the independent clause. A result clause follows the independent clause in a sentence.

RESULT SUBORDINATORS	EXAMPLES
so + (adjective / adverb) + that	Joanne's cookie business is so successful that **she hired three new employees last week.**
	New orders are coming in so rapidly that **she has expanded her production facilities.**
such (a / a[n]) + (noun) + that	Joanne's cookies are such a success that **she is considering franchising the business.**
so much / many + (noun) + that	Running the business takes so much time now that **Joanne no longer does the baking herself.**
	There were so many orders for her holiday cookies that **her workers were baking 24 hours a day.**
so little / few + (noun) + that	Joanne's employees have so little free time that **they are beginning to complain.**
	Her cookies contain so few calories that **even people on diets can enjoy them.**

A Combine each pair of sentences using a result clause. Add a comma if necessary. Circle the subordinator. Do not change the order of the clauses.

1. Anthropological museums have realistic displays. A visitor can gain insight into the lifestyles of ancient people.

   Anthropological museums have (such) realistic displays (that) a visitor can gain

   insight into the lifestyles of ancient people.

2. The Ancient Peru exhibit was popular. It was held over for two weeks.

   _____

   _____

3. The artifacts[1] were of historic value. Anthropologists from several universities came to study them.

   _____

   _____

4. The exhibits were precious. A museum guard was posted in every room.

   _____

   _____

5. Computer graphics allowed the exhibit's curators[2] to present the lives of ancient Peruvians realistically. You felt you were actually there.

   _____

   _____

6. There were not many exhibits. We were able to see all of them in an hour.

   _____

   _____

---

[1] **artifacts:** objects such as tools, weapons, pottery, and clothing

[2] **curators:** keepers of museums who plan and care for exhibits and collections

B Complete the sentences in the story with result clauses.

Science museums can be a valuable addition to the education of young people. By visiting these museums, students receive valuable hands-on experience with scientific thinking and can become more motivated to learn. In some cities, science museums are (1) _____ *so* _____ popular *that schools must make appointments for field trips at least a year in advance*.

Biology classes often visit animal exhibits. At many museums, a curator meets the students and takes them to see exhibits. In one popular snake exhibit, a museum employee sits on a chair with a very large boa constrictor around his neck. He feeds the snake its weekly meal of mice. Sometimes, students are concerned by this demonstration of the circle of life and start shrieking when they see a mouse disappear into the boa constrictor's open jaws. One museum curator reports that, on one visit, the students shrieked (2) _____ loudly _____ .

Another museum offers students a chance to hold its largest snake. It is (3) _____ a large and heavy snake _____ . The few students who are brave enough to hold it often comment that its skin is surprisingly dry and smooth.

Other museums invite students to visit the insect room. These rooms often hold an impressive array of different species. One frequently visited museum has (4) _____ many different _____ . At the insect exhibits, teachers often assign each student an insect to draw in detail. Sometimes finding the insect can take longer than drawing it. During one recent visit, a student spent (5) _____ time trying to find her assigned insect among the millions _____ . By the time the student had found her insect and sketched it, she was starved. In fact, she was (6) _____ hungry _____ !

PURPOSE CLAUSES

An **adverb purpose clause** states the purpose of the action in the independent clause. A purpose normally follows the independent clause, but you may put it at the beginning of a sentence if you want to especially emphasize it.

PURPOSE SUBORDINATORS	EXAMPLES
so that	Farmers use chemical pesticides so that **they can get higher crop yields[1].**
in order that	In order that **consumers can enjoy unblemished[2] fruits and vegetables**, farmers also spray their fields.

Notes

- *In order that* is formal.
- The modals *may / might, can / could, will / would,* or *have to* usually occur in a purpose clause.
- We often use the phrase *in order to* + a base verb or simply *to* + a base verb when the subjects of both the independent clause and the purpose clause are the same person or thing. We prefer *to* + verb over *in order to* + verb because it is shorter. The first example above could be written as follows because the two subjects (*farmers* and *they*) refer to the same people.

   Farmers use chemical pesticides **in order to get** higher crop yields.

   Farmers use chemical pesticides **to get** higher crop yields.

In the second example, the two subjects (*farmers* and *consumers*) are different, so it is not possible to use an *in order to* + verb or a *to* + verb phrase.

---

[1] **crop yields:** amounts of a crop that a farmer can sell
[2] **unblemished:** perfect, without spots or marks

Using Purpose Clauses

A Match each action with a purpose. Then write sentences by combining each action sentence with the appropriate purpose using a purpose clause. Add commas as needed. Circle the subordinators.

ACTIONS	PURPOSES
___e___ 1. Chemists create food products in the laboratory.	a. They can avoid food with chemicals.
_____ 2. For example, an artificial food called "bacon bits" was invented.	b. They can increase crop yields.
_____ 3. Chemicals are added to many foods.	c. They can produce organic[1] crops.
_____ 4. Most farmers use chemical fertilizers and pesticides.	d. The foods will stay fresh longer.
_____ 5. Some farmers use only natural pest control methods.	e. Consumers can have substitutes for scarce, expensive, or fattening natural foods.
_____ 6. People like to buy organic farm produce.	f. Consumers could enjoy the taste of bacon without the fat.

1. *Chemists create food products in the laboratory (so that) consumers can have substitutes for scarce, expensive, or fattening natural foods.*

2. _____

_____

3. _____

_____

4. _____

_____

5. _____

_____

6. _____

_____

---

[1] **organic:** grown without chemicals

B Decide which three sentences in Part A you can rewrite using *in order to* + simple verb or *to* + simple verb. Write the new sentences.

1. _____

_____

2. _____

_____

3. _____

_____

CONTRAST CLAUSES

There are two types of adverb clauses that express contrast: **direct opposition clauses** and **concession clauses**.

Direct Opposition Clauses

In this type, the information in the adverb clause and the information in the independent clause are in direct contrast. Note that the subordinators *while* and *whereas* have the same meaning and are interchangeable.

DIRECT OPPOSITION SUBORDINATORS	EXAMPLES
whereas	San Francisco is cool during the summer, whereas **Los Angeles is generally hot**.
while	**While most homes in San Francisco do not have air conditioning,** it is a necessity in Los Angeles.

Notes

- Use a comma between the two clauses no matter which order they are in. (This is an exception to the comma rule for adverb clauses.)
- Since the two ideas are exact opposites, you can put the subordinator with either clause, and the clauses can be in either order. Thus, the examples can be written in four ways with no change in meaning:

San Francisco is cool during the summer, whereas Los Angeles is generally hot.

Whereas Los Angeles is generally hot during the summer, San Francisco is cool.

While San Francisco is cool during the summer, Los Angeles is generally hot.

Los Angeles is generally hot during the summer, while San Francisco is cool.

Concession (Unexpected Result) Clauses

A concession clause means "This idea is true, but the idea in the independent clause is more important."

These clauses are sometimes called "unexpected result" clauses because the information in the independent clause is surprising or unexpected based on the information given in the concession clause.

CONCESSION SUBORDINATORS	EXAMPLES
although	**Although** I had studied all night, I failed the test.
even though	Our house is quite comfortable **even though** it is small.
though	**Though** the citizens had despised the old regime, they disliked the new government even more.

Notes

- *Although*, *even though*, and *though* have almost the same meaning. *Though* is less formal. *Even though* is a little stronger than *although*.
- Some writers follow the normal comma rule for adverb clauses: Use a comma only when the concession clause comes before the independent clause. Other writers use a comma between the two clauses no matter which order they are in.
- Be careful about which clause you use the subordinator with. Sometimes you can use it with either clause, but not always.

> CORRECT He loves sports cars, although he drives a sedan.

> CORRECT Although he loves sports cars, he drives a sedan.

> CORRECT I went swimming, even though the water was freezing.

> NOT POSSIBLE Even though I went swimming, the water was freezing.

PRACTICE 7   Using Contrast Clauses

Don't forget that there are other ways to express contrast. Refer to the section on contrast signal words in Chapter 7, pages 143–144.

A Combine the two sentences in each item using a contrast clause. Decide if the new sentence will express direct opposition or concession and choose an appropriate contrast subordinator. (There are four of each.)

1. Modern Olympic horse-related events emphasize style. The ancient Greek events emphasized speed.

   Modern Olympic horse-related events emphasize style, whereas the ancient

   Greek events emphasized speed.

2. Both the common cold and the flu are caused by viruses. Only the flu can be prevented through immunization.

_____

_____

3. A cold develops gradually, and any fever that develops will be low-grade (101°F or less). The flu often comes on abruptly, with a sudden high fever.

_____

_____

4. Ludwig van Beethoven became totally deaf in midlife. He wrote some of the Western world's greatest music.

_____

_____

5. South Korea is becoming an economic superpower. It is a small country with few natural resources.

_____

_____

6. In some areas of the Northwest United States, rainfall averages over 50 inches annually. Some areas of the Southwest average less than 10 inches per year.

_____

_____

7. Scientists know why earthquakes happen. They are still not able to predict them.

_____

_____

8. Smokers claim the right to smoke in public places. Nonsmokers claim the right to breathe clean air.

_____

_____

Complete the sentences. In some cases, you will have to add an independent clause. In others, simply complete the dependent clause.

1. **a.** A robot cannot think creatively, even though *it can make logical decisions* _____
   based on input data. _____

   b. A robot cannot think creatively, whereas *a human worker can.* _____

2. **a.** Though it seldom snows in the desert, _____
   _____

   b. While it seldom snows in the desert, _____
   _____

3. **a.** The IT (information technology) manager did not submit next year's budget on
   time, although _____
   _____

   b. The IT (information technology) manager did not submit next year's budget on
   time, whereas _____
   _____

4. **a.** In recent years, Asian medical techniques such as acupuncture have gained
   acceptance in the West, even though _____
   _____

   b. In recent years, Asian medical techniques such as acupuncture have gained
   acceptance in the West, while _____
   _____

5. **a.** Even though SUVs are dangerous to drive, _____
   _____

   b. Whereas SUVs are dangerous to drive, _____
   _____

CONDITIONAL CLAUSES

A **conditional clause** states a condition for a result to happen or not happen. In the sentence *If it rains tomorrow, we will not go to the beach,* the condition is the weather. The result is going or not going to the beach. A conditional clause can come before or after an independent clause.

CONDITIONAL SUBORDINATORS	EXAMPLES
if	If **you study,** you will get good grades.
	The mayor would have lost the election if **the labor unions had not supported him.**
unless	Unless **you study,** you will not get good grades.
	The mayor cannot govern unless **the labor unions support him.**

Note

- *Unless* means "if not."

> You cannot get a refund **unless you have a receipt.**
> *(You cannot get a refund if you do not have a receipt.)*

There are four basic patterns of conditional sentences. Each pattern has a different combination of verb forms depending on whether the time is present, future, or past, and on whether the condition is true or not true. The chart summarizes the four patterns. There are many variations to these basic patterns; consult a grammar book for more complete information.

PATTERN	VERB FORM IN THE *IF* CLAUSE	VERB FORM IN THE INDEPENDENT CLAUSE
1. Present time, true condition	**present** If (when) you **have** a college education,	**present** you **earn** more money.
2. Future time, true condition	**present** If you **get** at least 90% on the final exam,	**future** you **will get** an A in the course.
3. Present or future time, untrue condition	**simple past** If Paul **were** not so lazy, *(Paul is lazy.)*	*would* + **base form** he **would get** better grades.
4. Past time, untrue condition	**past perfect** If the test **had been** easier, *(The test was hard.)*	*would have* + **past participle** all of us **would have gotten** As.

Using Conditional Clauses

Complete the sentences. In some sentences, you will have to add an appropriate independent clause. In others, just complete the conditional clause. If necessary, refer to the preceding chart to select verb tenses.

1. The company will have to declare bankruptcy unless _its sales improve soon._

2. If the company does not increase it profits, _____.

3. The company would increase its profits if _____.

4. Unless _____, all the employees will lose their jobs.

5. The company president would not have resigned if _____.

6. The vice president will also resign unless _____.

Individuals make personal decisions that affect their lives. On a separate sheet of paper, write six sentences using conditional clauses. Write three sentences about decisions you are facing now or that you will face in the near future and three sentences about decisions you made in the past.

EXAMPLES

If I get married, I will not be free to travel as much as I want to.

If I had not finished high school, I would still be working at a minimum-wage job.

EDITING PRACTICE

Edit the essay "Net Addiction" on page 241 for 10 more errors in adverb clauses. Look for these kinds of errors.

TOO MANY CONNECTORS Even though I am studying five hours a night, ~~but~~ I am still getting low grades.

OR

~~Even though~~ I am studying five hours a night, but I am still getting low grades.

COMMA ERROR He does not eat meat͵ because he is a vegetarian.

WRONG SUBORDINATOR _If_ ~~Unless~~ his father were not the owner of the store, he would not be working here.

Net Addiction

1 A lot of people enjoy surfing the Net. 2 They look for interesting websites and chat with people all over the world. 3 However, some people spend ~~such~~ *so* many hours online that they are Internet addicts. 4 Although an average person spends about 12 hours per week, but an addict may spend 8 to 12 hours per day online. 5 Because addicts spend so much time interacting with the computer so their lives are negatively affected. 6 They become socially isolated, because they stop going out and talking to people face-to-face. 7 They avoid real-life social situations, preferring instead to be in a dimly lit room with only the glowing screen to light up their lives.

8 Internet addiction affects not only the addicts themselves but also the people around them. 9 For example, John Davis's marriage to his wife, Marta, broke up until he insisted on spending so many hours on the Net. 10 As soon as he arrived home from work he was at his computer. 11 While he finished dinner, he would disappear into his computer room again. 12 He paid so little attention to Marta, that she finally divorced him.

13 Since college students are especially technologically skilled they can easily become nonstop Net-surfers. 14 Many students have their own computers. 15 Moreover, most colleges provide computers at several locations around campus, so that students can use them at any time day or night.

16 As a result, students can spend too much time surfing the Net instead of reading their assignments for classes. 17 Last semester, nine freshmen at East Berkshire State University flunked out although they became Internet addicts.

18 In short, even though the Internet is an excellent source of information and entertainment, but we must not let it take over our lives.

On a separate sheet of paper, write a paragraph that uses adverb clauses. Use at least eight adverb clauses in your paragraph, with a variety of clause types—time, reason, contrast, purpose, result, frequency, conditional, and so on. Choose one of the prompts to write about.

Prompts

- Overcoming a fear
- The lifestyle of the future
- Recommendations for vacation / trip / adventure
- Characteristics of a good pet

After you have written a draft of your paragraph, look carefully at each sentence and consider these questions:

- Does your paragraph have a strong topic sentence?
- Do all the other sentences relate to the topic sentence?
- Have you used at least eight adverb clauses?
- Did you use a variety of adverb clause types?
- Does each adverb clause use appropriate word order, verb tense, and punctuation?
- Do your sentences flow smoothly from one sentence to the next?

Edit your paragraph as needed to improve it.

SELF-ASSESSMENT

In this chapter, you learned to:

○ Recognize kinds of adverb clauses

○ Punctuate sentences with adverb clauses

○ Use adverb clauses to express concepts such as time, place, manner, reason, result, purpose, and contrast

○ Write a paragraph that includes sentences with adverb clauses

Which ones can you do well? Mark them ✓

Which ones do you need to practice more? Mark them ✗

ADJECTIVE CLAUSES

OBJECTIVES

To write academic texts, you need to master certain skills.

In this chapter, you will learn to:

- Form adjective clauses with relative pronouns and adverbs

- Position adjective clauses properly in a sentence

- Make subjects and verbs agree in adjective clauses

- Form adjective clauses, using relative pronouns as subjects and objects

- Use adjective clauses to show possession, quantity, quality, time, and place

- Write a paragraph that includes sentences with adjective clauses

Traditional foods like turkey are a reminder of the first Thanksgiving feast.

In Chapter 12, you learned to form sentences with adverb clauses. In this chapter, you will learn to use adjective clauses. An **adjective clause** is a dependent clause that functions as an adjective. That is, it modifies (gives more information about) a noun or pronoun.

Adjective clauses are one way to improve your writing style because they use subordination to connect ideas. Subordination, rather than coordination (using lots of *ands* and *buts* to connect ideas) is the mark of a mature writing style. However, take care not to use too many adjective clauses. A paragraph or essay that is filled with too many uses of *who* and *which* is not good either.

At the end of the chapter, you will write a paragraph that includes sentences with adjective clauses.

ANALYZING THE MODEL

The writing model describes the legend of the first Thanksgiving in the United States. The model contains several boldfaced adjective clauses.

Read the model. Then answer the questions.

✎ **Writing Model**

The First Thanksgiving

1 According to legend, the first Thanksgiving feast in the United States, **which took place in 1621**, lasted three days. 2 The participants included Pilgrims, or settlers from Europe, as well as Native Americans. 3 Everyone **who came to the feast** enjoyed the celebration. 4 The food **that they ate** was native to the American continent, and some popular dishes included maize (corn) and wild birds. 5 The first Thanksgiving celebrated the Pilgrims' survival in America and the help **that they had received from the Native Americans**. 6 When modern Americans have Thanksgiving dinner, they remember that first celebration. 7 They give thanks for the food **that they eat**, for the friends and family **who are gathered around them**, and for their good fortune in surviving any hardships of the previous year. 8 In the twenty-first century, as in the seventeenth century, the Thanksgiving feast is a time for gratitude.

Questions about the Model

1. What is the adjective clause in the first sentence? What phrase does it modify?

2. What is the adjective clause in the third sentence? What word does it modify? Is this word a noun or a pronoun?

3. What is the adjective clause in the fourth sentence? What word does it modify?

4. Which adjective clause in the seventh sentence repeats the adjective clause in the fourth sentence? How are the two clauses different?

RELATIVE PRONOUNS AND ADVERBS

An adjective clause begins with a **relative pronoun** or **relative adverb**.

PRONOUNS

who, **whom**, **whose**, **that** refer to people

which, **whose**, **that** refer to animals and things

ADVERBS

when, **where** refer to a time or a place

POSITION OF ADJECTIVE CLAUSES

Notice the adjective clause in the first sentence of the model: *which took place in 1621*. This adjective clause gives more information about the noun phrase: *the first Thanksgiving feast in the United States*. The noun phrase is called the **antecedent** of the adjective clause. The word *antecedent* refers to whatever noun(s) or pronoun(s) an adjective clause modifies. To avoid confusion, an adjective clause should come right after its antecedent.

> CONFUSING He left the gift in his friend's car **that he had just bought**.
>
> *(It is not clear whether the adjective clause modifies car or gift.)*

> CORRECTED He left the gift **that he had just bought** in his friend's car.
>
> *(The adjective clause clearly modifies gift.)*

In these next sentences, notice that the adjective clause comes immediately after the antecedent *scientists* no matter where *scientists* appears in the sentence.

> Scientists **who study fossils** are called paleontologists.

> The government awards large contracts each year to scientists **who do research for the government**.

Occasionally, other words may come between the antecedent and the adjective clause.

> Recently, a friend of mine at the University of Toronto, **who is majoring in electrical engineering**, received a government grant to study airport runway lighting.

> Yesterday I spent an hour in the library reading the article from *Scientific American* **that the instructor had put on reserve**.

Sometimes an adjective clause modifies an entire sentence. In this case, it comes at the end of the sentence. The relative pronoun is always *which*.

> The team won the championship, **which shocked the opponents**.

VERB AGREEMENT IN ADJECTIVE CLAUSES

The verb in an adjective clause agrees in number with its antecedent. Compare these two sentences:

An employee **who works part-time** usually receives no benefits.

(The verb works *is singular to agree with the singular antecedent* employee.*)*

Employees **who work part-time** usually receive no benefits.

(The verb work *is plural to agree with the plural antecedent* employees.*)*

RESTRICTIVE AND NONRESTRICTIVE ADJECTIVE CLAUSES

Adjective clauses are either **restrictive** (necessary) or **nonrestrictive** (unnecessary).

- A restrictive clause is necessary because it identifies its antecedent for the reader. Do not use commas with restrictive clauses.
- A nonrestrictive clause is not necessary to identify its antecedent; it merely gives the reader some extra information about it. Because you can omit a nonrestrictive clause without loss of meaning, separate it from the rest of the sentence with commas.
- The relative pronoun *that* is used in restrictive clauses only. *Which* is used in nonrestrictive clauses only. The other relative pronouns and adverbs can be used in both restrictive and nonrestrictive clauses.

PUNCTUATION OF ADJECTIVE CLAUSES

Punctuation is important to indicate whether a clause is restrictive or nonrestrictive.

RESTRICTIVE (NECESSARY): The professor **who teaches my biology class** won a
NO COMMAS Nobel Prize two years ago.

(Which professor won a Nobel Prize two years ago? The clause who teaches my biology class *is necessary to identify the professor.)*

He won the prize for research **that might lead to a cure for AIDS**.

(For which research did he win the prize? We need the clause that might lead to a cure for AIDS *to tell us.)*

NONRESTRICTIVE (UNNECESSARY): Professor Jones, **who teaches my biology class**,
COMMAS won a Nobel Prize two years ago.

(The person who won a Nobel Prize is identified by his name, so the clause who teaches my biology class *is extra, unnecessary information about Professor Jones. If it were omitted, we would still know which person won the Nobel Prize.)*

He won the prize for his research into the structure of T-cells, **which might lead to a cure for AIDS**.

(We already know which research he won the prize for: his research into the structure of T-cells. *The information* which might lead to a cure for AIDS *is not necessary to identify the research; it merely gives us extra information about it.)*

Recognizing Restrictive and Nonrestrictive Clauses

Underline the adjective clause or clauses in each sentence. Label them *R* (restrictive clause) or *NR* (nonrestrictive clause). Add commas to the nonrestrictive clauses.

___R___ 1. Families whose incomes are below a certain level pay no income tax.

___NR___ 2. The Rodriguez family, whose income is more than $50,000, pays more in taxes than some of their neighbors.

_____ 3. The sun which in 40 minutes can produce enough solar energy to meet humankind's needs for a year is one of Earth's potential sources of power.

_____ 4. We are at the beginning of a medical computer revolution, according to an article that appeared online.

_____ 5. A medical computer is a machine that analyzes the results of laboratory tests and electrocardiograms.

_____ 6. A physician who feeds a patient's symptoms into a computer receives a list of diseases that fit the symptoms of that patient.

_____ 7. Laser beams which are useful in both medicine and industry were first predicted in science fiction stories 75 years ago.

_____ 8. According to the International Monetary Fund, the country that has the highest income per person is not the United States which is in fourth place.

_____ 9. It was a thrilling experience to meet the author of the book that we had been reading all semester.

_____ 10. My brother-in-law who is from Italy moves his hands a lot when he is talking.

KINDS OF ADJECTIVE CLAUSES

There are different types of adjective clauses. In each different type, the relative pronoun has a different function. It may be a subject or an object in its own clause, or it may replace a possessive word.

RELATIVE PRONOUNS AS SUBJECTS

A relative pronoun can be the subject of its own clause.

SUBJECT RELATIVE PRONOUNS	EXAMPLE
who, which, that	American football, **which is** the most popular sport in the United States, began at Harvard University.

In this pattern, *who*, *which*, and *that* can be either singular or plural. Make the verb agree with the antecedent.

I have not read the **magazine** that **is lying** on the coffee table.

(*The verb* is lying *is singular to agree with the singular antecedent* magazine.)

I have not read the **magazines** that **are lying** on the coffee table.

(*The verb* are lying *is plural to agree with the plural antecedent* magazines.)

The examples in the charts show you how to combine two sentences to make a new sentence containing a subject pattern adjective clause.

FOR PEOPLE	EXAMPLES
Restrictive who, that	People save time and energy. ~~They~~ use microwave ovens. People **who use microwave ovens** save time and energy. People **that use microwave ovens** save time and energy. (*informal*)
Nonrestrictive who	Microwave cooking is not popular with most professional chefs. ~~Professional chefs~~ say that fast cooking does not allow flavors to blend. Microwave cooking is not popular with most professional chefs, **who say that fast cooking does not allow flavors to blend**.

FOR ANIMALS AND THINGS	EXAMPLES
Restrictive that	Ovens are capable of cooking food quickly. ~~They~~ use microwave energy. Ovens **that use microwave energy** are capable of cooking foods quickly.
Nonrestrictive which	An electron tube in the oven produces microwaves. ~~Microwaves~~ cook by agitating[1] the water molecules in food. An electron tube in the oven produces microwaves, **which cook by agitating the water molecules in food**.

PRACTICE 2 **Using Relative Pronouns as Subjects**

A Combine the two sentences in each pair to make a new complex sentence containing an adjective clause in the subject pattern. Place the adjective clause as close to its antecedent as possible. Add commas as needed.

1. John Fish explained the complex structure of DNA. He is a research chemist.

John Fish, who is a research chemist, explained the complex structure of DNA.

---

[1] **agitating:** moving very quickly

2. While he lectured, he showed us a slide. The slide diagrammed the double helix structure of DNA.

_____

_____

3. Words in English are often difficult for foreigners to pronounce. They begin with the consonants *th*.

_____

_____

4. Foreigners also have difficulty with English spelling. English spelling is not always consistent with its pronunciation.

_____

_____

5. Anyone must have a logical mind. He or she wants to be a computer programmer.

_____

_____

6. Fans quickly lose interest in a sports team. The team loses game after game.

_____

_____

B Write six sentences that contain adjective clauses in the subject pattern. Use the following prompts.

EXAMPLE:

I do not know anyone who _does not like chocolate ice cream._____

1. I do not know anyone who _____

2. The president, who _____.

3. _____ is a sport that _____.

4. _____ is soccer, which _____.

5. The school subject that _____.

6. The school subjects that _____.

RELATIVE PRONOUNS AS OBJECTS

A relative pronoun can be an object in its own clause.

Object Relative Pronouns	Example
whom, which, that, Ø (no pronoun)	The address **that he gave me** was incorrect.

Note

It is sometimes possible to omit *that* or *whom* in object pattern clauses.

   The address **he gave me** was incorrect.

The examples in the chart show you how to combine two sentences to make a new sentence containing an object pattern adjective clause.

For People	Examples
Restrictive whom, that, Ø	The professor is chair of the English Department. You should see ~~the professor.~~
	The professor **whom you should see** is chair of the English Department.
	The professor **that you should see** is chair of the English Department. (*informal*)
	The professor **you should see** is chair of the English Department.
Nonrestrictive whom	Dr. White is an ecologist. You met ~~Dr. White~~ in my office.
	Dr. White, **whom you met in my office,** is an ecologist.

For Animals and Things	Examples
Restrictive that, Ø	The book was written in German. The professor translated ~~the book.~~
	The book **that the professor translated** was written in German.
	The book **the professor translated** was written in German.
Nonrestrictive which	Environmental science is one of the most popular courses in the college. Dr. White teaches ~~environmental science.~~
	Environmental science, **which Dr. White teaches,** is one of the most popular courses in the college.

Using Relative Pronouns as Objects

On a separate sheet of paper, combine the two sentences in each pair to make a new sentence containing an adjective clause in the object pattern. Place the new adjective clause as close to its antecedent as possible. Add commas as needed. Write the sentences as a paragraph.

1. Albert Einstein was a high school dropout. The world recognizes him as a genius.

   Albert Einstein, whom the world recognizes as a genius, was a high school dropout.

2. As a young boy, Einstein had trouble in elementary and high school. He attended these schools in Germany.

3. He did poorly in certain subjects such as history and languages. He disliked them.

4. The only subjects were mathematics and physics. He enjoyed them.

5. He developed theories. We use his theories to help us understand the nature of the universe.

6. Einstein is best known for his general theory of relativity. He began to develop this theory while living in Switzerland.

TRY IT OUT! Write five sentences of your own that contain adjective clauses in the object pattern. Use the prompts given, and then write two more sentences of your own. Use both restrictive and nonrestrictive clauses.

1. My mother, whom _____

   _____.

2. _____ the homework that

   _____.

3. _____ someone whom

   _____.

4. The islands of Hawaii, which _____

   _____.

5. The television program that _____

   _____.

6. _____

   _____.

7. _____

   _____.

POSSESSIVE ADJECTIVE CLAUSES

In possessive adjective clauses, the relative pronoun *whose* replaces a possessive word such as *Mary's, his, our, their, the company's,* or *its.* Possessive adjective clauses can follow the subject or the object pattern.

In the subject pattern, the *whose* + noun phrase is the subject of the adjective clause. In the object pattern, the *whose* + noun phrase is the object in the adjective clause.

Notes

- Some writers feel that *whose* should be used to refer only to people. For animals and things, they recommend using *of which.* Compare:

  I returned the book **whose cover** was torn.

  I returned the book, **the cover of which** was torn.

  Other writers use *whose* in all but the most formal writing (such as legal documents).

- You have learned that the verb in an adjective clause agrees with the antecedent.

  The **student** who **is working** alone is a friend of mine.

  The **students** who **are working** together are also friends of mine.

Now learn the exception: When *whose* + noun is the subject of an adjective clause, the verb agrees with that noun.

  She takes care of two children whose mother **works** at night.

  (The verb works *is singular to agree with* mother.*)*

  She takes care of two children whose parents **work** at night.

  (The verb work *is plural to agree with* parents.*)*

The examples in the chart show you how to combine two sentences to make a new sentence containing a subject pattern possessive adjective clause.

SUBJECT PATTERN	EXAMPLES
Restrictive	Opportunities are increasing for graduates. ~~Graduates'~~ degrees are in computer engineering.
whose	Opportunities are increasing for graduates **whose degrees are in computer engineering**.
Nonrestrictive	Santa Claus is the symbol of Christmas gift-giving. ~~His~~ jolly figure appears everywhere during the Christmas season.
whose	Santa Claus, **whose jolly figure appears everywhere during the Christmas season,** is the symbol of Christmas gift-giving.

These examples show you how to combine two sentences to make a new sentence containing an object pattern possessive adjective clause.

OBJECT PATTERN	EXAMPLES
Restrictive whose	The citizens protested. The government had seized ~~their~~ property. The citizens **whose property the government had seized** protested.
Nonrestrictive whose	*Consumer Reports* magazine publishes comparative evaluations of all kinds of products. Shoppers trust ~~the magazine's~~ research. *Consumer Reports*, **whose research shoppers trust,** publishes comparative evaluations of all kinds of products.

PRACTICE 4   **Possessive Adjective Clauses**

A Combine the two sentences in each pair to make a new sentence containing a possessive adjective clause in the subject pattern. Place the new adjective clause as close to its antecedent as possible. Add commas as needed. (*Hint:* Replace the possessive form in the second sentence with *whose*.)

1. A manufacturer can offer lower prices. Its costs are lower because of mass production.

   A manufacturer whose costs are lower because of mass production can offer

   lower prices.

2. Securities Corporation's president has a degree in business. His knowledge of financial matters is well known.

   _____

   _____

3. First National Bank tries to attract customers of all ages and income levels. The bank's president comes from my neighborhood.

   _____

   _____

4. Companies conduct market research to discover trends among consumers. Consumers' tastes change rapidly.

   _____

   _____

5. Maya Angelou tells about her early life in her book *I Know Why the Caged Bird Sings*. Her childhood was difficult.

   _____

   _____

B Now combine the two sentences in each pair to make a new sentence containing a possessive adjective clause in the *object* pattern.

1. Maya Angelou is one of the most famous poets in the United States. We have been reading Maya Angelou's poetry in our English class.

   Maya Angelou, whose poetry we have been reading in our English class, is one

   of the most famous poets in the United States.

2. John is dating Eileen's sister. I keep forgetting her name.

   _____

   _____

3. Any company has a better chance of success. Consumers easily recognize its logo or symbol.

   _____

   _____

4. McDonald's has restaurants all around the globe. Most people recognize its golden arches.

   _____

   _____

C Write three sentences containing possessive adjective clauses in either the subject or the object pattern. Use these prompts.

1. the lost child, whose photograph

   _____

   _____

2. my cousin, whose car

   _____

   _____

3. teachers whose classes

   _____

   _____

RELATIVE PRONOUNS AS OBJECTS OF PREPOSITIONS

A relative pronoun can be the object of a preposition in its own clause. These adjective clauses are formed with two patterns: a formal pattern and an informal pattern.

OBJECT RELATIVE PRONOUNS	EXAMPLE
whom, which, that, Ø (no pronoun)	The address **to which** I sent my application was incorrect.

(a) In the formal pattern, the preposition and relative pronoun are together at the beginning of the clause:

for whom I did a favor	**to which** I sent my application
with whom I shared a secret	**in which** the gift was wrapped

(b) In the informal pattern, the pronoun comes at the beginning and the preposition at the end of the clause:

whom I did a favor **for**	**which** I sent my application **to**
whom I shared a secret **with**	**that** the gift was wrapped **in**

When should you use the informal pattern, and when the formal pattern? In all but the most formal writing (master's theses, PhD dissertations, legal documents, or business reports, for example), the informal pattern is probably acceptable. English has no academic or governmental authority that issues rules about correctness. Standards vary. In your classes, some teachers will require you to use only the formal pattern, while others will accept informal usage. Always ask if you are not sure.

The chart shows you how to combine two sentences using an adjective clause in which the relative pronoun is the object of the preposition. Sentence (a) is formal; all of the (b) sentences are informal.

FOR PEOPLE	EXAMPLES
Restrictive whom, that, Ø	The candidate lost the election. I voted for ~~the candidate.~~ (a) The candidate **for whom I voted** lost the election. (b) The candidate **whom I voted for** lost the election. The candidate **that I voted for** lost the election. The candidate **I voted for** lost the election.
Nonrestrictive whom	Mayor Pyle lost the election. I voted for ~~Mayor Pyle.~~ (a) Mayor Pyle, **for whom I voted**, lost the election. (b) Mayor Pyle, **whom I voted for**, lost the election.

(continued on next page)

FOR ANIMALS AND THINGS	EXAMPLES
Restrictive which, that, Ø	No one had read the book. He quoted from the ~~book~~. (a) No one had read from the book **from which he quoted**. (b) No one had read the book **which he quoted from**. No one had read the book **that he quoted from**. No one had read the book **he quoted from**.
Nonrestrictive which	The President's Scholarship was awarded to someone else. John had applied for the ~~President's Scholarship~~. (a) The President's Scholarship, **for which John had applied**, was awarded to someone else. (b) The President's Scholarship, **which John had applied for**, was awarded to someone else.

PRACTICE 5   **Using Relative Pronouns as Objects of Prepositions**

A Combine the two sentences in each pair to make a new sentence, changing the sentence with the underlined prepositional phrase to an adjective clause. Write each new sentence twice, (a) in the formal pattern and (b) in any of the possible informal patterns.

1. Finding reasonably priced housing in big cities is a problem. Many young people are concerned <u>about the problem</u>.

   (a) _Finding reasonably priced housing in big cities is a problem about which many young people are concerned._

   (b) _Finding reasonably priced housing in big cities is a problem that many young people are concerned about._

2. Affordable apartments are scarce. Young people would like to live <u>in them</u>.

   (a) _____

   (b) _____

3. Of course, many young people share apartments, but they have to take care in choosing the people. They will share living space and expenses <u>with these people</u>.

   (a) _____

   (b) _____

4. Living with people can be stressful, but it can also be fun. You are not related <u>to the people</u>.

   (a) _____

   (b) _____

5. In many countries, young people continue to live with their parents in the same house. They grew up in that house.

(a) _____

(b) _____

6. In the United States, many young people choose not to live with their parents. They may declare their independence from their parents at age 18.

(a) _____

(b) _____

B Complete the relative clause in each sentence with your own ideas.

1. **Informal pattern**

(a) The package that _____ for finally arrived.

(b) Uncle Charlie, whom _____ with, is going to spend Thanksgiving with his friends this year.

2. **Formal pattern**

(a) I have received no response from your Customer Service Department, to

which _____ .

(b) The person to whom _____ called me yesterday with a job offer.

RELATIVE PRONOUNS IN PHRASES OF QUANTITY AND QUALITY

A relative pronoun can occur in phrases of quantity and quality.

QUANTITY RELATIVE PRONOUNS	EXAMPLES
all of whom some of whom both of which each of which	The top students, all of whom **graduated with honors,** received scholarships. He gave two answers, both of which **were correct**.
QUALITY RELATIVE PRONOUNS	EXAMPLES
the oldest of whom the best of whom the most important of which	She has three daughters, the oldest of whom **is studying abroad**. The committee received many reports about the situation, the most important of which **were published in the minutes**.

These adjective clauses can follow either the subject or the object pattern, and they are always nonrestrictive; that is, they are always used with commas.

The examples show you how to combine two sentences to make a new sentence containing an adjective clause with an expression of quantity or quality. Notice that the relative pronoun is always *of whom* or *of which*.

FOR PEOPLE	EXAMPLES
Nonrestrictive of whom	The citizens of Puerto Rico are well educated. Ninety percent of ~~them~~ are literate. The citizens of Puerto Rico, **ninety percent of whom are literate**, are well educated.

FOR ANIMALS AND THINGS	EXAMPLES
Nonrestrictive of which	There are many delicious tropical fruits in Puerto Rico. I have never tasted most of ~~them~~ before. There are many delicious tropical fruits in Puerto Rico, **most of which I have never tasted before**.

PRACTICE 6   **Using Adjective Clauses with Phrases of Quantity and Quality**

Ⓐ **Combine the two sentences in each pair, changing the second sentence into an adjective clause with a phrase of quantity or quality.**

1. There is a chain of islands in the Caribbean Sea. The most interesting of the islands is Puerto Rico.

    There is a chain of islands in the Caribbean Sea, the most interesting of which

    is Puerto Rico.

2. Puerto Rico attracts thousands of visitors. Most of them come for the sunny weather, the beautiful beaches, and the Spanish atmosphere.

    _____

    _____

3. Puerto Rico has many historic sites. The most famous of them are in the Old San Juan area of the capital city.

    _____

    _____

4. Puerto Rico's economy is strong compared to other economies in the region. The most important sector of the economy is services, such as tourism and finance.

    _____

    _____

5. Puerto Ricans have strong ties to the United States. All of them are U.S. citizens.

    _____

    _____

B Complete the phrases of quantity or quality. Use your own ideas.

1. The presidential candidate spoke about his qualifications, the most impressive of

   which _____ .

2. The doctors in the free clinic, most of whom _____

   _____ .

ADJECTIVE CLAUSES OF TIME AND PLACE

Adjective clauses can also be introduced by the relative adverbs *when* and *where*.

RELATIVE ADVERBS	EXAMPLES
when, where	Ramadan is the month **when devout Muslims fast**. The Saudi Arabian city of Mecca, **where Mohammed was born,** is the holiest city in Islam.

These clauses refer to a time or a place, and they can be restrictive or nonrestrictive. In the examples in the chart, notice how *when* and *where* replace entire prepositional phrases such as *during that night* and *in Berlin*.

TIME	EXAMPLES
Restrictive when	The lives of thousands of Germans suddenly changed on that night. East German soldiers began building the Berlin Wall ~~during that night~~. The lives of thousands of Germans suddenly changed on the night **when East German soldiers began building the Berlin Wall**.
Nonrestrictive when	On November 9, 1989, their lives changed again. The wall was torn down ~~on November 9, 1989~~. On November 9, 1989, **when the wall was torn down,** their lives changed again.
PLACE	**EXAMPLES**
Restrictive where	The city was suddenly divided. Citizens had lived, worked, and shopped relatively freely ~~in the city~~. The city **where citizens had lived, worked, and shopped relatively freely** was suddenly divided.
Nonrestrictive where	Berlin was suddenly divided. Citizens had lived, worked, and shopped relatively freely ~~in Berlin~~. Berlin, **where citizens had lived, worked, and shopped relatively freely,** was suddenly divided.

It is also possible to write time and place clauses with the relative pronoun *which, that,* or Ø and a preposition. These patterns are possible:

March 31, 1980, was the day
- when I was born.
- on which I was born.
- which I was born on.
- that I was born on.
- I was born.

Cody, Wyoming, is the town
- where I grew up.
- in which I grew up.
- which I grew up in.
- that I grew up in.
- I grew up in.

PRACTICE 7 **Using Adjective Clauses of Time and Place**

A Combine the two sentences in each pair, changing the second sentence into an adjective clause of time or place. Add commas if necessary.

1. Germany had been divided into two countries since 1945. It was defeated in World War II in 1945.

   Germany had been divided into two countries since 1945, when it was defeated in World War II.

2. Nineteen eighty-nine was the year. The Berlin Wall was torn down in that year.

3. In 1990, Germany became one country again. East and West Germany were reunited in 1990.

4. East Germany became part of the Federal Republic of Germany. People had lived under communist rule in East Germany.

5. There was rejoicing in areas. Germans looked forward to being reunited with their fellow citizens in some areas.

6. There was anxiety in places. People feared losing their jobs in some places.

_____

_____

7. Berlin, the new capital of Germany, is a city. Many important historical events have taken place there.

_____

_____

8. 1994 was the year. Russian and Allied troops finally left Berlin in that year.

_____

_____

B Write sentences with adverbial adjective clauses: two with *when* and two with *where*. Try to write both restrictive and nonrestrictive clauses. Use the prompts given for sentences 1 and 2. Use your own ideas in 3 and 4.

1. My grandmother enjoys telling about the time when _____

_____.

2. _____ my hometown, where

_____.

3. _____

_____

4. _____

_____

Find and correct eleven more errors in adjective clauses in this essay. Look for these kinds of errors:

INCORRENT RELATIVE PRONOUN	I telephoned the student ~~who his~~ *whose* wallet I found in the parking lot.
DISAGREEMENT OF VERB AND ANTECEDENT	People who ~~lives~~ *live* in earthquake zones need earthquake insurance.
INCORRECT REPETITION OF NOUNS OR PRONOUNS	My friend whom I loaned my car to ~~him~~ returned it with several dents.
INCORRECT COMMA USAGE	Cell phones, which always seem to ring at inappropriate times, should be turned off during concerts, lectures, and naps.

El Niño

1 Scientists have been studying an ocean event who is the cause of drastic changes in weather around the world. 2 This event is an increase in the temperature of the Pacific Ocean that ~~occur~~ *occurs* around Christmas off the coast of Peru. 3 Hence, the Peruvian fishermen whom first noticed it named it El Niño, a name that means "the Christ child" in Spanish. 4 The causes of this rise in ocean temperatures are unknown, but its effects are obvious and devastating.

5 For example, El Niño threatens Peru's anchovy harvest, which could mean higher prices for food. 6 The warm water of El Niño keeps the nutrient-rich cold water which provides anchovies with food down at the bottom of the ocean. 7 Anchovies are the primary source of fish meal which is the main ingredient in animal feed.

8 In addition, guano[1] from birds who feed off the anchovies is a major source of fertilizer. 9 As a result of decreasing supplies of anchovies and guano, the prices of animal feed, and fertilizer rise. 10 This causes farmers, who they must pay more for feed and fertilizer, to charge more for the food they produces. 11 Food prices have soared as a result of El Niños in past years.

12 El Niño has other global effects. 13 It can cause heavy rains, floods, and mudslides along the coasts of North and South America and droughts in other parts of the world. 14 In the 1982–1983 El Niño, West Africa suffered a terrible drought which caused crop failures and food shortages. 15 Lack of rain also created problems for Indonesia whose forests burned for months during the 1997–1998 El Niño. 16 Indeed, El Niño is an unpredictable and uncontrollable phenomenon of nature, that we need to study it in order to prepare for and perhaps lessen its devastating effects in the future.

[1] **guano:** droppings from birds and bats

On a separate sheet of paper, write a paragraph in which you use at least five adjective clauses. Try to include different patterns if possible. Use the writing model on page 244 to help you. Choose one of the prompts to write about.

Prompts

- An important event in your country's history
- An important event in your family's history
- A room in a house that you have lived in
- A photograph you have seen

After you have written a draft of your paragraph, look carefully at each sentence and consider these questions:

- Does your paragraph have a strong topic sentence?
- Do all the other sentences relate to the topic sentence?
- Have you used adjective clauses?
- Does each adjective clause use appropriate word order, verb tense, and punctuation?
- Do your sentences flow smoothly from one sentence to the next?

Edit your paragraph as needed to improve it.

SELF-ASSESSMENT

In this chapter, you learned to:

- ○ Form adjective clauses with relative pronouns and adverbs
- ○ Position adjective clauses properly in a sentence
- ○ Make subjects and verbs agree in adjective clauses
- ○ Form adjective clauses, using relative pronouns as subjects and objects
- ○ Use adjective clauses to show possession, quantity, quality, time, and place
- ○ Write a paragraph that includes sentences with adjective clauses

Which ones can you do well? Mark them ✓

Which ones do you need to practice more? Mark them ✗

CHAPTER 14

PARTICIPLES AND PARTICIPIAL PHRASES

OBJECTIVES

To write academic texts, you need to master certain skills.

In this chapter, you will learn to:

- Identify participles and participial phrases

- Form reduced adjective and adverb clauses

- Position and punctuate participial phrases

- Form present and past participial phrases

- Use participial phrases to improve your writing style

- Write a paragraph that includes participles and participial phrases

Despite cramped seats and crowded theaters, many people still prefer to watch performances live rather than on television or video.

In this chapter, you will learn about participles and participial phrases. Understanding how to use participles and participial phrases can help you become a better writer. A **participle** is an adjective formed from a verb. There are two kinds of participles: *-ing* participles (called present participles) and *-ed* participles (called past participles).

a **sleeping** baby   a **used** car

a **frightening** experience   a **frightened** child

A **participial phrase** is a phrase that contains a participle plus other words. Participial phrases can be used to modify nouns and pronouns. At the end of the chapter, you will write a paragraph that includes a variety of participles and participial phrases.

ANALYZING THE MODEL

The writing model tells how a fire alert system helped save people's lives in a theater. The paragraph includes several boldfaced participles and participial phrases.

Read the model. Then answer the questions.

✏ Writing Model

A Life-Saving System

1 Automated fire alert systems can save lives, even when the fire goes unnoticed at its location. 2 For example, at the performance of a new opera, a fire broke out. 3 The audience, **listening intently to the music**, failed to notice the fire. 4 **The fascinated audience** did not see what was happening. 5 They weren't aware of the fire **starting to smolder¹ in the back of the auditorium**. 6 Luckily, the automatic system detected the fire, **alerting the local fire station**. 7 The firefighters responded quickly, **arriving at the theater within minutes**. 8 Once there, they sprang into action. 9 They evacuated the theater, **saving the lives of all inside**. 10 **Having rescued the audience** and put out the blaze, the firefighters returned to their station.

---

¹ **smolder:** burn slowly with no flame

Questions about the Model

1. What is the participle in sentence 3? Underline it.

2. Is the participle in sentence 4 a present or past participle? How do you know?

3. What word does the participle in sentence 5 modify?

4. Is the participle in sentence 6 a present or past participle? How do you know?

5. What word begins the participial phrase in sentence 7? What word ends the participial phrase in sentence 7?

6. What does the participial phrase in sentence 9 modify?

KINDS OF PARTICIPLES

The two kinds of participles—present and past—come from either active or passive voice verbs.

- An active voice verb becomes a present participle.

VERBS	PRESENT PARTICIPLES
The custom **fascinates** me.	The **fascinating** custom has been the subject of many books.
The essay **won** an award.	Jacob wrote the **winning** essay.
The baby **will sleep** until eight.	Try not to wake a **sleeping** baby.

- A passive voice verb becomes a past participle.

VERBS	PAST PARTICIPLES
Some movies **are rated G**.	**G-rated** movies are suitable for general audiences.
My leg **was broken** in three places.	My **broken** leg is healing slowly.

- There are also perfect forms.

VERBS	PERFECT PARTICIPLES
The students **had solved** most of the problems without any help.	**Having solved** most of the problems without any help, the students were exhilarated.

PARTICIPLE FORMS

The most commonly used participle forms are shown in this chart.

DESCRIPTION	-ING FORMS	-ED FORMS
The **general forms** do not indicate time. Time is determined by the verb in the independent clause.	VERB + -ING **opening**	VERB + -ED, -EN, -T, -D **opened** **taken** **bought** **sold**
The **perfect forms** emphasize that the action happened before the time of the independent clause verb.	HAVING + PAST PARTICIPLE **having opened**	

PARTICIPIAL PHRASES

As you read previously, a participial phrase includes both a participle and other words. It can be used to modify nouns and pronouns. Participial phrases can be formed by reducing adjective clauses and adverb clauses. For this reason, they are sometimes called **reduced clauses**.

Students **planning to graduate in June** must make an appointment with the registrar.

Airport security will question anyone **found with a suspicious object in their baggage**.

REDUCED ADJECTIVE CLAUSES

You can reduce a subject pattern adjective clause as follows:

- Delete the relative pronoun (*who*, *which*, or *that*).
- Change the verb to a participle.
- Keep the same punctuation (commas or no commas).
- Put the word *not* at the beginning of a participial phrase to make it negative.

ADJECTIVE CLAUSES	PARTICIPIAL PHRASES
A pedestrian **who had been hit by a speeding taxi** was lying in the street.	A pedestrian **hit by a speeding taxi** was lying in the street.
An ambulance **that was summoned by a bystander** came quickly.	An ambulance **summoned by a bystander** came quickly.
The taxi driver, **who did not realize what had happened**, continued on.	The taxi driver, **not realizing what had happened**, continued on.

POSITION AND PUNCTUATION OF PARTICIPIAL PHRASES

Participial phrases, like adjective clauses, can be restrictive (necessary) or nonrestrictive (unnecessary). If the original clause is nonrestrictive, the phrase is nonrestrictive also. A nonrestrictive phrase is separated from the rest of the sentence by commas. Restrictive phrases use no commas.

The position of a participial phrase in a sentence depends on whether it is restrictive or nonrestrictive, or whether it modifies an entire clause.

- A restrictive participial phrase can only follow the noun it modifies and does not have commas.

    RESTRICTIVE A woman hurrying to catch a bus tripped and fell.

- A nonrestrictive participial phrase can precede or follow the noun it modifies and is separated by a comma or commas from the rest of the sentence.

    NONRESTRICTIVE Teresa, hurrying to catch a bus, stumbled and fell.

    Hurrying to catch a bus, Teresa stumbled and fell.

Caution! When you begin a sentence with a participial phrase, make certain that the phrase modifies the subject of the sentence. If it does not, your sentence is incorrect.

INCORRECT Hoping for an A, my exam grade disappointed me.

(*The participial phrase* Hoping for an A *cannot modify* my exam grade. *A grade cannot hope.*)

CORRECT Hoping for an A, I was disappointed in my exam grade.

- Sometimes a participial phrase modifies an entire independent clause. In this case, it follows the clause and requires a comma.

    The team won the championship, shocking their opponents.

PRESENT PARTICIPIAL PHRASES

A present participle may come from present, past, or future tense verbs.

VERB TENSE	SENTENCE WITH ADJECTIVE CLAUSE	SENTENCE WITH PARTICIPIAL PHRASE
Simple present	Many students **who study at this university** are from foreign countries.	Many students **studying at this university** are from foreign countries.
Present progressive	Students **who are taking calculus** must buy a graphing calculator.	Students **taking calculus** must buy a graphing calculator.
Simple past	The team members, **who looked happy after their victory,** were cheered by the fans.	The team members, **looking happy after their victory,** were cheered by the fans.
Past progressive	The crowd, **which was cheering wildly as the game ended,** would not leave the stadium.	**Cheering wildly as the game ended,** the crowd would not leave the stadium.
Future	Everyone **who will take the TOEFL next month** must preregister.	Everyone **taking the TOEFL next month** must preregister.

PRACTICE 1   **Using Present Participial Phrases**

Ⓐ Rewrite the sentences, reducing the adjective clause to a participial phrase. Rewrite sentences 4 and 5 in two ways: once with the participial phrase before the noun it modifies and once with it after the noun. Add commas as needed.

1. Robotics is a complex field that combines electronics, computer science, and mechanical engineering.

    Robotics is a complex field combining electronics, computer science, and

    mechanical engineering.

2. The number of students who are studying robotics is growing.

3. Soon, robots that work in assembly plants will be able to follow voice commands.

_____

_____

4. Robots, which have the ability to withstand extreme temperatures and radiation levels, can perform jobs that are too dangerous for humans.

a. _____

b. _____

5. Robots, which do not need to eat, sleep, or take breaks, can work nonstop.

a. _____

b. _____

B Complete the sentences with a present participial phrase formed from the words in parentheses. Add commas if necessary.

1. The industries ___*using the most robots*___ are those with assembly lines, such as automobile manufacturing. (**use / the most robots**)

2. In the field of medicine, it will soon be normal to find robots

_____. (**perform / surgery**)

3. With one kind of robotic device, a human surgeon _____ directs the robot. (**sit / in front of a video screen**)

4. The surgeon controls three robotic arms _____ with joysticks similar to those used in video games. (**hold / surgical tools above the patient**)

5. _____ robots are very valuable for surgery on infants. (**allow / surgeons to make tiny incisions and to use small tools**)

PAST PARTICIPIAL PHRASES

The past participle is the third form of a verb: _opened_, _spoken_, _sold_, _caught_. It comes from both present and past tense passive voice verbs.

VERB TENSE	SENTENCE WITH ADJECTIVE CLAUSE	SENTENCE WITH PARTICIPIAL PHRASE
Simple present	Lab reports **that are not handed in by Friday** will not be accepted.	Lab reports **not handed in by Friday** will not be accepted.
Simple past	The proposed law, **which was opposed by the majority of the people,** did not pass.	The proposed law, **opposed by the majority of the people,** did not pass.

A Rewrite the sentences, reducing the adjective clause to a participial phrase. Keep the commas in sentences that have them.

1. Cigarette companies, which have been long criticized for their advertising tactics, have been looking for new ways to sell their products.

   Cigarette companies, long criticized for their advertising tactics, have been

   looking for new ways to sell their products.

2. One company plans to try out a new approach that is aimed at young adults.

   _____

   _____

3. The new approach suggests that smokers, who are often scorned for continuing to smoke despite health risks, are daring rebels.

   _____

   _____

4. The company hopes that the image that is projected by the new marketing campaign will succeed half as well as another image succeeded in the 1950s.

   _____

   _____

5. This image, which was pictured in hundreds of ads over the years, portrayed a ruggedly handsome cowboy smoking a cigarette.

   _____

   _____

B Use the words in parentheses to write past participial phrases. Add commas if necessary.

1. The languages _spoken most widely in Switzerland_ are German, French, and Italian. (**speak / most widely in Switzerland**)

2. Switzerland _____ has tried to remain neutral throughout its history. (**situate / between four sometimes warring countries**)

3. Children _____ have an advantage over monolingual children. (**raise / in bilingual families**)

4. A new treatment for malaria _____ will soon be available. (**develop / ABC Pharmaceutical Company**)

5. _____ the public responded generously. (**ask / to donate food and clothing to the hurricane victims**)

PERFECT FORM PARTICIPIAL PHRASES

Perfect forms emphasize the completion of an action that takes place before the action of the main verb. You can change both present perfect and past perfect verbs into perfect participles.

Note that there is also an -ed perfect form (*having been* + a past participle). However, the perfect -ed form is often shortened to the general -ed form with no difference in meaning. For example, *having been elected* becomes *elected*: *The president, (having been) elected by a large majority, promised to lower taxes.*

VERB TENSE	SENTENCE WITH ADJECTIVE CLAUSE	SENTENCE WITH PARTICIPIAL PHRASE
Present perfect	The secrets of the universe, **which have fascinated people for centuries,** are slowly being revealed.	The secrets of the universe, **having fascinated people for centuries,** are slowly being revealed.
Past perfect	The senator, **who had heard that most people opposed the new law,** voted against it.	**Having heard that most people opposed the new law,** the senator voted against it.

PRACTICE 3   **Using Perfect Form Participial Phrases**

A Rewrite each sentence by changing the adjective clause to a participial phrase. Since all of the clauses in these sentences are nonrestrictive, use commas. For practice, write at least two of the sentences with the participial phrase at the beginning of the sentence, as in the second example in the chart above.

1. Women around the world, who have traditionally been without political power, are beginning to gain influence in politics and government.

   Having traditionally been without political power, women around the world are

   beginning to gain influence in politics and government.

   OR

   Women around the world, having traditionally been without political power, are

   beginning to gain influence in politics and government.

2. Ireland, which had never chosen a woman leader in its entire history, elected two consecutive female presidents in the 1990s. (*Put* never *in front of the participle.*)

   _____

   _____

3. India and the Philippines, which have elected women prime ministers in the past, have been more progressive in this area than the United States.

   _____

   _____

B Complete the sentences with perfect form participial phrases. Use the words in parentheses. Add commas as needed.

1. _Having saved for many years,_ the young couple could finally buy their first home. (**save / for many years**)

2. In my opinion, the New York Yankees baseball team

_____ is the best baseball team in the United States. (**win / the World Series more times than any other team**)

3. Janice _____ decided to hide one in a potted plant outside her front door. (**forget / her house key for the third time in a week**)

4. _____ my father found it difficult to quit. (**smoke / for 40 years**)

PARTICIPIAL PHRASES AND WRITING STYLE

Use participial phrases to improve your writing style.

- If you write sentences with many uses of *which*, *who*, and *that*, consider reducing some adjectives clauses to participial phrases.
- If you write short, choppy sentences, consider combining them by using participial phrases.
- Vary your sentence openings by occasionally starting a sentence with a participial phrase.

SHORT, CHOPPY SENTENCES	First-born children are often superachievers. They feel pressure to behave well and to excel in school.
IMPROVED	First-born children, who feel pressure to behave well and to excel in school, are often superachievers.
	First-born children, feeling pressure to behave well and to excel in school, are often superachievers.
	Feeling pressure to behave well and to excel in school, first-born children are often superachievers.

Sentence Combining

Match the related sentences in the two columns. Then combine the two sentences by changing the second sentence to a participial phrase. Add commas as needed. (There is more than one way to combine some of the sentences.)

___d___ 1. Eskimos are distant cousins of modern Asians.

_____ 2. Eskimos have adapted well to their harsh environment.

_____ 3. A problem concerns the rights of native Alaskans.

_____ 4. Some Eskimos reject the ways of the modern world. (Delete *some* in your sentence.)

_____ 5. On the other hand, some Eskimos hope that they can combine both worlds—old and new. (Delete *some* in your sentence.)

a. A problem is being discussed by the Alaskan government.

b. Eskimos want to improve their standard of living.

c. Eskimos want to preserve their traditional way of life.

d. Eskimos had migrated across a land bridge from Asia.

e. Eskimos have lived in Alaska for thousands of years.

1. *Having migrated across a land bridge from Asia, Eskimos are distant cousins of modern Asians.*

2. _____

_____

3. _____

_____

4. _____

_____

5. _____

_____

TRY IT OUT! On a separate sheet of paper, write eight sentences about yourself or another person, using a participial phrase in each.

> *Having six athletic brothers and sisters, I have always been interested in sports.*
> *My father always had time to play with us, even after working 12-hour days in his small shop.*

REDUCED ADVERB CLAUSES

Just as you can reduce some adjective clauses, you can reduce some adverb clauses to participial phrases.

Sentence with Adverb Clause	Sentence with Participial Phrase
When you enter a theater, you should turn off your cell phone.	**When entering a theater,** you should turn off your cell phone.
Because he had read that the company needed workers, John applied for a job.	**Having read** that the company needed workers, John applied for a job.

A participial phrase from an adverb clause may occupy several positions in a sentence. If a participial phrase from a reduced adverb clause comes in front of or in the middle of the independent clause, punctuate it with commas. If it comes after the independent clause, do not use commas.

To reduce an adverb clause, you will usually follow the steps below. These are general guidelines and do not cover every situation.

Rules	Examples
1. Make sure that the subject of the adverb clause and the subject of the independent clause are the same.	While **technology** creates new jobs in some sectors of the economy, **it** takes away jobs in others.
2. Delete the subject of the adverb clause. If necessary, move it to the subject position in the independent clause.	While **technology** creates new jobs in some sectors of the economy, ~~it~~ takes away jobs in others.
3. Change the adverb clause verb to the appropriate participle.	While **creating** new jobs in some sectors of the economy, technology takes away jobs in others.

In reduced adverb clauses with participial phrases, the subordinator is sometimes retained and sometimes deleted. Some of the more common situations appear in the chart.

Rules	Examples
1. Retain *before*	Before a student chooses a college, he or she should consider several factors.
	Before choosing a college, a student should consider several factors.
	A student should consider several factors **before choosing a college**.

RULES	EXAMPLES
2. Retain *since* when it is a time subordinator.	Carlos has not been back home since he came to the United States three years ago.
	Since coming to the United States three years ago, Carlos has not been back home.
	Carlos has not been back home **since coming to the United States three years ago**.
3. Delete *because*, *since*, *as* when they are reason subordinators.	Because Carlos came from a very conservative family, he was shocked at the U.S. system of coed[1] dormitories.
	Coming from a very conservative family, Carlos was shocked at the U.S. system of coed dormitories.
4. Delete *as* when it is a time subordinator.	As he gradually got used to the way of life in the United States, he became less homesick.
	Gradually getting used to the way of life in the United States, he became less homesick.
5. Retain *after*, *while*, and *when* if the participial phrase follows the independent clause.	He became a freshman in college **after passing the TOEFL exam.**
	He lived with a family **while preparing for the TOEFL.**
	Carlos studied hard **when preparing for the TOEFL**.
6. When the phrase is in another position, you may either retain or delete the subordinators *after*, *while*, and *when*	**After passing the TOEFL**, he became a freshman in college.
	Having passed the TOEFL, he became a freshman in college.
	While preparing for the TOEFL, he lived with a family.
	Preparing for the TOEFL, he lived with a family.
	When asked about his life in the United States, Carlos said that he was enjoying himself.
	Asked about his life in the United States, he said that he was enjoying himself.

Note

Placing the participial phrase at the end of the sentence does not always work well. In this example, it sounds as if the dormitories come from a conservative family.

Carlos was shocked at the American system of coed dormitories coming from a very conservative family.

---

[1] **coed:** coeducational, shared by men and women

A Rewrite the sentences, changing the adverb clause in each to a participial phrase. If possible, write the sentence in more than one way.

1. After I had received my B.A., I went to graduate school for two years.

   After receiving my B.A., I went to graduate school for two years.

   Having received my B.A., I went to graduate school for two years.

2. I enjoyed living in a big city while I was studying at the University of Chicago.

   _____

   _____

3. Before I left home, I promised my parents that I would return.

   _____

   _____

4. Because I am the eldest son, I am responsible for taking care of my parents.

   _____

   _____

5. Since they have spent most of their savings to send me and my sisters to college, my parents may not have enough money for their retirement.

   _____

   _____

B Use the words in parentheses to complete the sentences. Use participial phrases. Add commas if necessary.

1. _____ automobile manufacturers want to replace assembly line workers with robots. (**hope / to save labor costs**)

2. Labor unions _____ are resisting the introduction of robots into factories. (**fear / loss of jobs for their members**)

3. Union members _____ went on strike. (**protest / loss of jobs**)

Improve the short essay by changing the underlined adjective and adverb clauses to participial phrases. Rewrite the essay on a separate sheet of paper.

Global Warming

1   One of the biggest problems <u>that faces humankind in the next few decades</u> is the problem of global warming. In the past 150 years, global temperatures have risen approximately 1°C (1.8°F). The warmest year <u>that has ever been recorded</u> occurred in this century. If temperatures continue to rise, the consequences could be catastrophic. As Earth's temperature rises, polar ice will melt, <u>which will cause the water level of the oceans to rise</u>. Rising ocean levels, in turn, will cause flooding along the coasts. Global warming will also cause major changes in climate that will affect agriculture. For example, crops <u>that were previously grown in Guatemala</u> may not do so well because it will become too hot.

2   <u>Because they believe</u> that the increase in carbon dioxide in Earth's atmosphere is the primary cause of global warming, scientists have urged action to decrease CO_2 levels. They are asking the world's governments to sign an agreement <u>that will control the amount of CO_2 that is released into the atmosphere</u>. Thus far, not all governments have committed to doing so. <u>After each government signs such an agreement</u>, each government will have to enforce it. Individuals, corporations, and government officials will all have a responsibility to help keep our planet safe from harm.

On a separate sheet of paper, write a paragraph about an interesting, exciting, or surprising event you witnessed or experienced. Include at least three participial phrases in your paragraph. Use the writing model on page 265 to help you.

After you have written a draft of your paragraph, look carefully at each sentence and consider these questions:

- Does your paragraph have a strong topic sentence?
- Do all the other sentences relate to the topic sentence?
- Have you used participial phrases?
- Does each participial phrase use appropriate word order, verb tense, and punctuation?
- Do your sentences flow smoothly from one sentence to the next?

Edit your paragraph as needed to improve it.

SELF-ASSESSMENT

In this chapter, you learned to:

○ Identify participles and participial phrases

○ Form reduced adjective and adverb clauses

○ Position and punctuate participial phrases

○ Form present and past participial phrases

○ Use participial phrases to improve your writing style

○ Write a paragraph that includes participles and participial phrases

Which ones can you do well? Mark them ✓

Which ones do you need to practice more? Mark them ✗

APPENDICES

READING FOR CHAPTER 3 WRITING ASSIGNMENT

Read "How Technology Aids Language," which is adapted from a news article that was published online. The reading discusses the role of technology in language learning and preservation. When you have read the article, return to page 70 to complete the writing assignment for Chapter 3.

How Technology Aids Language

1   In the past, learning a language could be difficult, if not impossible, unless you were able to travel to a foreign country or study with a skilled teacher. But now, with web-based training and software available, learning a new language is possible for almost anyone with Internet access. Indeed, the boom in technology has helped millions to speak, read, and write foreign languages. For example, one popular software program offers training in more than 30 languages for tourists and businesses alike.

2   Along with teaching language, technology is also being used to translate languages. These include ones that can be difficult for native English language speakers to learn, such as Arabic and Urdu. Many tools are available on the Internet for quick and easy translations. In addition, experts are working on advanced software to translate the subtle meanings and nuances of different languages. One such program is currently being used to analyze and translate Twitter feeds from Urdu into English (Joyce). With so few Americans fluent in Asian and Arabic languages, this type of technology can help close that language gap.

3   One very significant use of technology has been to preserve dying or endangered languages. Through technology, dictionaries of diverse languages can be recorded and preserved online for generations to come. In the United States and Canada, experts are working with several Native American tribes, including the Inuit and Siletz peoples, to help record and preserve their languages (Banse). Microsoft has also begun translating its operating system and software programs into several languages. Language activists helped inspire this initiative. They believe that using an endangered language every day on computers can help revive a language.

4   Despite these remarkable accomplishments, technology alone can't spread or revitalize a language. Keeping a language alive and viable requires a group of people who communicate in the language on an everyday basis.

Sources:
1. Article adapted from Spitbaum, Anna. "How Technology Aids Language."
2. Banse, Tom. "Digital Technologies Give Dying Languages New Life: All Tech Considered: NPR."
3. Joyce, Christopher. "Computer Translator Reads between the Tweets: NPR."

Read "The Challenge of Many Languages," which is adapted from a college textbook. The passage discusses the issues faced by nations in which many different languages are spoken. Answer the questions that follow it. When you have read the passage and answered the questions, return to page 72 to complete the Expansion assignments for Chapter 3.

The Challenge of Many Languages

1   When many different languages are spoken within one country, there are often political and social consequences. In the United States, for example, English has remained the primary language over a long period of time. Immigrants to the United States have historically been required to learn English in order to participate in society. In the past, schools offered classes only in English. Similarly, television programs were almost always in English. And, of course, work for the government and business also required English. The English-only policy was not without social consequences, however. For example, children of immigrants, who were born in the United States and grew up speaking mostly English outside the home, often lost their ability to speak the language of their parents fluently. In their eagerness to become more "American," people lost sight of the fact that being able to speak two languages well is actually a very valuable skill.

2   In recent years in the United States, there has been a change in the English-only pattern. Now, throughout the country, there are many people for whom English is not the primary language. As a result, teaching staffs are multilingual. In addition, government offices provide services to non-English speakers. Even cable television has entertainment and news programming in Spanish, Chinese, Japanese, Arabic, and so on.

3   In some countries, political agreements recognize the role of multiple languages in the government and educational systems. Canada has two official languages: English and French. Belgium uses three: French, German, and Flemish. In Singapore, English, Mandarin, Malay, and Tamil are all official languages. India has more than a dozen.

4   When India was established in 1948, one of the major problems concerned a national language. Although Hindi was spoken by the largest number of people, the majority of people did not speak it. India's solution was to identify sixteen national languages. The constitution permitted government, schools, and commerce to operate in any of them. However, even that solution has not eased the concerns of non-Hindi speakers. In the mid-1950s, there was political agitation to redraw boundaries based on the languages in particular regions. Even now, political upheavals occur in India over language issues.

5   Language is an important part of most people's identities. Therefore, a great deal of emotion is attached to political choices about language. Political solutions to a diversity of languages require a delicate balance. It is not easy to preserve harmony among different groups.

Source:
    Passage adapted from Lustig, Myron W. and Jolene Koester. *Intercultural Competence.*

Questions about the Reading

1. What is the main idea of "The Challenge of Many Languages"?

2. What example does the author give in paragraph 1 to show a problem with the English-only policy?

3. What reason does the author give in paragraph 4 for the controversy around choosing an official language in India?

READING FOR CHAPTER 6 EXPANSION

Read "Nice by Nature?". It is adapted from an essay that appeared in an academic journal and was later reprinted in a college textbook. The essay discusses the capacity for fairness in monkeys. Answer the questions that follow it. When you have read the essay and answered the questions, return to page 132 to complete the second expansion assignment for Chapter 6.

Nice by Nature?

1   Try paying one monkey with a delicious grape and another with a ho-hum cucumber for the same amount of work. You may be surprised at the results! The monkey who got the lesser reward will probably quit working for you. He may even throw the vegetable back at you, even though monkeys are usually happy to receive cucumbers, says Sarah Brosnan, PhD, a psychology professor at Georgia State University. That experiment by Brosnan and collaborator Frans de Waal, PhD, published in 2003 in *Nature*, was one of the first to show that animals may have an appreciation for fairness—a moral sense that many researchers previously thought was the sole domain of humans. Since then, a slew of intriguing results suggest that animals—particularly those that depend on cooperation for their survival—may have underpinnings of justice and altruism.

2   For example, a chimpanzee is quick to let another chimp out of his cage. They also happily retrieve out-of-reach objects for their human handlers. Monkeys will spontaneously share rewards with others who worked toward the goal. And, in the fairness realm, dogs will quit participating in a task if they see another animal receive a better reward.

3   "Fairness and altruism didn't develop *de novo* in humans," Brosnan says. "It's likely something that began in social species, including primates, and evolved to us."

4   Research indicates that some animals—particularly ones that hunt together—divvy up the rewards of a spoil. One study even found that animals will occasionally deliver a better reward to a collaborator than they themselves receive. In a 2006 study by Brosnan and her colleagues published in the *American Journal of Primatology*, two capuchin monkeys had to work together to pull a tray of food to their cages. But before they began pulling, the monkeys had to decide which one would receive a grape and which one would get a less coveted apple slice. Instead of fighting over the grape or always letting the dominant monkey eat it, the animals generally alternated roles across trials, so they both earned some grapes and some apple slices, Brosnan found. In the few cases where the dominant monkey hogged the good food, the other monkey tended to quit participating. The second monkey would rather go without a reward than be paid unfairly.

5   That tendency to share rewards, says Brosnan, probably developed as a result of the way capuchins work together to hunt. "If we are hunting and I am not giving you much of the kill, you would be better off finding another partner," she says.

6   Monkeys that were sensitive to unfair situations were more likely to demand their fair share of meat. With more meat, they were more likely to survive. The survivors then reproduced, thereby passing to their offspring a genetic predisposition to seek equitable situations, Brosnan hypothesizes.

7   Yale psychology professor Laurie Santos, PhD, and her colleagues got a similar result with capuchin monkeys. In a 2008 study published in *Current Biology*, they found that, when given the choice of delivering an average or a special reward (an apple vs. a marshmallow) to a monkey in an adjacent cage, the monkeys more often chose to deliver the tasty marshmallow. They made this choice for no apparent reason and even without receiving a reward.

8   From these studies, one overarching theme is emerging: Many animals seem to act with the others' well-being in mind, Santos says. "All pro-sociality is not unique to humans," she says. "Our close living primate relatives are very nice to each other."

Source:
    Essay adapted from Dingfielder, Sadie F. "Nice by Nature?"

Questions about the Reading

About the Introduction and Conclusion

1. The thesis statement for this essay is the last sentence of which paragraph? (*Hint:* Rereading the conclusion will help you answer this question.)

   a. paragraph 1

   b. paragraph 2

   c. paragraph 3

2. What does the conclusion do?

   a. It summarizes the main ideas.

   b. It repeats the thesis statement in different words.

About the Organization

3. What is mainly discussed in the essay?

   a. the causes of animals being nice to each other

   b. effects of animals being nice to each other

   c. both the causes and the effects

4. Chain organization is used in which paragraphs?

   a. 2 and 3

   b. 5 and 6

   c. 7 and 8

About the Support

5. What is the topic sentence for paragraph 4?

   a. the first sentence

   b. the second sentence

   c. There is no topic sentence.

6. Paragraph 4 supports the point made in which paragraph?

   a. 6

   b. 2

About Coherence

7. What cause/effect signal word is used in the:

   a. fifth sentence of paragraph 4? _____

   b. first sentence of paragraph 5? _____

   c. third sentence of paragraph 6? _____

8. What key nouns appear frequently throughout this essay?

   _____ and _____

Read "Marital Exchanges," which is adapted from a college textbook. The essay discusses cultural differences in the custom of exchanging gifts at a marriage. Answer the questions that follow it. When you have read the essay and answered the questions, return to page 151 to complete the second Expansion assignment for Chapter 7.

Marital Exchanges

1   In most cultures, the marriage of a man and a woman is accompanied by some kind of transfer of goods or services. These marital exchanges are used to create in-law relationships, compensate a family for the loss of one of its members, provide for the new couple's support, or provide a daughter with an inheritance that helps attract a desirable husband.

2   Marital exchanges take numerous forms, including the North American custom of wedding showers and wedding gifts. In these, the presents given by relatives and friends supposedly help the newlyweds establish an independent household. We give things that are useful to the couple jointly, with tools for food preparation and other household utensils easily the most common type of gift. Many couples even register at stores so that their relatives and friends will provide the items they want.

3   From a cross-cultural perspective, the most unusual feature of North American marital exchange is that nothing is transferred between the relatives of the groom and bride: The couple treats the gifts as their private property. Like most of our other customs, this seems natural to us. Of course the gifts go to the couple—what else could happen to them?

4   Plenty else, as we shall see in a moment. For now, notice that the fact that the couple receives the gifts fits with several other features of Euro-American marriage.

5   First, in addition to creating new nuclear families, marriage is the bond through which new independent households are started. So the husband and wife "need their own stuff." If, in contrast, the newlyweds moved in with one of their relatives, they would not have as great a need for their own pots and pans, wine glasses, silver candlesticks, and other "stuff."

6   Second, our marriage-gift customs fit with the value our culture places on the privacy of the marital relationship: It is a personal matter between the husband and wife, and their relatives should keep their noses out. If the in-laws get along and socialize, that's great, but our marriages generally do not create strong bonds between families of the bride and groom. (In fact, the two families often compete for the visits and attention of the couple and their offspring.) . . . The fact that the in-laws do not exchange gifts with each other is a manifestation of the absence of a necessary relation between them after the wedding. If, in contrast, the marriage created an alliance between the two sets of relatives, some kind of an exchange would probably occur between them to symbolize and cement their new relations.

7   Third, gifts are presented to the couple, not to the husband or wife as individuals, and are considered to belong equally and jointly to both partners. But there are marriage systems in which the property of the wife is separate from that of her husband; if divorce should occur, there is no squabbling over who gets what and no need for prenuptials.

8   With this background in mind, consider what kinds of marital exchanges occur in other cultures.

9   **Bridewealth** *Bridewealth* is the widespread custom that requires a man and his relatives to transfer wealth to the relatives of his bride. It is easily the most common of all marital exchanges, found in more than half the world's cultures. The term *bridewealth* is well chosen because the goods transferred usually are among the most valuable symbols of wealth in the local culture. In sub-Saharan Africa, cattle and sometimes other livestock are the most common goods used for bridewealth. Peoples of the Pacific Islands and Southeast Asia usually give their bridewealth in pigs or shell money and ornaments.

(continued on next page)

10   **Brideservice** As the term implies, *brideservice* is the custom whereby a husband is required to spend a period of time working for the family of his bride. A Yanomamo (a member of a tribe living in the rain forests of the Amazon) son-in-law is expected to live with his wife's parents, hunting and gardening for them until they finally release control over their daughter. Among some !Kung bands (a tribe living in the Kalahari desert of Africa), a man proves his ability as a provider by living with and hunting for his wife's parents for three to ten years, after which the couple is free to camp elsewhere.

11   Brideservice is the second most common form of marital exchange; it is the usual compensation given to the family of a bride in roughly one-eighth of the world's cultures. However, sometimes it occurs alongside other forms of marital exchange and occasionally is used to reduce the amount of bridewealth owed.

12   **Dowry** A marital exchange is called *dowry* when the family of a woman transfers a portion of their own wealth or other property to their daughter and her husband. The main thing to understand about dowry is that it is not simply the opposite of bridewealth; that is, it is not "groomwealth." It is, rather, ordinarily the share of a woman's inheritance that she is allowed to take into her marriage for the use of her new family, although her parents are still alive. The woman and her family do not acquire marital rights over her husband when they provide a dowry, as they would if dowry were the opposite of bridewealth; rather, the bride and her husband receive property when they marry, rather than when the bride's parents die. By doing so, parents give their female children extra years of use of the property and also publicly demonstrate their wealth.

13   Dowry is a relatively rare form of marital exchange, occurring in only about 5 percent of the societies recorded by anthropology. Dowry today is common in parts of India, where it includes jewelry, household utensils, women's clothing, and money. Much of the dowry is presented to the bride on her wedding day, but her parents and maternal uncle often provide gifts periodically throughout the marriage. Dowry, then, is not always a one-time expense for a family, but may represent a continual drain on their resources.

14   There are other forms of exchanges that occur at marriages, including some in which both sets of relatives exchange gifts as a material symbol of the new basis of their relationship. And the three forms discussed above are not mutually exclusive. For example, in most of traditional China, both bridewealth and dowry occurred at most marriages. The groom's family would make a payment to the bride's family and the bride's family would purchase some furniture and other household goods for their daughter to take with her when she moved into her husband's household. For wealthier families, dowry was usually displayed by being transported ostentatiously over the streets between the households of the bride and groom. Dowry thus became a Chinese "status symbol." Sometimes, if the bride's family was substantially poorer than the groom's, part of the bridewealth payment would be spent on purchasing goods for the woman's dowry. This was legal and common until after the Communist Revolution in 1949, when the leaders outlawed both bridewealth and dowry, though both continue in some places to this day.

Source:
    Essay adapted from Peoples, James, and Garrick Bailey. "Marriage, Family, and Residence."

Questions about the Reading

1. In which paragraphs do the authors describe the North American form of marital exchange?

    a. 1–7

    b. 2–7

    c. 1–4

    d. 2–4

2. Excluding the North American form of marital transfer, what other forms do the authors discuss? List them in order:

    a. _____

    b. _____

    c. _____

    Why are they discussed in this particular order? In other words, what pattern did the authors use to organize this part of the reading?

3. Which two paragraphs contain the phrase *in contrast*?

    Paragraphs _____ and _____

    a. In the first paragraph containing the phrase *in contrast*, what is contrasted?

    b. What is contrasted in the second paragraph containing *in contrast*?

4. What is contrasted in paragraph 7?

    Is there a contrast signal word in this paragraph? If so, what is it?

5. In which paragraphs do the authors contrast the customs of *bridewealth* and *dowry*?

    a. 9, 10, 12, 14

    b. 9 and 12

    c. 12 only

Read "Why We Should Send a Manned Mission to Mars" and "Let's Not Go to Mars: Why a Staffed Mission Is Impractical." These two articles discuss whether or not the United States should attempt to send humans to Mars. The first article argues in favor of such a mission. The second article argues against doing so. Answer the questions that follow each article. When you have read both articles and answered the questions, return to page 166 to complete the writing assignment for Chapter 8.

Reading 1

Why We Should Send a Manned Mission to Mars

1   Mars has fascinated Earth-bound humans since prehistoric times, due to its captivating red hue and proximity and similarity to Earth. The romance of space travel and the exploration of new worlds is a major argument in favor of a manned mission to Mars. Supporters claim that exploring and colonizing the moon and Mars will give us a better understanding of our own home planet, Earth. Other supporters are motivated by feelings of national pride, saying the prestige of the United States is at stake. Still others believe that the research required by such a complex mission will help the United States retain its position as a leader in science and technology.

2   The success of the Apollo program in the 1960s and 1970s created a generation of astronaut heroes that inspired the nation. "In 1969, America sent men to the moon, not machines," Ben Wattenberg said on PBS's *Think Tank*. "[H]uman beings are exploratory creatures . . . mankind needs big ideas and big projects to ennoble and inspire society. Don't our little boys and girls need heroes and heroines to say, 'Look at him, look at her, she's there'?" President George W. Bush once said in an address to the nation, "Mankind is drawn to the heavens for the same reason we were once drawn to unknown lands and across the open sea. We choose to explore space because doing so improves our lives and lifts our national spirit."

3   Many supporters of manned travel to Mars argue that because of its similarity to Earth, Mars offers opportunities to discover the origins of life and ways to protect the environment on Earth. "We cling to the hope of a neighboring planet that harbors . . . at least some primitive forms of life. If Mars contains even nanobacteria—or indisputable evidence of past life of the simplest forms—this will profoundly change our conception of our place in the universe," wrote Thomas Gangale, an author who has written articles and books about outer space. "If Mars is dead now, but was once alive, understanding how Mars died may give us a crucial understanding of how close we are coming to killing the Earth."

4   The Mars Society (a group that supports Mars exploration) shares that opinion. In its Founding Declaration, the society wrote, "As we begin the twenty-first century, we have evidence that we are changing the Earth's atmosphere and environment in significant ways. . . . Mars, the planet most like Earth, will have even more to teach us about our home world. The knowledge we gain could be key to our survival."

5   And, despite the excitement over the successful landing of the unmanned Mars rover "Curiosity" in 2012, many scientists assert that the best way to attain that knowledge is with human scientists. "Robots can do a lot," Chris Welch, a lecturer in space technology at Kingston University, told the BBC. "But having multiple trained human beings there would tell us so much more." Dava Newman, associate professor of aeronautics at the Massachusetts Institute of Technology, agreed. "It's risky and it's also very costly, but there's just so much humans can do as explorers that we don't have any other way to accomplish."

6   China, Russia, and the European Union have all announced plans to boost their space programs in coming years, including sojourns to the moon and Mars. Some people believe it's essential to U.S. international status that the United States leads the way in space exploration. "Republican officials said conservative lawmakers who might balk at the cost (of a manned mission to Mars) are likely to be lured by the chance to extend the U.S. military supremacy in space when China is pursuing lunar probes and Russia is considering a Mars mission," Mike Allen and Eric Pianin wrote in *The Washington Post*.

7   The European Space Agency (ESA) has developed a long-term plan—known as Aurora—that uses robotics to first explore low-Earth orbit and then move farther out into planetary excursions, including Mars. The ESA intends to send a rover to Mars by 2018 and is hoping to send a manned mission to the moon in the future that "would significantly extend surface exploration opportunities by enabling enhanced human mobility, extended human lunar surface presence and new surface exploration opportunities." The final step in the Aurora program is a human mission to Mars.

8   Regaining the top position in science and technology is another reason to support a Mars mission. According to *The New York Times*, the dominance the United States once had in science and innovation has declined in recent years as the number of international prizes and journal publications awarded to European and Asian researchers has increased. Jennifer Bond, vice president for international affairs for the Council on Competitiveness said, "Many other countries have realized that science and technology are key to economic growth and prosperity. They're catching up to us." She warned that people in the United States should not "rest on their laurels." A poll by the Associated Press seems to indicate that many people in the United States agree with her. Most respondents in the poll deemed it important for the United States to be the "leading country in the world in the exploration of space."

9   "America is not going to remain at peace, and we're not going to remain the most prosperous nation, and we're not going to remain a free nation unless we remain the technological leader of the world," said Representative Dana Rohrabacher, who served as chairman of the House Subcommittee on Space and Aeronautics. "And we will not remain the technological leader of the world unless we are the leaders in space."

Source:
  Essay adapted from Joulwan, Melissa. "You Decide: Manned Mission to Mars."

Questions about Reading 1

1. What are four reasons given in paragraph 1 to explain why the United States should send a manned mission to Mars? List them here.

   a. _____

   b. _____

   c. _____

   d. _____

2. Which paragraph discusses the first reason?

   _____

3. Which paragraph(s) discuss(es) the second reason? _____

   Summarize the reason here.

   _____

   _____

   _____

   _____

4. Which paragraph(s) discuss(es) the third reason? _____

   Summarize the reason here.

   _____

   _____

   _____

   _____

5. Which paragraph(s) discuss(es) the fourth reason? _____

   Summarize the reason here.

   _____

   _____

   _____

   _____

Reading 2

Let's Not Go to Mars: Why a Staffed Mission Is Impractical

1   "By the mid-2030s, I believe we can send humans to orbit Mars and return them safely to Earth, and a landing on Mars will follow. And I expect to be around to see it," said President Obama during a 2010 speech at NASA's Kennedy Space Center in Florida ("NASA—President"). He is certainly not alone in looking forward with enthusiasm to this event. The possibility of a human expedition to Mars is thrilling to many people. It would be an amazing achievement, and it is widely agreed that it could contribute to advancing our understanding of life in the universe. Recently, in fact, Mars has become the new frontier for space exploration (including the widely celebrated unmanned Mars rover "Curiosity" in 2012) and programs for staffed missions are being planned in the United States and other countries around the world. Nevertheless, there are several reasons why it is impractical to attempt sending people to Mars by the mid-2030s.

2   Although a staffed mission to Mars would indeed be an incredible feat, the costs associated with such a mission would be enormous, ranging from $20 to $450 billion over the next 20 years (Sherriff). NASA's yearly budget of a mere $17.7 billion is hardly enough to cover the expenses of the Mars project along with other NASA programs ("NASA FY2013"). Additionally, estimates of the cost vary widely. No one knows how much the real cost of the program could be. It could increase during the project because of unforeseen complications.

3   Along with financial concerns, a trip to Mars poses great risks to the health of astronauts, reports journalist Eric Niiler in *Discovery News*. Landing humans on the moon was a memorable accomplishment, but landing them on Mars would be a far more formidable task. Unlike a trip to the moon, which only takes a few days, a trip to Mars would take around 2.5 years. (It would take about 6 months to get to Mars, followed by an 18-month stay, and 6 months to get back to Earth). The longer journey would mean longer exposure to the hazards of space travel. During a 2.5 year period, the astronauts would be exposed to excessive amounts of radiation from both the sun and cosmic rays, which could lead to cancers and other debilitating diseases. This radiation could also damage the food supply and destroy vitamins that the astronauts need for nutrition, further endangering the health of the crew (Niiler).

4   Spending a long time in zero gravity could lead to many other health-related complications as well, notes Niiler. Zero gravity can cause muscles to become weaker and atrophy. It can also cause the bones to become more brittle and break down. Zero gravity also has an effect on the brain—astronauts might develop cognitive problems such as loss of memory or brain function over time.

5   Astronauts could also face psychological challenges from being in space for an extended period of time. Isolation from family and friends for extended periods can cause psychological stress. While there would be other crew members with whom an astronaut could socialize, the potential for conflict among the members of the team might increase because they would be spending such a long time together in close quarters.

6   Along with health concerns, there are other reasons why a manned mission to Mars is impractical. First, in order to protect the astronauts from radiation, the space shuttle would need to have a thick protective layer of lead and water (Easterbrook). This would make the shuttle heavier, so it would have to be built in space instead of being launched from Earth. While this seems like a plausible solution, the amount of time, energy, and money spent building a spacecraft in space seems frivolous and unrealistic. It would be important to develop new launch systems and other forms of advanced technology before attempting a human landing (Easterbrook).

7   Other problems with the plan also lie in the expertise needed to make the mission successful. The astronauts themselves would need to be able to perform a multitude of highly specialized tasks in order to survive. Not only would they need to pilot the shuttle, they would also have to be able to grow their own food on the shuttle and on Mars, make any repairs and maintenance to the shuttle, build a shelter on Mars, and treat any injuries or medical emergencies. These responsibilities are in addition to the real purpose of the mission: gathering scientific data about the planet. Even with a diverse crew in place, the loss of one member could be potentially devastating for the whole mission.

8   Today, unmanned crafts, or probes, are being launched to Mars. These probes are very effective at collecting data about Mars, and are also less expensive than a staffed mission and do not risk human lives. When you consider all of the problems with the economy and the environment here on Earth, spending billions of dollars and over 20 years on a mission with so many pitfalls seems irresponsible (Easterbrook).

(continued on next page)

9   For the human race, having a successful staffed trip to Mars is an undeniably huge technologic and scientific accomplishment. Nevertheless, the technology today is not advanced enough to guarantee that a staffed mission would be successful, while at the same time containing costs and minimizing the risk to human life. Perhaps a manned mission to Mars is in our future, but until the technology is advanced enough to make the mission faster, cheaper, and safer, a trip to Mars may be in the distant, rather than the near future.

Sources:

1. Essay adapted from Willbrook, Tianna. "The Problem with Manned Space Travel."
2. Easterbrook, Greg. "Why We Shouldn't Go to Mars: Someday people may walk on the planet, but not until it makes technological sense."
3. "NASA—President Outlines Exploration Goals, Promise."
4. "NASA FY 2013 President's Budget Request Summary."
5. Niiler, Eric. "How a Mission to Mars Could Kill You: Discovery News."
6. Sherriff, Lucy. "NASA reveals manned Mars mission plans."

Questions about Reading 2

1. What is one important event that President Obama believes will happen by the mid-2030s? Rewrite his direct quotation in paragraph 1 as a paraphrase. Be sure to include a reporting phrase.

2. What two things are contrasted in paragraph 2?

3. What is the thesis statement of the article? Underline it.

4. What are the main reasons why a manned mission to Mars would not work, according to the article?

Coordinators

Coordinating conjunctions connect grammatically equal elements. One way to remember the seven coordinating conjunctions is to use the expression "Fan Boys". Each letter of the expression represents the first letter of one of the conjunctions: *for, and, nor, but, or, yet, so.*

CONJUNCTION	FUNCTION	EXAMPLE
for	Connects a reason to a result	I am a little hungry, **for** I didn't eat breakfast this morning.
and	Connects equal similar ideas	John likes to fish **and** hunt.
nor	Connects two negative sentences	She does not eat meat, **nor** does she drink milk.
but	Connects equal different ideas	I like to eat fish **but** not to catch them.
or	Connects two equal choices	Do you prefer coffee **or** tea?
yet	Connects equal contrasting ideas	It is sunny **yet** cold.
so	Connects a result to a reason	I did not eat breakfast this morning, **so** I am a little hungry.

Correlative (Paired) Conjunctions

Correlative conjunctions are always in pairs. Like coordinating conjunctions, they connect grammatically equal elements. (Please also read the section Parallel Structure in Sentences on pages 191–192.)

CONJUNCTION PAIRS	EXAMPLE
both . . . and	**Both** San Francisco **and** Sydney have beautiful harbors.
not only . . . but also	Japanese food is **not only** delicious to eat **but also** beautiful to look at.
either . . . or	Bring **either** a raincoat **or** an umbrella when you visit Seattle.
neither . . . nor	My grandfather could **neither** read **nor** write, but he was a very wise person.
whether . . . or	The newlyweds could not decide **whether** to live with her parents **or** to rent an apartment.

Subordinators

A subordinator is the first word in a dependent clause. The following charts illustrate some common subordinators.

SUBORDINATORS FOR ADVERB CLAUSES

TIME (WHEN?)	
after	**After** we ate lunch, we decided to go shopping.
as, just as	**Just as** we left the house, it started to rain.
as long as	We waited **as long as** we could.
as soon as	**As soon as** the front door closed, I looked for my house key.
before	I thought I had put it in my coat pocket **before** we left.
since	I have not locked myself out of the house **since** I was 10 years old.
until	**Until** I was almost 12, my mother pinned the key to my coat.
when	**When** I turned 12, my mother let me keep the key in my pocket.
whenever	I usually put the key in the same place **whenever** I come home.
while	**While** I searched for the key, it rained harder and harder.
PLACE (WHERE?)	
where	I like to shop **where** prices are low.
wherever	I try to shop **wherever** there is a sale.
anywhere	You can find bargains **anywhere** you shop.
everywhere	I use my credit card **everywhere** I shop.
MANNER (HOW?)	
as, just as	I love to get flowers(,) **as** many people do.*
as if	You look **as if** you didn't sleep at all last night.
as though	She acts **as though** she doesn't know us.
DISTANCE (HOW FAR? HOW NEAR? HOW CLOSE?)	
as + (adverb) + as	We will hike **as far as** we can before it turns dark.
	The child sat **as close as** she could to her mother.
	The child sat **as close** to her mother **as** she could.
FREQUENCY (HOW OFTEN?)	
as often as	I call my parents **as often as** I can.
REASON (WHY?)	
as	I can't take evening classes(,) **as** I work at night.*
because	I can't take evening classes **because** I work at night.
since	I can't take evening classes **since** I work at night.

PURPOSE (FOR WHAT PURPOSE?)	
so that	Many people emigrate **so that** their children can have a better life.
in order that	Many people emigrate **in order that** their children can have a better life.

RESULT (WITH WHAT RESULT?)	
so + (adjective) + that	I was **so tired** last night **that** I fell asleep at dinner.
so + (adverb) + that	She talks **so softly that** the other students cannot hear her.
such a(n) + (adjective) + (noun) + that	It was **such an easy test that** most of the students got A's.
so much/many/little/few + (noun) + that	He is taking **so many classes that** he has no time to sleep.

CONDITION (UNDER WHAT CONDITION?)	
if	We will not go hiking **if** it rains.
unless	We will not go hiking **unless** the weather is perfect.

PARTIAL CONTRAST	
although	I love my brother **although** we disagree about almost everything.
even though	I love my brother **even though** we disagree about almost everything.
though	I love my brother **though** we disagree about almost everything.

CONTRAST (DIRECT OPPOSITES)	
while	My brother likes classical music, **while** I prefer hard rock.
whereas	He dresses conservatively, **whereas** I like to be a little shocking.

*This is an exception to the usual rule for commas. Many writers use a comma before *as*.

SUBORDINATORS FOR ADJECTIVE CLAUSES

The first word in an adjective clause is usually a relative pronoun or relative adverb.
However, when the relative pronoun is the object of the clause, it can sometimes be omitted.

TO REFER TO PEOPLE	
who, whom	People **who** live in glass houses should not throw stones. My parents did not approve of the man (**whom**) my sister married.
whose	An orphan is a child **whose** parents are dead.
that (informal)	The man **that** is on the left in the photo is my brother.

TO REFER TO ANIMALS AND THINGS	
which	My new computer, **which** I bought yesterday, stopped working today.
that	Yesterday I received an email (**that**) I did not understand.

TO REFER TO A TIME OR A PLACE	
when	Thanksgiving is a time **when** families travel great distances to be together.
where	An orphanage is a place **where** orphans live.

SUBORDINATORS FOR NOUN CLAUSES

Noun clauses are introduced by the words *that*, *if*, or *whether* or by a *Wh-* word.

THAT CLAUSES	
that	Do you believe **that** there is life in outer space?
IF / WHETHER CLAUSES	
whether	I can't remember **whether** I locked the door.
whether or not	I can't remember **whether or not** I locked the door.
whether . . . or not	I can't remember **whether** I locked the door **or not**.
if	I can't remember **if** I locked the door.
if . . . or not	I can't remember **if** I locked the door **or not**.
QUESTION CLAUSES	
who, whoever, whom	**Whoever** arrives at the bus station first should buy the tickets.
which, what	Do you know **which** bus we need to take?
where, when, why, how	We should ask **when** the bus arrives.
how much, how many	Do not worry about **how much** they cost.
how long, how often, etc.	He didn't care **how long** he had to wait.

Notice that some subordinators can introduce different kinds of dependent clauses. *That* can introduce either noun clauses or adjective clauses, and *where* can introduce a noun, an adjective, or an adverb clause. It normally is not important to know the kind of clause.

> I can't remember **where** I put the house key.
> (noun clause; direct object of *remember*)

> It's not in the place **where** I usually put it.
> (adjective clause; tells *which place*)

> I always put it **where** I will see it when I go out the front door.
> (adverb clause; tells *where I put it*)

Conjunctive Adverbs

Conjunctive adverbs can appear at the beginning, in the middle, or at the end of one independent clause, but we often use them to connect two independent clauses.

Remember to put a semicolon before and a comma after the conjunctive adverb if an independent clause follows.

CONJUNCTIVE ADVERBS	FUNCTION	EXAMPLE
also, besides, furthermore, in addition, moreover	To add a similar idea	Community colleges offer preparation for many jobs; **in addition**, they prepare students to transfer to four-year colleges.
however, nevertheless, nonetheless, still	To add an unexpected or surprising continuation	The cost of attending a community college is low; **however**, many students need financial aid.
in contrast, on the other hand	To add a complete contrast	Most community colleges do not have dormitories; **in contrast**, most four-year colleges do.
as a result, consequently, therefore, thus	To add a result	Native and nonnative English speakers have different needs; **as a result**, most schools provide separate classes for each group.
meanwhile, afterward, then, subsequently	To list ideas in chronological order	Police kept people away from the scene of the accident; **meanwhile**, ambulance workers tried to pull victims out of the wreck. The workers put five injured people into an ambulance; **afterward**, they found another victim.
for example, for instance	To give an example	Colors can have different meanings; **for example**, white is the color of weddings in some cultures and of funerals in others.
similarly, likewise	To show similarities	Hawaii has sunshine and friendly people; **similarly**, Mexico's weather is sunny and its people hospitable.
instead, on the contrary, rather	To indicate an alternative	The medicine did not make him feel better; **instead**, it made him feel worse.
instead	To indicate a substitution	They had planned to go to Hawaii on their honeymoon; **instead**, they went to Mexico. We ordered hamburgers; they brought us pizza **instead**.*
on the other hand, alternatively	To give another possibility	You can live in a dorm on campus; **on the other hand**, you can rent a room with a family off campus.
otherwise	To give a result, often bad (meaning "if not")	Students must take final exams; **otherwise**, they will receive a grade of Incomplete.
in other words, that is	To add an explanation	Some cultures are matriarchal; **in other words**, the mothers are the head of the family.
indeed, in fact	To make a statement stronger	Mangoes are a very common fruit; **indeed**, people eat more mangoes than any other fruit in the world.

* When it indicates substitution, *instead* can go at the end of the sentence.

Transition Signals

Transition Signals and Conjunctive Adverbs	Coordinators and Paired Conjunctions	Subordinators	Others: Adjectives, Prepositions, Verbs
To list ideas in order of time			
first, . . . first of all, . . . second, . . . third, . . . next, . . . then . . . after that, . . . meanwhile, . . . in the meantime, . . . finally, . . . last, . . . last of all, . . . subsequently, . . .		before after until when while as soon as since	the first (reason, cause, step, etc.) the second . . . the third . . . another . . . the last . . . the final . . .
To list ideas in order of importance			
first, . . . first of all, . . . first and foremost, . . . second, . . . more important, . . . most important, . . . more significant, . . . most significant, . . . above all, . . . most of all, . . .			the first . . . (reason, cause, step, etc.) an additional . . . the second . . . another . . . a more important (reason, cause, step, etc.) the most important . . . the most significant . . . the best/the worst . . .
To add a similar or equal idea			
also, . . . besides, . . . furthermore, . . . in addition, . . . moreover, . . . too as well	and both . . . and not only . . . but also		another . . . (reason, cause, step, etc.) a second . . . an additional . . . a final . . . as well as

TRANSITION SIGNALS AND CONJUNCTIVE ADVERBS	COORDINATORS AND PAIRED CONJUNCTIONS	SUBORDINATORS	OTHERS: ADJECTIVES, PREPOSITIONS, VERBS
To add an opposite idea			
however, . . . on the other hand, . . . nevertheless, . . . nonetheless, . . . still, . . .	but yet	although even though though	despite in spite of
To explain or restate an idea			
in other words, . . . in particular, . . . (more) specifically, . . . that is, . . .			
To make a statement stronger			
indeed, . . . in fact, . . .			
To give another possibility			
alternatively, . . . on the other hand, . . . otherwise, . . .	or either . . . or whether . . . or		
To give an example			
for example, . . . for instance, . . .			such as an example of to exemplify
To express an opinion			
according to . . . in my opinion, . . . in my view, . . .			to believe (that) to feel (that) to think (that)
To give a reason			
for this reason, . . .	for	because	as a result of because of due to

(continued on next page)

Transition Signals *(continued)*

TRANSITION SIGNALS AND CONJUNCTIVE ADVERBS	COORDINATORS AND PAIRED CONJUNCTIONS	SUBORDINATORS	OTHERS: ADJECTIVES, PREPOSITIONS, VERBS
To give a result			
accordingly, . . . as a consequence, . . . as a result, ... consequently, ... for these reasons, . . . hence, . . . therefore, . . . thus, . . .	so		the cause of the reason for to cause to result (in) to have an effect on to affect
To add a conclusion			
all in all, . . . in brief, . . . in short, . . . to conclude, . . . to summarize, . . . in conclusion, . . . in summary, . . . for these reasons, . . .			
To show similarities			
likewise, . . . similarly, . . . also	and both . . . and not only . . . but also neither . . . nor		alike, like, just like as, just as as well as well as compared with or to in comparison with or to to be similar (to) too
To show differences			
however, . . . in contrast, . . . instead, . . . on the contrary, . . . on the other hand, . . . rather, . . .			instead of

Using correct punctuation is important because punctuation conveys meaning just as words do. Consider these two sentences:

> Eat children.

> Eat**,** children.

Both sentences are commands, but the first sentence would be correct only in a society of cannibals[1]! Learn and practice the rules of punctuation until you are confident about using them correctly.

Commas[2]

Commas are sometimes troublesome to learners of English because they are used differently in other languages. There are many comma rules in English, but you may remember them more easily if you realize that they can be organized into just four main groups: **introducers**, **coordinators**, **inserters**, and **tags**. Each group of commas relates to independent clauses in a particular way, except the coordinator group. Coordinator commas link not just independent clauses but any coordinate (equal) elements in a sentence.

Study the examples for each comma group, and notice the kinds of elements that can be introducers, coordinators, inserters, and tags.

Introducer Commas

An introducer comma follows any element that comes in front of the first independent clause in a sentence.

WORDS   Therefore**,** I plan to quit smoking.

Nervously**,** I threw away my cigarettes.

PHRASES   As a result**,** I feel terrible right now.

After 16 years of smoking**,** it is not easy to quit.

Having smoked for 16 years**,** I find it difficult to quit.

DEPENDENT CLAUSES   Because I have a chronic cough**,** my doctor recommended that I quit immediately.

DIRECT QUOTATIONS   "Stop smoking today**,**" she advised.

---

[1] cannibals: people who eat human flesh

[2] Thanks to Anne Katz for permission to adapt her presentation of comma rules.

Coordinator Commas

Together with a coordinating conjunction, a comma links coordinate (equal) elements in a sentence.

COMPOUND SENTENCE WITH 2 INDEPENDENT CLAUSES

She has a good job, yet she is always broke.

They were tired, so they went home early.

SERIES OF 3 OR MORE WORDS

He does not enjoy skiing, ice-skating, or sledding.

Cecille speaks English, Spanish, French, and Creole.

(No comma with only two items: Chen speaks Mandarin and Taiwanese.)

SERIES OF 3 OR MORE PHRASES

A nurse has to work at night, on weekends, and on holidays.

We ran into the airport, checked our luggage, raced to the boarding gate, gave the attendant our boarding passes, and collapsed in our seats.

Inserter Commas

An inserter comma is used before and after any element that is inserted into the middle of an independent clause.

WORDS

My uncle, however, refuses to go on a diet.

PHRASES

My father, on the other hand, has always eaten lightly.

There is no point in living, according to my uncle, if you do not do what you enjoy.

NONRESTRICTIVE PHRASES AND CLAUSES

My aunt, his wife, was very obese and died of heart attack.

My cousins, grieving over their mother's death, resolved to eat a healthier diet.

My mother, who just celebrated her fiftieth birthday, enjoys an occasional piece of chocolate cake.

REPORTING VERBS IN DIRECT QUOTATIONS

"I have tried to quit dozens of times," she says, "but I can't."

Tag Commas

A tag comma is used when adding certain elements to the end of a sentence.

WORDS

My uncle believes in drinking coffee several times a day, too.[1]

He appears to be in good health, however.

PHRASES

He swims for an hour every day, for example.

He also plays tennis, beating me most of the time.

It is not logical, is it?

---

[1] Many writers do not use a comma before *too*.

Using Commas

Add commas wherever they are necessary. Note that not all sentences need them. Then label the function of each comma *Int* (introducer), *Co* (coordinator), *Ins* (inserter), or *T* (tag).

Ins   1. The advertising industry, which is one of the largest industries in the United States, employs millions of people and spends billions of dollars.

_____   2. A company that wants to be successful must spend a great deal of money to advertise its products.

_____   3. Advertising is essential to the free enterprise system yet it can sometimes be very annoying.

_____   4. Every minute of the day and night people are exposed to ads on television on billboards in the newspapers and in magazines.

_____   5. You cannot even avoid advertising in the privacy of your own car or your own home because advertisers have begun selling their products in those places too.

_____   6. In the last few years advertising agencies have started to hire young people to hand out circulars on street corners and in parking lots.

_____   7. You can often find these circulars stuck on your windshield thrust through the open windows of your car stuffed in your mailbox or simply scattered on your front doorstep.

_____   8. Many people object to ads that encourage the use of cigarettes and alcohol.

_____   9. Many ads that sell these products imply that you will have a better social life and be more attractive if you buy the product.

_____   10. The women in such ads are often dressed in beautiful clothes and they are surrounded by handsome men.

_____   11. Smoking and drinking as everyone knows do not make you more attractive or improve your social life.

_____   12. You know that drinking makes you fat and smoking makes you sick don't you?

Semicolons

Using semicolons is not difficult if you remember that a semicolon (;) is more like a period than a comma. It is a very strong punctuation mark. Semicolons are used in three places:

- Between two sentences that are closely connected in idea
- Before conjunctive adverbs and some transition phrases when they are followed by an independent clause
- Between items in a series when the items themselves contain commas

Between Sentences

Use a semicolon to join two independent clauses that are closely connected in meaning. You could also use a period, but a semicolon indicates the close connection.

┌──────── INDEPENDENT CLAUSE ────────┐┌──────── INDEPENDENT CLAUSE ────────┐
Andrew did not accept the job offer; he wants to go to graduate school.

Computer use is increasing; computer crime is, too.

The meeting ended at dawn; nothing had been decided.

Before Connectors

Use a semicolon before conjunctive adverbs such as *however, therefore, nevertheless, moreover,* and *furthermore.* Also use a semicolon before transition phrases such as *for example, as a result, that is,* or *in fact* when they are followed by an independent clause.

```
                                    CONJUNCTIVE
                                    ADVERB, OR
                                    TRANSITION
┌──── INDEPENDENT CLAUSE ────┐ ┌──── PHRASE ────┐┌──────── INDEPENDENT CLAUSE ────────┐
```
Skiing is a dangerous sport; nevertheless, millions of people go skiing every winter.

I have never been to Asia; in fact, I have never been outside the country.

Between Items in a Series

Semicolons are used to separate items in a series when some of the items already contain commas.

I cannot decide which car I like best: the Ferrari, with its quick acceleration and sporty look; the midsize Ford Taurus, with its comfortable seats and ease of handling; or the hybrid Prius, with its economical fuel consumption.

PRACTICE 2   **Using Semicolons and Commas**

A Add semicolons and commas where necessary. Then label the function of each semicolon as *1* (between two closely connected independent clauses), *2* (before a conjunctive adverb or transition phrase), or *3* (between items in a series in which the items already have commas).

_____2_____ 1. Professor Smith is at a conference; however, Dr. Jones will be glad to see you.

_____ 2. Grace works for a prestigious law firm she is their top criminal lawyer.

_____ 3. My favorite leisure-time activities are going to movies especially musicals reading novels especially stories of love and adventure listening to music both rock and classical and participating in sports particularly tennis and volleyball.

_____ 4. The future of our wild animals is uncertain for example illegal shooting and chemical poisoning threaten many birds.

_____ 5. Homework is boring therefore I never do it.

_____ 6. The freeways are always crowded during the busy rush hours nevertheless people refuse to take public transportation.

_____ 7. The Smiths' marriage should succeed they share the same interests.

_____ 8. Hoping that he would pass the course he stayed up all night studying for the final exam unfortunately he overslept and missed the test.

_____ 9. In general I enjoy my English class the amount of homework our teacher assigns is definitely not enjoyable however.

_____ 10. If you are a college student, an average day is filled with challenges: you have to avoid running into Professor Jones whose class you missed because you overslept you have to race across the campus at high speed to reach your next class which is always at the other side of the campus and you have to secretly prepare your homework assignment during class hoping all the time that the teacher will not catch you.

B Punctuate the following sentences by adding semicolons and commas. Use semicolons wherever possible.

1. My bus was late therefore I missed my first class.

2. The politician was discovered accepting bribes as a result his political career was ruined.

3. My father never cries in fact he never shows any emotion at all.

4. The restaurant was closed consequently we went home to eat.

5. Some people feel that grades are unnecessary on the other hand some people feel that grades motivate students.

6. Technology is changing our lives in harmful ways for example the computer is replacing human contact.

7. The computer dehumanizes business nevertheless it has some real advantages.

8. Writing essays is easy it just takes a little practice.

9. North Americans love pets every family seems to have at least one dog or cat.

10. The life expectancy of North Americans is increasing for example the life expectancy of a person born in 2012 was 79 years which is an increase of about 30 years since 1900.

C Write one original sentence for each type of semicolon.

1. Between closely connected sentences

_____

2. Before conjunctive adverbs and some transition phrases

_____

3. Between items in a series

_____

Colons

Using a colon at the end of an independent clause focuses attention on the words following the colon. After a colon, we often write lists, appositives, and direct quotations.

Before Lists

Use a colon to introduce a list.

Libraries have two kinds of periodicals: bound periodicals and current periodicals.

I need the following groceries: eggs, milk, and coffee.

The causes of the U.S. Civil War were as follows: the economic domination of the North, the slavery issue, and the issue of states' rights versus federal intervention.

Before Appositives

Use a colon after an independent clause to direct attention to an appositive (a word or word group that renames another word or word group).

He had one great love in his life: himself.

A doctor has two important abilities: the ability to listen and the ability to analyze.

Before Long Quotations

Use a colon to introduce a quotation longer than three lines. This type of quote begins on a new line and is indented on both sides. No quotation marks are used.

As Albert C. Baugh and Thomas Cable state in their book *The History of the English Language*:

> There is no such thing as uniformity in language. Not only does the speech of one community differ from that of another, but the speech of different individuals of a single community, even different members of the same family, is marked by individual peculiarities.

Before Subtitles

Use a colon between the main title and the subtitle of a book, article, or play.

A popular book on nonverbal communication is Samovar and Porter's *Intercultural Communication: A Reader*.

The title of an article from *The New York Times* is "Man on Mars: Dream or Reality?"

In Expressions of Time of Day

Use a colon between the numbers for hours and minutes when indicating the time of day.

6:30   11:41

After Formal Salutations

Use a colon after the salutation of a formal letter.

Dear Professor Einstein**:**

Dear Customer Relations**:**

Dear Ms. Smith**:**

To Whom It May Concern**:**

In informal letters, use a comma.

Dear Mom**,**   Dear Mark**,**

PRACTICE 3   ### Using Punctuation Marks

A Add commas, semicolons, and colons as needed.

1. The library offers many special services the Student Learning Center where students can receive individual tutoring special classes where they can improve their math reading writing and computer skills and group study rooms where they can meet with classmates to discuss assignments.

2. Dear Dr. Patterson

   Dear Jacob

   Dear Mr. Carter

3. To check a book out of the library you should follow this procedure Write down the call number of the book find the book take it to the circulation desk fill out the card and show your student I.D.

4. The principal sources of air pollution in our cities are factories airplanes and automobiles.

5. I have a dental appointment at 330 today. Please pick me up at 300.

B Write a sentence in which you list two pieces of advice that you have received from someone older, such as a parent or a teacher. Use a colon to direct attention to them.

_____

_____

C Rewrite the title and subtitle of the book correctly. Remember to underline the full title.

TITLE	SUBTITLE
Paris	A Visitor's Guide to Restaurants

_____

Quotation Marks

Quotation marks ("...") have three basic uses: to enclose direct quotations, to enclose unusual words, and to enclose titles of short works.

Around Direct Quotations

Use quotation marks around a direct quotation that is shorter than three lines. A direct quotation states the *exact* words of a speaker and is usually introduced by a reporting phrase such as *he said* or *as the report stated*.

Punctuation with quotation marks can be a little tricky. Here are some rules to follow:

- Separate a quoted sentence from a reporting phrase with a comma.

    The receptionist said, "The doctor is unavailable right now. Please wait."

    "We have already been waiting for an hour," we answered.

- Periods and commas go inside the second quotation mark of a pair.

    "I thought he was responsible," he said, "but he isn't."

- Colons and semicolons go outside quotation marks.

    "Give me liberty or give me death": These are famous words.

- Exclamation points (!) and question marks (?) go inside quotation marks if they are a part of the quotation; otherwise, they go outside.

    "Is it eight o'clock?" she asked.

    Did she say, "It is eight o'clock"?

- Begin each quoted sentence with a capital letter. When a quoted sentence is divided into two parts, the second part begins with a lowercase letter unless it is a new sentence.

    "We thought he was responsible," he said, "but he isn't."

    "We think he is responsible," he said. "Look at his fine work."

- Use single quotation marks ('...') to enclose a quotation within a quotation.

    As John F. Kennedy reminded us, "We should never forget the words of Martin Luther King, Jr., who said, 'I have a dream.'"

Around Unusual Words

Use quotation marks around words with an unusual, especially ironic, meaning.

The "banquet" consisted of hot dogs and soft drinks.

The little girl proudly showed her "masterpiece": a crayon drawing of a flower.

Around Titles of Short Works

Use quotation marks around the titles of articles from periodical journals, magazines, and newspapers; chapters of books; short stories; poems; and songs.

In the article "The Future of Manned Space Travel," published in the July 19, 2004, issue of *Space*, the authors explore the problems of a manned flight to Mars.

The British newspaper *The Times* recently published an article entitled "Who Needs the Monarchy?" which discussed the relevancy of the English monarchy.

Note: Underline or *italicize* titles of books, journals, magazines, newspapers, and movies.

PRACTICE 4 **Using Quotation Marks**

On a separate sheet of paper, write five sentences about any article in a newspaper or magazine that you enjoy reading. Include a quotation, the name of the newspaper or magazine, and the title of the article in each sentence. (For practice using quotation marks, see Chapter 3, Practice 4, page 55.)

PRACTICE 5 **Editing Practice**

Add punctuation to the following paragraphs.

Aging

1 People are more likely to live long enough to get old in wealthy countries than in poor countries. 2 In rich countries people have nutritious food modern medical care good sanitation and clean drinking water but poor countries lack these things. 3 As a result the mortality rate especially infant mortality is very high. 4 Citizens of Congo Liberia Zimbabwe and Burundi which are the world's poorest countries[1] each have an average life expectancy of less than 60 years.[2] 5 Citizens of Monaco Macau Japan Singapore Hong Kong and Australia in contrast have an average life span of more than 81 years. 6 Monaco a very wealthy country has the highest life expectancy at more than 89 years Chad a relatively poor country has the lowest at 48 years. 7 One exception is South Africa which falls in the middle of the list for wealth. 8 Having an average life expectancy of 49 years South Africans live only slightly longer than citizens of Chad. 9 Surprisingly the United States is not among the highest rated nations having an average life expectancy of only 79 years.

10 Compared to other mammals, humans have a relatively long life span.

11 The average life span of elephants is 70 years of dogs 18 years of cats 14 years and of horses 20 years. **12** The life spans of other species are as follows eagles parrots and owls 60 years parakeets 12 years guppies 5 years and box tortoises 100 years. **13** Some plants such as trees live much longer than animals. **14** Redwood trees for example live more than 3,000 years and bristlecone pine trees can live over 4,000 years.

15 The life expectancy of people who live in industrialized societies is increasing rapidly in fact it has doubled in the past hundred years. **16** When comparing males and females one finds that women generally live longer than men. **17** The person who had the longest lifespan was a French woman Jeanne Calment.[3] **18** At her death Madame Calment was 122 years old[4] and both blind and deaf but she never lost her sharp wit for which she had become quite famous. **19** Near the end of her life, she was asked what kind of future she expected she replied A very short one. **20** Bragging about her smooth skin she said I've only had one wrinkle in my life and I'm sitting on it.

Sources:
1–2. https://www.cia.gov/library/publications/the-world-factbook/rankorder/2102rank.html
3. http://www.guinnessworldrecords.com/records-5000/oldest-person/
4. http://www.chron.com/CDA/archives/archive.mpl/1997_1396376/world-s-oldest-person-marks-122nd-birthday.html

Symbol	Meaning	Example of Error	Corrected Sentence
P	punctuation	_P_ _P_ I live, and go to school here	I live and go to school here.
^	missing word	_am_ I working in a restaurant. ^	I am working in a restaurant.
—	rewrite as shown	_some of my_ I go with ~~my some~~ friends.	I go with some of my friends.
cap	capitalization	_cap_ It is located at <u>main</u> and _cap_ _cap_ _cap_ <u>baker</u> <u>streets</u> in the <u>City</u>.	It is located at Main and Baker Streets in the city.
vt	wrong verb tense	_vt_ I never <u>work</u> as a cashier _vt_ until I <u>get</u> a job there.	I never worked as a cashier until I got a job there.
s/v agr	subject-verb agreement	_s/v agr_ The manager <u>work</u> hard. _s/v agr_ He <u>have</u> five employees.	The manager works hard. He has five employees.
pron agr	pronoun agreement	Everyone works hard _pron agr_ at <u>their</u> jobs.	All the employees work hard at their jobs.
⌣	connect to make one sentence	We work together. ⌢So we have become friends.	We work together, so we have become friends.
sp	spelling	_sp_ The <u>maneger</u> is a woman.	The manager is a woman.
sing/pl	singular or plural	She treats her employees _sing/pl_ like <u>slave</u>.	She treats her employees like slaves.
✕	unnecessary word	My boss ~~she~~ watches everyone all the time.	My boss watches everyone all the time.
wf	wrong word form	_wf_ Her voice is <u>irritated</u>.	Her voice is irritating.
ww	wrong word	The restaurant has great _ww_ food. <u>Besides</u>, it is always crowded.	The restaurant has great food. Therefore, it is always crowded.

(continued on next page)

Symbol	Meaning	Example of Error	Corrected Sentence
ref	pronoun reference error	The restaurant's specialty is ref fish. They are always fresh. The food is delicious. ref Therefore, it is always crowded.	The restaurant's specialty is fish. It is always fresh. The food is delicious. Therefore, the restaurant is always crowded.
wo OR ~	wrong word order	Friday always is our busiest night.	Friday is always our busiest night.
ro	run-on sentence	ro [Lily was fired she is upset.]	Lily was fired, so she is upset.
cs	comma splice	cs [Lily was fired, she is upset.]	
frag	fragment	frag She was fired. [Because she was always late.] frag [Is open from 6:00 P.M. until the last customer leaves.] frag [The employees on time and work hard.]	She was fired because she was always late. The restaurant is open from 6:00 P.M. until the last customer leaves. The employees are on time and work hard.
prep	preposition	We start serving prep dinner 6:00 P.M. ^	We start serving dinner at 6:00 P.M.
conj	conjunction	Garlic shrimp, fried conj clams, broiled lobster ^ are the most popular dishes.	Garlic shrimp, fried clams, and broiled lobster are the most popular dishes.
choppy	choppy writing	choppy I like the work. I do not like my boss. I want to quit.	Even though I like the work, I do not like my boss, so I want to quit.
not //	not parallel	Most of our regular customers are not // friendly and generous tippers.	Most of our regular customers are friendly and tip generously.

Symbol	Meaning	Example of Error	Corrected Sentence
sub	subordinate	sub The tips are good, and all the employees share them.	The tips, which all of the employees share, are good.
art	article	Diners in the United States art expect glass of water when they first sit down.	Diners in the United States expect a glass of water when they first sit down.
Ⓣ	add a transition	The new employee was Ⓣ careless. She frequently spilled coffee on the table.	The new employee was careless. For example, she frequently spilled coffee on the table.
¶	start a new paragraph		
nfs/nmp	needs further support/needs more proof. You need to add some specific details (examples, facts, quotations) to support your points.		

When you need to research a topic, two places where you can look for information are the library and the Internet.

Types of Sources

You can find these kinds of sources in a library:

- **Reference books, such as dictionaries, encyclopedias, and atlases.**
  There are general encyclopedias like the *Encyclopedia Americana* and specialized encyclopedias like the *Film Encyclopedia*. There are also general dictionaries and specialized dictionaries like *A Dictionary of Botany*. Reference books are in the reference room or reference area of the library. You cannot check them out and take them home; you must use them inside the library.

  Note: Although encyclopedias are a good place to get basic information about your topic, many college instructors will not allow them as sources in college research papers.

- **Books**
  Libraries usually list their books in a computerized catalog. You can search for books by title, by author's last name, or by subject. If you are searching by subject, you may have to look under several subjects at first. To find books on IQ tests, for example, look under the subject "IQ tests." If there are no books listed, try looking under the subjects "intelligence testing" or "testing" and "intelligence" separately.

  When you find a book that you think might be useful, write down the title, the name of the author, and the book's call number. A call number is a book's address in the library. You must know this number to find the book on the library shelves.

- **Articles in magazines and newspapers**
  To find articles from periodicals, such as magazines and newpapers, you can search an index, such as *The Reader's Guide to Periodical Literature*. You can search for articles by author, title, or subject. In the past, the *Reader's Guide* was published in book form; however, it is now available as an online database hosted by EBSCO, which can be found at most libraries. The database includes all articles published after 1983. There are also other indexes for specialized subjects such as pychology or business. Since many, if not most, magazines and newspapers are now available in online format, you may be able to access the material electronically.

  Note: Be cautious about using information from popular magazines and some newspapers. They may not be appropriate or reliable sources for academic purposes. This also applies to some Internet sources. For more on this see the next section, Evaluating Sources.

- **Scholarly journals**
  For students in graduate school who do advanced research, scholarly journals are important sources of information. Scholarly journals are magazines that publish academic articles, usually about a specific field of study, either in print or online. These journals are also called periodicals or periodical journals. Examples of scholarly journals are *Journal of Educational Psychology* and *New England Journal of Medicine*. Instructors in undergraduate classes do not usually require students to use scholarly journals.

Searching the Internet is a convenient way to do research, but it takes practice to do it efficiently. There are several ways to find information. One way is to type in keywords. Keywords are words that name your specific topic, such as *tattoos* or *poisonous snakes*. Search programs like Google and Bing will search the Internet and display websites containing your keywords. The more specific your keywords are, the more selective the search will be. For example, the keyword *snakes* will produce an enormous number of sites. The keywords *poisonous snakes* will give fewer, and *Central American poisonous snakes* will give the fewest.

Your instructor may also allow you to gather information on your topic by performing an experiment, taking a survey, or interviewing people. If you do this, make sure to take good notes and keep careful records of the people you talk to and what each person says.

Evaluating Sources

Before you use information from an outside source, you should first determine if the information is reliable. There is a lot of outdated, biased, and false information in print and on the Internet. Your sources should be reliable, which means that the information should be current, unbiased, and true. You can judge a source's reliability by checking the following:

- Check the date. Your sources of information should be current unless your topic is a historical one. For example, if your topic is space exploration, a source dated before 1960 would probably not have very useful information.
- Check the reputation of the author. What do you know about him or her? At the very least, you should find out the author's occupation. A reliable author is not necessarily famous; he or she just has to have special knowledge about your topic. For example, if your topic is the conditions in U.S. prisons, a letter or article written by a prisoner might be reliable. However, the same prisoner would probably not be a reliable source on the topic of the history of U.S. prisons.
- Check the reputation of the publisher. What company or organization published the information? Is it nationally or internationally known?
- What is the purpose of the publication or website? Is it to sell a product, support one side of a controversy, promote a political point of view, or merely provide information?
- Check the content. Is it mostly fact, opinion, or propaganda? Does it seem strongly biased? Are the ideas supported by reliable evidence?
- Check the language. Does the source seem well written? Is it free from emotion-arousing words? Do you notice any errors in spelling or grammar? These would indicate that it is probably not a reliable source.
- Check the quality of the presentation. Is the quality of the printing good? Is the website well organized? Does it offer links to other sites? Check them out.

If you aren't sure about a source, ask your instructor or a reference librarian for help in evaluating it. There are also sites on the Internet that can help. Find them by searching the keywords "evaluating Internet information."

Evaluating Sources

Check (✓) the sources that might be useful and reliable for research on the topic of body art (body painting, tattooing, and piercing) in ancient and modern cultures.

PRINT SOURCES

☐ 1. *Tattoo History: A Source Book by Stephen G. Gilbert.* A collection of historical writings on tattooing. Includes accounts of tattooing in the Ancient World, Polynesia, Japan, the pre-Columbian Americas, nineteenth-century Europe and the United States. Published in 2001.

☐ 2. *The Rose Tattoo.* A play by Tennessee Williams, made into a movie starring Anna Magnani and Burt Lancaster. The story of a widow whose loyalty to her dead husband is tested by a handsome truck driver.

☐ 3. "Tattooing among the Maoris of New Zealand." An article by William Oldenburg in the June 1946 issue of *Journal of Cultural Anthropology.*

☐ 4. "Regulating the Body Art Industry." A doctor proposes laws to ensure the safe practice of tattooing and body piercing in the state of New York. An article written by Dr. Evan Whitman in the February 10, 2001, issue of *The New York Times.*

☐ 5. "Tattoo Arts and Their Cultural Connections." An article by Soriyya Bawa in the October 2011 issue of *Anokhi* magazine. Tattooing is becoming popular with Canadians of South Asian descent, but their immigrant parents often disapprove.

☐ 6. *Tattoo World* by Michael Kaplan. A collection of photographs of tattoos from around the world. Published in 2011.

INTERNET SOURCES

☐ 1. Tattoos.com. A website that provides information about tattooing and links to other sites.

☐ 2. "Tattoo." An article in the online *Encyclopedia Britannica*, found at britannica.com.

☐ 3. Body Piercing Shop. A website offering titanium, surgical steel, silver, and gold body jewelry. Also semiprecious gemstones and Austrian crystal. Best prices.

☐ 4. "Body-Marking." An article in the online *Columbia Encyclopedia* on body-marking, painting, tattooing, or scarification (cutting and burning) of the body for ritual, esthetic, medicinal, magic, or religious purposes.

☐ 5. Getting Pierced Safely. A website that explains health factors. All the facts you need if you are thinking of body piercing. Choosing a safe practitioner. Risks.

☐ 6. "The Human Canvas." A report on body art throughout history. *Discovery Online*, Expeditions series, produced in cooperation with the American Museum of Natural History.

Documentation of Sources

In academic classes, instructors may ask you to document the sources of outside information you use in a paper. There are two steps to this process.

1. Insert a short reference in the body of your paper. This is called an in-text citation.

2. Prepare a list describing all your sources completely. This list is titled Works Cited and appears as the last page of your paper.

The next few pages will show you only the basics of the MLA style[1] of formal documentation. Consult the *MLA Handbook for Writers of Research Papers* for detailed information. You can find this book and others like it in the reference area of any library.

In-Text Citations

The purpose of an in-text citation is to refer the reader to the works-cited list at the end of your paper. In-text citations are also called parenthetical references because they are enclosed in parentheses. Place in-text citations immediately after the borrowed information, usually at the end of a sentence, before the final period.

> A universal language could bring countries together culturally and economically as well as increase good feelings among them (Kispert).

The name *Kispert* in parentheses at the end of the sentence tells us that the ideas in the sentence came from a work written by a person whose last name is Kispert. No page number is given, which indicates that the work is an Internet source.

If readers want more information about this source, they can turn to the works-cited list at the end of the essay, report, or paper and find this entry:

> Kispert, Robert J. "Universal language." World Book Online Reference Center. 2004. World Book, Inc. 12 5 Sep. 2004. Web. 12 Sep. 2004. <http://www.aolsvc.worldbook.aol.com/wb/ Article?id=ar576960>.

In-text citations are as short as possible. They contain only enough information to allow the reader to find the full reference in the list of works cited at the end of your paper. Here are some guidelines.

ONE AUTHOR

Use the last name of the author and a page number (or numbers, if the borrowed information appears on more than one page). Use no punctuation.

> (Clinton 17)

TWO OR MORE AUTHORS

If there are two or three authors, give all the names. If there are four or more, use the first author's name and the Latin abbreviation *et al.* ("and others") followed by a period.

> (Bamberger and Yaeger 62)   (Singleton *et al.* 345)

AUTHOR ALREADY MENTIONED

If you have already mentioned the author's name in the text, or if you are citing two consecutive pieces of borrowed information from the same source, do not repeat the name in your citation. For example, if you introduced the borrowed information with a phrase such as "According to Clinton," give only the page number.

> (18)

NO AUTHOR

If there is no author, use a short title in quotation marks.

> ("2002 Olympics")

---

[1] The MLA (Modern Language Association) style is used in English and other language classes. Other fields of study, such as the social sciences, physical sciences, and business, use other styles.

QUOTED QUOTATION

If you use someone's words that are quoted in a source written by a different person, begin the in-text citation with the abbreviation *qtd. in* (for *quoted in*).

(qtd. in Herper 1)

ENCYCLOPEDIA ARTICLE WITH NO AUTHOR

For an encyclopedia article, use the author's name if possible. If not, use the title of the article in quotation marks. You do not need a page number since encyclopedia articles are arranged alphabetically and a reader will be able to find the source easily.

("Global Warming")

ELECTRONIC SOURCE

For an electronic source (online or CD-ROM), follow the same system as for print sources. If there are no page numbers, do not write a number.

(Kidder)   ("2000 Olympics")

Works-Cited Lists

The second step in citing sources is to list all the sources you actually used in your paper. (Do not include sources that you read but did not use.) List them alphabetically by last name of the author or, if there is no author, by the first word of the title (disregarding *A*, *An*, and *The*). Include information about each source as described here. Pay close attention to punctuation and capitalization, and indent the second line 5 spaces. For kinds of sources not included here, consult a more comprehensive English handbook, such as the MLA Handbook.

BOOK WITH ONE AUTHOR (READ IN PRINT, NOT ONLINE)

Use this form for a basic book reference. Divide the information into three parts: (1) name of the author, (2) title of the book, (3) publishing information. Put a period and one space after each part.

- Write the author's last name first and put a comma after it. Do not include a person's titles.
- Write the city of publication, a colon, the name of the publishing company, a comma, the year of publication, and a period. Get this information from the title page or the back of the title page inside the book, not from the book's cover. Use the first city listed if there are several. Include an abbreviation for a state or country if the city is unfamiliar or in any way unclear. Use the most recent year. Shorten the name of the publisher by omitting words like *Press*, *Publishers*, *Books*, *Inc.*, and *Co*.
- Finish with the word *Print*.

Lahiri, Jhumpa. *Unaccustomed Earth*. New York: Vintage Books, 2008. Print.

BOOK WITH TWO OR MORE AUTHORS

Use reverse order for the first author's name, and then write all other authors' names in normal order. Put a comma after the last name of the first author and also between authors. Put a colon between the title and subtitle, and underline both.

Hamilton, Tyler, and Daniel Coyle. *The Secret Race: Inside the Hidden World of the Tour de France: Doping, Cover-ups, and Winning at All Costs*. New York: Bantam Books, 2012. Print.

Book with More Than One Edition

Put the number and the abbreviation "ed." (2nd ed., 3rd ed., 4th ed., and so on) after the title, followed by a period.

> Slavin, Robert. *Educational Psychology: Theory and Practice*. 10th ed. Boston: Pearson, 2012. Print.

Encyclopedia Article

Use the author's name if it is given. If there is no author, put the title of the article first. Enclose the title in quotation marks. Underline or italicize the title of the encyclopedia. Put the edition number if there is one; if there is none, use the year.

> "Intelligence Test." *New Encyclopedia Britannica: Micropedia.* 15th ed. Print.

Magazine Article

Put the title of the article inside quotation marks. Underline or italicize the name of the magazine. Include the day, month, and year for weekly magazines followed by a colon and the page number or numbers on which the article appears. Abbreviate the names of months except May, June, and July.

> Rapoport, Abby. "School for Success." *Mother Jones.* July/Aug. 2012: 44-49. Print.

Newspaper Article

This article appeared on page A-22 of the newspaper.

> "An Unfinished Campaign Against Polio." Editorial. *The New York Times*. 29 Sep. 2012: A-22. Print.

Personal Interview

Give the person's name (last name first) and the date of the interview.

> Jones, John. Personal interview. 31 Oct. 2003.

Online Source

Citations for online sources need the same basic information as print sources: author, title, and date of publication. The date of publication for an online source is the date it was put online or the date it was last revised. Sometimes you cannot find an author or a publication date; in this case, just give information you are able to find.

At the end of your entry, write the word *Web* followed by the date you accessed the site. This shows which version of the website you used.

You may choose (or your teacher may ask you) to include the exact electronic address. Copy the address from the top of your computer screen and enclose it in angle brackets (< >). Copy the address of the webpage you used, not the home page. To divide an address that is too long to fit on a line, break it only at a slash mark (/).

> Kispert, Robert J. "Universal Language." *World Book Online Reference Center*. 2004. World Book, Inc. Web. 25 Mar. 2004. <http://www.aolsvc.worldbook.aol.com/wb/Article?id=ar576960>.

> Bonner, Jessie, and Heather Hollingsworth. "Single-Sex Classes Popular As More Public Schools Split Up Boys and Girls." *HuffingtonPost*. 8 July 2012. Web. 1 Oct. 2012. <http://www.huffingtonpost.com/2012/07/08/more-public-schools-split_0_n_1657505.html>.

A works-cited list is written or typed on a separate page, which is the last page of a paper. Use the following format.

- Capitalize the title of the Works-Cited list and center it on the page.
- Put the list in alphabetical order by author's last name (or title of the work, if there is no author).
- Double-space everything.
- Indent the second line of each citation 5 spaces or 1/2 inch.

Works Cited

Baugh, Albert C., and Thomas Cable. *A History of the English Language.* 5th ed. Upper Saddle River, NJ: Prentice Hall, 2002. Print.

Bonner, Jessie and Heather Hollingsworth. "Single-Sex Classes Popular As More Public Schools Split Up Boys and Girls." *Huffington Post.* 8 July 2012. Web. 1 Oct. 2012 <http://www.huffingtonpost.com/ 2012/07/08/more-public-schools-split_0_n_1657505.html>.

Bruce, Meredith. *Cybercrime.* New York: Wexler, 2004. Print.

Brunish, Cory. Letter. *Time* 16 Feb. 2004: 9. Print.

Clinton, Patrick. "Manned Mars Flight: Impossible Dream?" *Space Science* 15 Oct. 2003: 16–18. Print.

Downie, Andrew. "Brazil Considers Linguistic Barricade." *Christian Science Monitor* 6 Sep. 2000. Web. 13 Sep. 2004. <http://csmonitor.com/ cgi-bin/durableRedirect.pl?/durable/2000/09/06/fp7s2-csm.shtml>.

Hamilton, Tyler, and Daniel Coyle. *The Secret Race: Inside the Hidden World of the Tour de France: Doping, Cover-ups, and Winning at All Costs.* New York: Bantam Books, 2012. Print.

Henderson, Lynne, and Philip Zimbardo. "Shyness." *Encyclopedia of Mental Health*. San Diego: Academic Press, 19 pp. 4 May 2004. <http://www.shyness.com/encyclopedia.html>.

Herper, Matthew. "Performance Drugs Outrun the Olympics." *Forbes* 15 Feb. 2002. Print. 30 Mar. 2004. <http://www.forbes.com/2002/02/15/0215ped.html>.

Jones, John. Personal interview. 31 Oct. 2003.

Kispert, Robert J. "Universal language." *World Book Online Reference Center.* 2004. World Book, Inc. 12 Sep. 2004. Web. 12 Sep. 2004. <http://www.aolsvc.worldbook.aol.com/wb/Article?id=ar576960>.

Kluger, Jeffrey. "Mission to Mars: First the Rover Lands, and Now Bush Wants to Send People. We Can Do It Even Faster Than Planned, but Here Is What It Will Take." *Time* 26 Jan. 2004: 42–47. Print.

Rapoport, Abby. "School for Success." *Mother Jones.* July/Aug. 2012: 44-49. Print.

Slavin, Robert. *Educational Psychology: Theory and Practice*. 10th ed. Boston: Pearson, 2012. Print.

"The 2000 Olympics: Games of the Drugs?" *CBSNEWS.com* 9 Sep. 2000. Web. 30 Mar. 2004. <http://www.cbsnews.com/stories/2002/01/31/ health/main326667.shtml?CMP=ILC-SearchStories>.

On a piece of paper, write the heading "Works Cited." Then list each of the following sources in MLA style and in alphabetical order.

1. A book entitled *Learning Disorders* by Robert W. Henderson published by Morris & Burns in Chicago in 2005.

2. A magazine article entitled "How to Live to Be 100" by Richard Corliss and Michael D. Lemonick on pages 40–48 of the August 30, 2004, issue of *Time* magazine.

3. A newspaper article entitled "Biology of Dyslexia Varies with Culture, Study Finds" on page D7 of the September 7, 2004, issue of *The New York Times* newspaper. The author's name is Anahad O'Connor.

4. An article in an online encyclopedia. The title of the article is "Dyslexia." The site's address is http://www.aolsvc.worldbook.aol.com/wb/Article? id=ar171010. The author's name is Michel W. Kibby. The website is *World Book Online Reference Center*. The publisher is World Book, Inc., and the copyright date is 2004. Use today's date as your date of access.

5. A website published by the U.S. Food and Drug Administration's Center for Food Safety and Applied Nutrition. The website contains an article titled "Tattoos and Permanent Makeup." The website's address is http://www.cfsan.fda.gov/~dms/cos-204.html. The article was updated on July 1, 2004. Use today's date as your date of access.

Peer Review and Writer's Self-Check worksheets are designed to help you become a better writer.

Peer Review

Peer review is an interactive process of reading and commenting on a classmate's writing. You will exchange rough drafts with a classmate, read each other's work, and make suggestions for improvement. Use the worksheet for each assignment and answer each question. Write your comments on the worksheet or on your classmate's paper as your instructor directs. If you exchange rough drafts via email instead of hard copy, it may be easier to make comments in the document. Check with your instructor to find out how you should exchange and comment on drafts.

Advice for Peer Reviewers

- Your job is to help your classmate write clearly. Focus only on content and organization.
- If you notice grammar or spelling errors, ignore them. It is not your job to correct your classmate's English.
- Don't cross out any writing. Underline, draw arrows, circle things, but don't cross out anything.
- Make your first comment a positive one. Find something good to say.
- If possible, use a colored ink or pencil if you are working in hard copy.
- The writer may not always agree with you. Discuss your different opinions, but don't argue, and don't cause hurt feelings.

Here are some polite ways to suggest changes:

Do you think _____ is important/necessary/relevant?

I don't quite understand your meaning here.

Could you please explain this point a little more?

I think an example would help here.

This part seems confusing.

I think this part should go at the end/at the beginning/after XYZ.

Maybe you don't need this word/sentence/part.

Writer's Self-Check

Becoming a better writer requires that you learn to edit your own work. Self-editing means looking at your writing as a writing instructor does. The Writer's Self-Check worksheets contain questions about specific elements that your instructor hopes to find in your paragraph or essay—a strong thesis statement, clear topic sentences, specific supporting details, coherence, an effective conclusion, and so on. Self-editing also requires attention to every aspect of your writing. It involves proofreading to check for and correct errors in format, mechanics, grammar, and sentence structure. By answering the worksheet questions thoughtfully, you can learn to recognize the strengths (and weaknesses) in your rhetorical skills as well as to spot and correct errors.

Reader: _____   Date: _____

1. Is the paragraph interesting?   ☐ yes   ☐ no
   Write a comment about a part that is especially interesting to you.

   _____

2. Do you understand everything?   ☐ yes   ☐ no
   Circle or underline any part that you do not understand, and write a comment about it.

   _____

3. Copy the topic sentence here, and circle the topic and double-underline the controlling idea.

   _____

   _____

4. How many supporting sentences are there in the paragraph? Number: _____
   a. What kind of supporting details does the writer use (facts, examples, quotations, statistics, etc.)? _____

      Is there at least one example?   ☐ yes   ☐ no
   b. Would you like more information about anything?   ☐ yes   ☐ no

      If your answer is *yes*, write down what you would like to know more about.

      _____

5. Is there anything unnecessary or that seems "off topic?"   ☐ yes   ☐ no
   If your answer is *yes*, write a comment about this.

   _____

6. If the paragraph has a concluding sentence, copy it here and circle the end-of-paragraph signal (if there is one).

   _____

7. In your opinion, what is the best feature of this paragraph? In other words, what is this writer's best writing skill?

   _____

CHAPTER 1 WRITER'S SELF-CHECK

Writer: _____ Date: _____

Format

My paragraph has a title.   ☐ yes ☐ no

The title is centered.   ☐ yes ☐ no

The first line is indented.   ☐ yes ☐ no

There are margins on both sides of the page.   ☐ yes ☐ no

The paragraph is double-spaced or skips lines, if handwritten.   ☐ yes ☐ no

Mechanics

I put a period, a question mark, or an exclamation mark after
every sentence.   ☐ yes ☐ no

I used capital letters correctly.   ☐ yes ☐ no

I checked my spelling.   ☐ yes ☐ no

Content and Organization

My paragraph fits the assignment.   ☐ yes ☐ no

My paragraph has a topic sentence.   ☐ yes ☐ no

The topic sentence has both a topic and a controlling idea.   ☐ yes ☐ no

My paragraph contains several specific and factual
supporting sentences, including at least one example.   ☐ yes ☐ no

How many supporting sentences did I write?   number: _____

My paragraph ends with an appropriate concluding sentence.   ☐ yes ☐ no

All of my sentences are directly related to the topic.   ☐ yes ☐ no

Grammar and Sentence Structure

Every student has his or her own personal grammar trouble spots. Some students battle with verb tenses. For others, articles are the main enemy. Some find it hard to know where to put periods.

In the space, create your own personal checklist for items that you know are problems for you. Then, throughout the term, work on eliminating these errors. Delete items you have mastered and add new ones that you become aware of.

Errors to check for include verb tenses, subject-verb agreement, articles, pronoun agreement, sentence fragments, and run-on sentences/comma splices.

Number found and corrected

I checked my paragraph for _____ errors.   _____
                              (verb tense, article, etc.)

I checked my paragraph for _____ errors.   _____

I checked my paragraph for _____ errors.   _____

Reader: _____   Date: _____

1. Is the paragraph interesting? ☐ yes ☐ no
   Write a comment about a part that is especially interesting to you.

   _____

2. Do you understand everything? ☐ yes ☐ no
   Circle or underline any part that you do not understand, and write a comment about it.

   _____

3. Copy the topic sentence here, and circle the topic and double-underline the controlling idea.

   _____

4. How many supporting sentences are there in the paragraph? Number: _____
   a. What kind of supporting details does the writer use (facts, examples, quotations,

      statistics, etc.)? _____

   b. Would you like more information about anything? ☐ yes ☐ no
      If your answer is *yes*, write down what you would like to know more about.

      _____

5. **Unity:** Is there anything unnecessary or that seems "off topic?" ☐ yes ☐ no
   If your answer is *yes*, write a comment about it.

   _____

6. Does the paragraph have coherence; that is, does it flow smoothly from
   beginning to end? ☐ yes ☐ no
   a. What key noun is repeated? _____
   b. Are pronouns consistent? ☐ yes ☐ no
   c. What transition signals can you find?

      _____

   d. Are the ideas arranged in some kind of logical order? What kind?

      _____

7. If the paragraph has a concluding sentence, copy it here and circle the
   end-of-paragraph signal (if there is one).

   _____

8. In your opinion, what is the best feature of this paragraph? In other words,
   what is this writer's best writing skill?

   _____

CHAPTER 2 WRITER'S SELF-CHECK

Writer: _____   Date: _____

Format

My paragraph is correctly formatted (title centered, first
line indented, margins on both sides, double-spaced).   ☐ yes   ☐ no

Mechanics

I checked punctuation, capitalization, and spelling.   ☐ yes   ☐ no

Content and Organization

My paragraph begins with a topic sentence that has both
a topic and a controlling idea.   ☐ yes   ☐ no

My paragraph contains specific and factual supporting
sentences that explain or prove my topic sentence.   ☐ yes   ☐ no

How many supporting sentences does the paragraph have?   number: _____

Unity: All sentences are on the topic.   ☐ yes   ☐ no

My paragraph ends with an appropriate concluding sentence.   ☐ yes   ☐ no

Coherence: My paragraph flows smoothly from beginning
to end.   ☐ yes   ☐ no

I repeat key nouns where necessary.   ☐ yes   ☐ no

I use pronouns consistently.   ☐ yes   ☐ no

I use some transition signals. How many? _____   ☐ yes   ☐ no

My sentences are in some type of logical order.   ☐ yes   ☐ no

Grammar and Sentence Structure

Errors to check for include verb tenses, subject-verb agreement, articles, pronoun
agreement, sentence fragments, and run-on sentences/comma splices.

                                             Number found and corrected

I checked my paragraph for _____ errors.   _____
                          (verb tense, article, etc.)

I checked my paragraph for _____ errors.   _____

I checked my paragraph for _____ errors.   _____

Reader: _____   **Date:** _____

1. Does the summary correctly state the main idea of the original text?   □ yes   □ no
    Write a comment if the main idea is missing or incorrectly stated.

    _____

2. Do you understand everything?   □ yes   □ no
    Circle or underline any part that you do not understand, and write a
    comment about it.

    _____

3. Is the summary missing any of the main supporting points from the
    original text?   □ yes   □ no
    If your answer is *yes*, write a comment about this.

    _____

4. Does the summary include any unnecessary details from the
    original text?   □ yes   □ no
    If your answer is *yes*, write a comment about this.

    _____

5. Does the summary properly paraphrase the original text?   □ yes   □ no
    If you find any places where the summary is too similar to the original,
    underline them.

6. In your opinion, what is the best feature of this summary? In other words,
    what is this writer's best summarizing skill?

    _____

CHAPTER 3 WRITER'S SELF-CHECK

Writer: _____   Date: _____

Format

My summary is correctly formatted (title centered, first line indented, margins on both sides, double-spaced).   ☐ yes ☐ no

Mechanics

I checked punctuation, capitalization, and spelling.   ☐ yes ☐ no

Content and Organization

My summary begins with a topic sentence that states the main idea of the original text.   ☐ yes ☐ no

My summary contains all of the main supporting points from the original text.   ☐ yes ☐ no

My summary contains only the main supporting points from the original text.   ☐ yes ☐ no

I paraphrased the ideas from the original text by using synonyms and changing sentence structure.   ☐ yes ☐ no

My summary ends with an appropriate concluding sentence.   ☐ yes ☐ no

My summary contains transition signals and other strategies so that it flows smoothly from beginning to end.   ☐ yes ☐ no

My summary includes an in-text citation in proper format.   ☐ yes ☐ no

Grammar and Sentence Structure

Errors to check for include verb tenses, subject-verb agreement, articles, pronoun agreement, sentence fragments, and run-on sentences/comma splices.

Number found and corrected

I checked my paragraph for _____ errors.   _____
(verb tense, article, etc.)

I checked my paragraph for _____ errors.   _____

I checked my paragraph for _____ errors.   _____

Reader: _____   **Date:** _____

1. What kind of introduction does this essay have? (funnel, dramatic, etc.) _____

   What is the thesis statement? _____

   Where is the thesis statement placed? _____

   Does the introduction capture your interest?   ☐ yes   ☐ no

2. How many paragraphs are there in the body? Number: _____
   What are the topics of the body paragraphs?

   1. _____   3. _____

   2. _____   4. _____

3. What kind of supporting details does the writer use in each body paragraph?

   1. _____   3. _____

   2. _____   4. _____

4. Check each paragraph for unity. Are any sentences unnecessary or "off topic?"   ☐ yes   ☐ no
   If your answer is *yes*, write a comment about this.

   _____

5. Check each paragraph for coherence. Does each one flow smoothly from
   beginning to end?   ☐ yes   ☐ no

   What key nouns are repeated? _____

   What transition signals can you find? _____

   _____

6. What expressions does the writer use to link paragraphs? If there are none, write *none*.
   (Write the expressions and the numbers of the paragraphs each links.)

   _____   _____

   _____   _____

   _____   _____

7. What kind of conclusion does this essay have—a summary of the main points or a
   paraphrase of the thesis statement? _____

   Does the writer make a final comment?   ☐ yes   ☐ no

   What is it? _____

   Is this an effective ending (one that you will remember)?   ☐ yes   ☐ no

8. In your opinion, what is the best feature of this essay? In other words, what is this
   writer's best writing skill?

   _____

CHAPTER 4 WRITER'S SELF-CHECK

Writer: _____   Date: _____

Format

My essay is correctly formatted (title centered, first line of every
paragraph indented, margins on both sides, double-spaced).   ☐ yes ☐ no

Mechanics

I checked punctuation, capitalization, and spelling.   ☐ yes ☐ no

Content and Organization

My essay has all three parts: introduction, body, and conclusion.   ☐ yes ☐ no

Introduction: Type of introduction (funnel, historical background,

surprising statistics, dramatic story, etc.): _____

The introduction ends with my thesis statement.   ☐ yes ☐ no

Body: The body has _____ paragraphs.

The topics of the body paragraphs are as follows:

   1. _____   3. _____

   2. _____   4. _____

Unity: Each paragraph discusses only one main idea,
and there are no sentences that are "off topic."   ☐ yes ☐ no

Coherence: Each paragraph has coherence. My essay
flows smoothly from beginning to end.   ☐ yes ☐ no

I repeat key nouns.   ☐ yes ☐ no

I use transition signals to show relationships among ideas.   ☐ yes ☐ no

I use transitions to link paragraphs.   ☐ yes ☐ no

Conclusion: The conclusion (a) summarizes the main points or

(b) paraphrases the thesis statement. (Circle one.)

Grammar and Sentence Structure

Errors to check for include verb tenses, subject-verb agreement, articles, pronoun
agreement, sentence fragments, and run-on sentences/comma splices.

                                        Number found and corrected

I checked my essay for _____ errors.   _____
                  (verb tense, article, etc.)

I checked my essay for _____ errors.   _____

I checked my essay for _____ errors.   _____

Reader: _____   **Date:** _____

1. What kind of introduction does this essay have (funnel, entertaining story, etc.)?
   _____

   Does the thesis statement indicate that chronological order will be used to describe a process?   ☐ yes   ☐ no

   If your answer is *yes*, what words show this?

   _____

2. Does each body paragraph describe one step or a group of steps clearly and in chronological order?   ☐ yes   ☐ no

   What are the topics of the body paragraphs?

   1. _____   3. _____
   2. _____   4. _____

3. What details does the writer add to clarify the process in the body paragraphs?

   1. _____   3. _____
   2. _____   4. _____

4. Check each paragraph for unity. Are any sentences unnecessary or "off topic?"   ☐ yes   ☐ no

   If your answer is *yes*, write a comment about them.

   _____

5. Check each paragraph for coherence. Does each one flow smoothly from beginning to end?   ☐ yes   ☐ no

   What key nouns are repeated? _____

   What transition signals for chronological order can you find? _____

   _____

6. What expressions does the writer use to link paragraphs? If there are none, write *none*.

   _____   _____

   _____   _____

   _____   _____

7. What kind of conclusion does this essay have—a summary of the main

   points or a paraphrase of the thesis statement? _____

   Does the writer make a final comment?   ☐ yes   ☐ no

   If your answer is *yes*, what is it?

   _____

   Is this an effective ending (one that you will remember)?   ☐ yes   ☐ no

8. In your opinion, what is the best feature of this essay? In other words, what is this writer's best writing skill?

   _____

CHAPTER 5 WRITER'S SELF-CHECK

Writer: _____   Date: _____

Format

My essay is correctly formatted (title centered, first line of every
paragraph indented, margins on both sides, double-spaced).   ☐ yes   ☐ no

Mechanics

I checked punctuation, capitalization, and spelling.   ☐ yes   ☐ no

Content and Organization

My essay has all three parts: introduction, body, and conclusion.   ☐ yes   ☐ no

Introduction: Type of introduction I used (funnel, historical background,

surprising statistics, dramatic story, etc.): _____

The thesis statement indicates that I will use chronological
order to describe a process.   ☐ yes   ☐ no

Body: The body has _____ paragraphs. Each paragraph explains
one major step or one group of steps in the process I am writing about.
The topics of the body paragraphs are as follows:

1. _____   3. _____

2. _____   4. _____

Unity: In the body, no sentences are "off topic."   ☐ yes   ☐ no

Coherence: Each paragraph has coherence.
My essay flows smoothly from beginning to end.   ☐ yes   ☐ no

I repeat key nouns.   ☐ yes   ☐ no

I use transition signals to show chronological order.   ☐ yes   ☐ no

I use transitions to link paragraphs.   ☐ yes   ☐ no

Conclusion: The conclusion (a) summarizes the main points or

(b) paraphrases the thesis statement. (Circle one.)

Grammar and Sentence Structure

Errors to check for include verb tenses, subject-verb agreement, articles, pronoun
agreement, sentence fragments, and run-on sentences/comma splices.

                                                      Number found and corrected

I checked my essay for _____ errors.   _____
                        (verb tense, article, etc.)

I checked my essay for _____ errors.   _____

I checked my essay for _____ errors.   _____

Reader: _____   Date: _____

1. What kind of introduction does this essay have (funnel, entertaining story, etc.)?

    _____

    Is the thesis statement appropriate for a cause/effect essay?   ☐ yes   ☐ no
    Does it mention any subtopics? What are they?

    _____

2. What kind of organization does the essay use for the body paragraphs?
    Write *block*, *chain*, or *"unclear."* _____
    What are the topics of the body paragraphs?

    1. _____   3. _____
    2. _____   4. _____

3. What kind of supporting details does the writer use in each body paragraph?

    1. _____   3. _____
    2. _____   4. _____

4. Check each paragraph for unity. Are any sentences "off topic?"   ☐ yes   ☐ no
    If your answer is *yes*, write a comment about this.

    _____

5. Check each paragraph for coherence. Does each one flow smoothly?   ☐ yes   ☐ no
    What key nouns are repeated?

    _____

    What transition signals can you find?

    _____

6. What expressions does the writer use to link paragraphs? If there are none, write *none*.

    _____   _____

    _____   _____

    _____

7. What kind of conclusion does this essay have—a summary of the main points or a
    paraphrase of the thesis statement?

    _____

    Does the writer make a final comment?   ☐ yes   ☐ no
    What is it? _____
    Is this an effective ending (one that you will remember)?   ☐ yes   ☐ no

8. In your opinion, what is the best feature of this essay? In other words, what is this
    writer's best writing skill?

    _____

CHAPTER 6 WRITER'S SELF-CHECK

Writer: _____   Date: _____

Format

My essay is correctly formatted (title centered, first line of every
paragraph indented, margins on both sides, double-spaced).   ☐ yes   ☐ no

Mechanics

I checked punctuation, capitalization, and spelling.   ☐ yes   ☐ no

Content and Organization

My essay has all three parts: introduction, body,
and conclusion.   ☐ yes   ☐ no

Introduction: Type of introduction I used (funnel, historical background,

surprising statistics, dramatic story, etc.): _____

The introduction ends with my thesis statement.   ☐ yes   ☐ no

Body: The body has _____ paragraphs. The topics of the body paragraphs are as follows:

   1. _____   3. _____

   2. _____   4. _____

Unity: Each paragraph discusses only one main
idea, and there are no sentences that are "off topic."   ☐ yes   ☐ no

Coherence: Each paragraph has coherence.
My essay flows smoothly from beginning to end.   ☐ yes   ☐ no

I repeat key nouns.   ☐ yes   ☐ no

I use transition signals and cause/effect signal words
to show relationships among ideas.   ☐ yes   ☐ no

I use transitions to link paragraphs.   ☐ yes   ☐ no

Conclusion: The conclusion (a) summarizes the main points or (b) paraphrases the thesis
statement. (Circle one.)

Grammar and Sentence Structure

Errors to check for include verb tenses, subject-verb agreement, articles, pronoun
agreement, sentence fragments, and run-on sentences/comma splices.

Number found and corrected

I checked my essay for _____ errors.   _____
                        (verb tense, article, etc.)

I checked my essay for _____ errors.   _____

I checked my essay for _____ errors.   _____

Reader: _____   Date: _____

1. Analyze how the writer organizes his or her essay.

   a. Copy the thesis sentence here. Does it state the writer's opinion clearly?

   _____

   b. Does the essay use block or point-by-point organization?

   _____

2. List the writer's arguments:

   a. _____

   b. _____

   c. _____

3. List the opposing arguments and counterarguments (rebuttals):

   a. Opposing argument: _____

   Counterargument: _____

   b. Opposing argument: _____

   Counterargument: _____

   c. Opposing argument: _____

   Counterargument: _____

4. What is the writer's strongest and most convincing argument or counterargument?

   _____

   How does he or she support it?

   _____

   Is any argument or counterargument weak and unconvincing?   ☐ yes   ☐ no

   Why is it weak? _____
   Discuss with the writer possible ways to strengthen it.

5. Do you understand everything?   ☐ yes   ☐ no
   Circle or underline any part that you do not understand, and write a comment about it.

6. What kind of supporting details does the writer use (statistics, examples, quotations, paraphrases, summaries, etc.)?

   _____

7. How does the writer name the source of each piece of borrowed supporting information; that is, what phrases or verbs does the writer use to name the sources? Write them here.

   _____

8. Is this a convincing argumentative essay? In other words, does the writer persuade you that his or her opinion is the right one?   ☐ yes   ☐ no

CHAPTER 8 WRITER'S SELF-CHECK

Writer: _____   Date: _____

Format

My essay is correctly formatted.   ☐ yes ☐ no

Mechanics

I have checked for punctuation, capitalization, and spelling errors.   ☐ yes ☐ no

Content and Organization

My essay has all three parts: introduction, body, and conclusion.   ☐ yes ☐ no

I used block or point-by-point organization. (Underline one.)

Introduction: Type of introduction I used (funnel, historical background,

surprising statistics, dramatic story, etc.): _____

The thesis statement states my opinion clearly.   ☐ yes ☐ no

Body: The body has _____ paragraphs.

I give _____ arguments for my point of view

and _____ arguments for the opposing point of view.

I rebut each opposing argument.   ☐ yes ☐ no

I support each point with a specific supporting detail such as an
example, a statistic, a quotation, a paraphrase, or a summary.   ☐ yes ☐ no

I cite the source of all borrowed information.   ☐ yes ☐ no

Conclusion: The conclusion (a) summarizes my arguments or
(b) restates my opinion. (Circle one.)

Grammar and Sentence Structure

Errors to check for include verb tenses, subject-verb agreement, articles, pronoun
agreement, sentence fragments, and run-on sentences/comma splices.

Number found and corrected

I checked my essay for _____ errors.   _____
                        (verb tense, article, etc.)

I checked my essay for _____ errors.   _____

I checked my essay for _____ errors.   _____

INDEX

CREDITS

Photo Credits:

Page 1 jupeart/Shutterstock; **p. 2** Ian Shaw/Alamy; **p. 11** chewan/Fotolia; **p. 22** Corbis Cusp/Alamy; **p. 35** Cheryl Ann Quigley/Fotolia; **p. 36** Pat & Chuck Blackley/Alamy; **p. 46** Gunter Marx/PE/Alamy; **p. 50** WavebreakmediaMicro/Fotolia; **p. 59** mybaitshop/Fotolia; **p. 73** jupeart/Shutterstock; **p. 74** Rich Legg/Getty Images; **p. 88** Jim Wileman/Alamy; **p. 101** herculaneum79/Fotolia; **p. 102** Oxford Designers & Illustrators Ltd/Pearson Education Ltd; **p. 110** (top) Sunshine Pics/Fotolia, (bottom) ChmpagnDave/Fotolia; **p. 116** freshidea/Fotolia; **p. 120** ta samaya/Fotolia; **p. 133** Digital Vision/ Thinkstock; **p. 145** (left) vichie81/Fotolia, (right) qingwa/Fotolia; **p. 152** (top) branex/Fotolia, (bottom) Directphoto.org/Alamy; **p. 169** jupeart/Shutterstock; **p. 170** michaeljung/Shutterstock; **p. 189** OJO Images Ltd/Alamy; **p. 205** (top) Bryan Smith/ZUMA Press/Newscom, (bottom) dima266f/Fotolia; **p. 221** Blend Images/Hill Street Studios/Getty Images; **p. 243** Radius Images/Alamy; **p. 264** Hiroyuki Ito/Hulton Archive/Getty Images.

Text Credits:

Page 23: Public Health Successes. Adapted from Buckingham, Robert. *A Primer on International Health*, 1st Ed., © 2001. Reprinted and Electronically reproduced by permission of Pearson Education, Inc., Upper Saddle River, New Jersey.

Page 25: paragraphs 1 and 2. Adapted from Thieman, William J.; Palladino, Michael A., *Introduction to Biotechnology*, 2nd Ed., © 2009. Reprinted and Electronically reproduced by permission of Pearson Education, Inc., Upper Saddle River, New Jersey.

Page 27: The Health Consequences of Fear. Adapted from Karren, Keith J.; Smith, Lee; Hafen, Brent Q.; Frandsen, Kathryn J., *Mind/Body Health: The Effects of Attitudes, Emotions, and Relationships*. 4th Ed., © 2010. Reprinted and Electronically reproduced by permission of Pearson Education, Inc., Upper Saddle River, New Jersey.

Page 39: © 2012. Courtesy of California Avocado Commission. Get more facts about California Avocados, recipes, nutrition, and California Avocado grower stories at www.CaliforniaAvocado.com.

Page 41: paragraph 2. Adapted from Buckingham, Robert. *A Primer on International Health*, 1st Ed., © 2001. Reprinted and Electronically reproduced by permission of Pearson Education, Inc., Upper Saddle River, New Jersey.

Pages 58, 66: Excerpt from "Universal Language." WORLD BOOK REFERENCE CENTER © 2004. World Book, Inc. By permission of the publisher. All rights reserved. www.worldbookonline.com. This excerpt may not be reproduced in whole or in part in any form without prior written permission from the publisher.

Page 62: Passage from "Late-blooming or Language Problem" reprinted with permission from the American Speech-Language-Hearing Association. Available from www.asha.org/public/speech/disorders/lateblooming.htm. © Copyright 2012 American Speech-Language-Hearing Association. All rights reserved.

Page 63: Passage from "Speech and Language Disorders in the School Setting" reprinted with permission from the American Speech-Language-Hearing Association. Available from www.asha.org/public/speech/development/schoolsFAQ.htm. © Copyright 2012 American Speech-Language-Hearing Association. All rights reserved.

Page 63: Passage from "Editorial: Children can, and should, learn more than one language" courtesy of *The Houston Chronicle*.

Page 81: paragraph 2. Adapted from Eva Kras, "Mr. Wygard's Story" in *Management in Two Cultures: Bridging the Gap between U.S. and Mexican Managers.* Copyright © by Nicholas Brealey Publishing.

Page 88: Student-Centered Teaching. Adapted from Morrison, Gary R.; Lowther, Deborah L., *Integrating Computer Technology into the Classroom: Skills for the 21st Century*, 4th Ed., © 2010. Reprinted and Electronically reproduced by permission of Pearson Education, Inc., Upper Saddle River, New Jersey.

Page 117: The Biological and Environmental Causes of Shyness. Adapted from Henderson, Lynne, "Shyness." Copyright © The Shyness Institute. Reproduced by permission.

Page 161: Graph "Internet Users per 100 Inhabitants, 1997–2007" (Graph.) © International Telecommunication Union (ITU). http://itu.int.

Page 162: Graph "SMS Text Messages Sent Globally in Trillions" from the TomiAhonen Almanac 2010, by Tomi T. Ahonen. TomiAhonen Consulting (Creative Commons Attribution 2.0, http://creativecommons.org/licenses/by/2.0/).

Page 162: Graph. "Messages Sent Per Mobile Subscriber Per Month." From Mashable.com, © 2010 Mashable, Inc. All rights reserved. Used by permission and protected by the Copyright Laws of the United States. The printing, copying, redistribution or retransmission of this Content without express written permission is prohibited.

Page 164: Graph "Unique Visitors on Global Social Networking Sites" from "Chart of the Day: Facebook is Absolutely Crushing the Competition," Copyright © 2013 Business Insider, Inc.

Page 164: Graph "U.S., Non-U.S., and Worldwide Online Advertising Spending on MySpace and Facebook, 2009 and 2010 (millions and percent change)" courtesy of eMarketer.com.

Page 280: "The Challenge of Many Languages." Adapted from Lustig, Myron W.; Koester, Jolene, *Intercultural Competence: Interpersonal Communication Across Cultures*, 6th Ed., © 2010. Reprinted and Electronically reproduced by permission of Pearson Education, Inc., Upper Saddle River, New Jersey.

Page 281: "Nice by Nature?" Adapted from Dingfielder, S. (2009, September). Nice by Nature? Monitor on Psychology, 40(8). Retrieved from http://www.apa.org/monitor/. No further reproduction or distribution is permitted without written permission from the American Psychological Association.

Pages 283–284: "Marital Exchanges." Adapted from Peoples / Bailey, *Humanity: An introduction to Cultural Anthropology*, 6E. © 2003 Cengage Learning.

Pages 286–287: "Why We Should Send a Manned Mission to Mars." Adapted from Joulwan, Melissa. "You Decide: Manned Mission to Mars." KQED, 13 May 2004.

Pages 299–300: Presentation of comma rules adapted with permission from Anne Katz.

Illustration Credits:

TSI Graphics: pgs: 80, 115

Reader: _____ **Date:** _____

1. What kind of introduction does this essay have (funnel, entertaining story, etc.)?

   _____

   Does the thesis statement make clear what the essay is going to compare? ☐ yes ☐ no

   Where is the thesis statement placed? _____

   Does the introduction capture your interest? ☐ yes ☐ no

2. Does the essay use block or point-by-point organization?

   _____

3. If it uses block organization, is there a transition sentence or transition paragraph between the two blocks? ☐ yes ☐ no

4. How many paragraphs are there in the body? Number: _____
   What are the topics of the body paragraphs?

   1. _____   3. _____

   2. _____   4. _____

5. What kind of supporting details does the writer use in each body paragraph?

   1. _____   3. _____

   2. _____   4. _____

6. Check each paragraph for unity. Are any sentences unnecessary or "off topic"? ☐ yes ☐ no
   If your answer is *yes*, write a comment about this.

   _____

7. Check each paragraph for coherence. Does each one flow smoothly from beginning to end? ☐ yes ☐ no
   What comparison and contrast signals does the writer use to connect similar or different ideas?

   _____

8. What kind of conclusion does this essay have—a summary of the main points or a paraphrase of the thesis statement?

   _____

   Does the writer make a final comment? ☐ yes ☐ no
   What is it?

   _____

   Is this an effective ending (one that you will remember)? ☐ yes ☐ no

9. In your opinion, what is the best feature of this essay? In other words, what is this writer's best writing skill?

   _____

Writer: _____   Date: _____

Format

My essay is correctly formatted (title centered, first line of every paragraph indented, margins on both sides, double-spaced).   ☐ yes ☐ no

Mechanics

I checked punctuation, capitalization, and spelling.   ☐ yes ☐ no

Content and Organization

My essay has all three parts: introduction, body, and conclusion.   ☐ yes ☐ no

I used block/point-by-point organization. (Underline one.)

If I used block organization, I inserted a transition sentence or transition paragraph between the two blocks.   ☐ yes ☐ no

Introduction: Type of introduction I used (funnel, historical background, surprising statistics, dramatic story, etc.): _____

My thesis statement makes clear what the essay is going to compare.   ☐ yes ☐ no

Body: The body has _____ paragraphs. The topics are:

1. _____   3. _____

2. _____   4. _____

Unity: Each paragraph discusses only one main idea, and no sentences are "off topic."   ☐ yes ☐ no

Coherence: Each paragraph has coherence. My essay flows smoothly from beginning to end.   ☐ yes ☐ no

I use transition signals and comparison/contrast signal words to show relationships among ideas.   ☐ yes ☐ no

I use transitions to link paragraphs.   ☐ yes ☐ no

Conclusion: The conclusion (a) summarizes the main points or (b) paraphrases the thesis statement. (Circle one.)

Grammar and Sentence Structure

Errors to check for include verb tenses, subject-verb agreement, articles, pronoun agreement, sentence fragments, and run-on sentences/comma splices.

Number found and corrected

I checked my essay for _____ errors.   _____
                        (verb tense, article, etc.)

I checked my essay for _____ errors.   _____

I checked my essay for _____ errors.   _____